The Life and Rhymes of Ogden Nash

The Life and Rhymes of Ogden Nash

David Stuart

TAYLOR TRADE PUBLISHING
Lanham • Boulder • New York • London

All poems of Ogden Nash are from *Verses from 1929 On* by Ogden Nash, and are reprinted here by permission of Little, Brown and Co.

"Reflections on Ice-Breaking," "Spring on Murray Hill," and "A Necessary Dirge" are copyright 1930, 1935 by Ogden Nash. They first appeared in *The New Yorker*.

"Invocation," "Introspective Reflection," "Sedative Reflection," "More about People," "Old Men," and "Nuptial Reflection" are copyright 1931 by Ogden Nash.

"That Reminds Me," "Don't Cry, Darling, It's Blood All Right," and "Ask Daddy, He Won't Know" are copyright 1934, 1942 by Ogden Nash, and first appeared in *The Saturday Evening Post*.

"Barmaids Are Diviner Than Mermaids" and "My Trip daorbA" are copyright 1936, 1949 by Ogden Nash, and first appeared in the *New York American*.

"The Middle" is copyright 1949 by Ogden Nash. It first appeared in the *New York American*.

Excerpt from *The Portable Dorothy Parker*, edited by Brendan Gill, is copyright 1926, 1954 by Dorothy Parker. Reprinted by permission of Viking Penguin, Inc.

Published by Taylor Trade Publishing
An imprint of The Rowman & Littlefield Publishing Group, Inc.
4501 Forbes Boulevard, Suite 200, Lanham, Maryland 20706
www.rowman.com

16 Carlisle Street, London W1D 3BT, United Kingdom

Distributed by NATIONAL BOOK NETWORK

Copyright © 2000 by David Stuart
First Taylor Trade paperback edition 2014

British Library Cataloguing in Publication Information Available

The Library of Congress has cataloged the hardcover edition of this book as follows:

Stuart, David
    The life and rhymes of Ogden Nash / by David Stuart.
       p.   cm.
    Includes bibliographical references and index.
    1. Nash, Ogden, 1902–1971—Biography. 2. Poets, America—20th century—Biography.
  I. Nash, Ogden, 1902–1971. II. Title.
    PS3527.A637Z84 2000
    811'.52—dc20 [B]
    91-22056

ISBN 978-1-56833-127-0 (cloth : alk. paper)
ISBN 978-1-58979-959-2 (pbk. : alk. paper)
ISBN 978-1-4617-1036-3 (electronic)

♾ ™ The paper used in this publication meets the minimum requirements of American National Standard for Information Sciences—Permanence of Paper for Printed Library Materials, ANSI/NISO Z39.48-1992.

Printed in the United States of America

Contents

Acknowledgments

I want to thank a large number of people for help with this book, more or less in order of consultation and receipt of communications:

Benton Arnovitz, my editor at three publishing houses; Olga Hoyt, my personal editor; Dr. Howard Gotlieb, curator, and Margaret R. Goostray, Assistant Director of Special Collections, Mugar Memorial Library, Boston University; Dr. Neda M. Westlake, Rare Book Collection, University of Pennsylvania; Joyce Shue, Special Collections Assistant, Amherst College; Dorothy E. Mosakowski, Special Collections and Rare Books, Robert Hutchins Goddard Library, Clark University; Catherine Herbert, Rare Books Assistant, Cornell University Library; Susan Barbarossa, Library Assistant in Special Collections, Wellesley College Library; Gregory Johnson, Manuscripts Department, Alderman Library, University of Virginia; Constance Boquist, Harvard Alumni Association; Charles Schille, Curatorial Assistant, Harvard University Archives; James J. Lewis, Houghton Reading Room, the Houghton Library, Harvard University; Eleanor Howard, Director of Alumni Affairs and Annual Giving, St. George's School, Newport, R.I.; Frank R. Curtis, Rembar & Curtis, New York; Kenneth A. Lohf and Bernard R. Crystal, Butler Library, Columbia University; Robert J. Bertholf, Curator, The Poetry/Rare Books Collection, State University of New York at Buffalo; Shirley Viviano, Wesley Wilson, Enoch Pratt Free Library, Baltimore; James Oliver Brown, Curtis Brown Associates, Ltd.; Pearl London, New York; Cathy Henderson, Research Librarian, Seyed M. Moosavi, Research Associate, George Crandall, Patrice S. Fox, Ken Craven, Carolyn Cowper, Scott Collison, The Harry Ransom Humanities Research Center, the University of Texas at Austin; Arthur H. Thornhill, Jr., Little, Brown and Company; Diana Hoyt, Washington; Leo M.

Dolenski, Manuscripts Librarian, Bryn Mawr College Library; Carolyn A. Sheehy, Special Collections, The Newberry Library, Chicago; Herbert Cahoon, Curator of Autograph Manuscripts, The Pierpont Morgan Library, New York; Andrew Zaremba, Librarian, The Century Association, New York; Saundra Taylor, Curator of Manuscripts, The Lilly Library, Indiana University; Connell Gallagher, University Archivist and Curator of Manuscripts, Bailey Howe Library, University of Vermont; Evert Volkersz, Head, Department of Special Collections, State University of New York at Stony Brook; Karen Hoyle, Curator, Kerlan Collection, University of Minnesota Libraries; Barbara A. Filipac, Library Associate Specialist, Manuscripts Division, Brown University Library; Hilary Cummings, Manuscripts Curator, Special Collections, University of Oregon; Shelley Cox, Rare Books Cataloger, Special Collections, Morris Library, Southern Illinois University at Carbondale; Patience-Anne W. Lenk, Associate, Special Collections, Colby College, Waterville, Me.; E. B. White, who very kindly allowed me to quote his little poem on page 83; Samuel Hazo, International Poetry Forum, Pittsburgh; L. Szeldits, Curator, Berg Collection, New York Public Library; Richard A. Shrader, Reference Archivist, Wilson Library, the University of North Carolina at Chapel Hill; Gene M. Greesley, Director, Emmett D. Chisum, Research Historian, the University of Wyoming Archive of Contemporary History; Lilace Hatayama, Literary Manuscripts Assistant, Department of Special Collections, The University Library, University of California, Los Angeles; Susan M. Allen, Reference Librarian, the Ella Strong Denison Library, Claremont, Ca.; Tania Rizzo, Special Collections Librarian, Honnold Library, Ca.; Casindania P. Eaton, Library, American Academy and Institute of Arts and Letters, New York; Ed Lonergan, Local History Department, Springfield City Library, Ma.; Nora J. Quinlan, Head, Special Collections, Rare Books Room, University Libraries, University of Colorado at Boulder; Giuseppe Bisaccia, Curator of Manuscripts, Rare Books and Manuscripts, Boston Public Library; the Kent County Library of Maryland, Miller Library, Washington College, Chestertown, Md.; Nancy Oppel, the *Baltimore Sun*; Harriet Pilpel, attorney for the Edna Ferber estate, who kindly gave me permission to quote a poem Miss Ferber wrote to Ogden; Agent Liz Darhansoff of New York, who encouraged me to use material from S. J. Perelman; Agent Charlotte Sheedy of New York, who gave me permission to quote material from Dorothy Parker; and Irene Godlis, Viking-Penguin, who arranged permission to quote a few lines from Dorothy Parker.

Introduction

After Ogden Nash died in the spring of 1971, various critics and friends tried to assess his place in American letters. *The New York Times* said America had lost its Master of Light Verse. Archibald MacLeish, in the foreword to a collection of Nash's works, concluded that he was more than poet and master of light verse, he was also an important American philosopher and conscience of the people.

Ogden Nash's friend S. J. Perelman appeared at a memorial service to give a eulogy:

> That his poetry was so widely acclaimed and his audience so devoted never surprised me, for the man himself had all its qualities—wit, compassion, and the extraordinary ability to enchant his readers—in the highest degree. I am grateful to have known Ogden Nash, and only sorry that those who know him merely from the printed page cannot share my love.

Ogden's contemporaries of The Century Association did even better in delineating the man and the poet. Here is a bit of their tribute:

> . . . he used to say, "I do have a little joke," and the world is richer for his decision to let his sense of humor be his guide. . . . It should be said, moreover, that he had no use for practical jokes and no taste for the unprintable.

One of The Century Association members recalled that Ogden had never lost his temper. Another said he could not recall that Ogden ever had an enemy. Another recalled him as a family man, deeply involved with his wife and children all his married life long. Another said he was very religious, though not openly so. Still another recalled how Ogden had mellowed with age, how he was a charming, considerate host, and a delightful, warmhearted guest, given to writing bread-and-butter letters to people who had entertained him, and often including a poem written especially for them. Friends and acquaintances were known to frame those notes.

He was also inclined to sit down and dash off verses on occasions such as when his car was broken into and robbed while he was in Boston. He sent a poem to the *Boston Globe,* it was published, and one of The Century Association members saved it out of the paper, and it was included in the Association tribute to Nash after his death.

"But," continued The Century Association tribute, "it was his ability to make us laugh—especially at ourselves—that brought him fame. He carried so much to his writing: enormous range of interests, encyclopedic knowledge of the world and world affairs, politics, sports, learning, literature, birdwatching, travel, food, family life, English at its best—Shakespeare didn't write 'Like You Like It.' He would never be 'congratulated'; prime ribs of beef 'with au jus' would shock him. One thinks of a line in *Macbeth*: 'More is thy due than more than all can pay.' "

Finally, *The New Yorker* magazine, for which he wrote three hundred and fifty-three verses in forty-one years ran his last poem, "You Steer and I'll Toot," beneath a black line. "There is no way to comment adequately upon such an enormous body of joyful, surprising, pointed, and always gentle poetry, and no way to express gratitude for a man who gratified four generations of readers . . ."

There is a bit of hyperbole in those tributes. Ogden did lose his temper occasionally, even with his wife, and most notably with Little, Brown and Company.

No, Ogden Nash was not perfect. Sometimes he drank too much, a matter that caused difficulties in the family, as any careful reader of Ogden's will gather. He did have a taste for the unprintable—what used to be unprintable—especially limericks, and he often circulated these privately among his friends. He also wrote in his second book a poem about four prominent bastards, which was about as hairy as you could get in print in the 1930s.

He also abandoned an early sense of *ars gratia artis* shortly after he began writing for a living. When he first became a celebrity in 1931 a shoe company offered him money to write a poem commending their shoes. He refused disdainfully. But later, he succumbed to the lure of Hollywood's filthy lucre, and, even later, wrote poems in praise of the *Reader's Digest*, vermouth, and the New York Stock Exchange.

He was also a very proud man and more than a little resentful that the awarders of prizes in American society never saw fit to give him any. The behavior of the Pulitzer commities, in particular, is inexplicable, since at various times when they wanted to honor someone they simply invented a new category. But never for Ogden Nash.

No, Ogden Nash was not perfect. The above are the worst sins I could find in tracing his history. He was a man, and therefore he was full of foibles. Fortunately for the world, he recognized them better than anyone and wrote about them constantly, to the enrichment of the American language and the betterment of society. Here, in the following pages, is the story of this remarkable artist and American of the twentieth century.

> Tell me not, in mournful numbers
> Life is but an empty dream!
> For the soul is dead that slumbers,
> And things are not what they seem.
>
> Life is real! Life is earnest!
> And the grave is not its goal;
> Dust thou art, to dust returnest,
> Was not spoken of the soul.
>
> Not enjoyment, and not sorrow,
> Is our destined end or way;
> But to act, that each tomorrow
> Find us farther than today. . .
>
> "A Psalm of Life"
> Henry Wadsworth Longfellow

The Life and Rhymes of Ogden Nash

1

The Proper Boyhood of a WASP

To begin with, you would have to call him Scion of the Establishment. Frederic Ogden Nash, Scion of the Establishment. That is not to say that he was born with a gold spoon in his mouth, silver plate it turned out to be, or that the Nashes rivaled the Roosevelts and the Burdens in early American pedigree; they didn't, although the Nash history is long enough and respectable enough to qualify Nashes for various clubs and associations, mostly WASP and Confederate, if such still exist these days. But Establishment he was. His great-great-great grandfather was governor of North Carolina during the Revolutionary War. The governor's brother, Francis, founded Nashville, Tennessee.

Ogden's father was a Southern gentleman, a North Carolinian who had participated in the Civil War, in a way: Edmund Strudwick Nash had been twelve years old in 1865 and had patrolled the family estate with a shotgun, the only male left at home to protect his mother and sisters from looters and worse. After the war, sensing where the future lay, Edmund Nash had gone north to the very heart of Yankeeland, New York City, and there he had cast anchor in New York harbor, starting a business to sell North Carolina resin and turpentine to the Union navy and to private shipowners. Half the year was spent in the chandler's trade in New York and the other half in Savannah, where he arranged for supplies to sell up north. He married a Kentucky girl, Mathilde Chenault, whose father was a professor of classics. They moved for summers to the commuting town of Rye, New

1

York, on the New Haven Railroad's main line. Very Establishment, indeed.

After Mattie Chenault became Mrs. Edmund Nash, along came a clutch of children, in the middle of them Ogden, who was born on August 19, 1902, and properly baptized at Christ Episcopal Church in Rye on November 20.

As a boy, Ogden was unexceptionable. He collected frogs, and hated girls properly, and did all the usual boyish things. At home he acquired manners of a sort common among upper-middle-class Americans of the first quarter of the twentieth century; he learned about spoons and shaking hands and white gloves and the waltz. The summers in Savannah instilled in Ogden a southern courtliness that would mark him forever. From the church he acquired the outer trappings of Anglican Christianity, proper reverence for bishops, and more; he was a churchman all his life, although not a flamboyant one.

In his education one bit stood out: his appreciation of the American English language. He attributed this to his education. That began with his mother, who had received her standards from Professor Chenault. So Ogden and his siblings grew up exposed at home to the classics. It was the family's intention to send him to good boarding schools, but naval architecture intervened. The U.S. Navy began in the late nineteenth century to convert from sail to steam and from wooden hulls to steel, and the need for resin and turpentine began to dry up. Also Edmund Nash fell at odds with the U.S. government, which began a series of lawsuits against his firm, which played hob with the assets. The family's finances rocked with the shocks. Ogden went to day school in Rye for a time, and when he was about ten years old the family went to Europe, and he was sent to a boys' boarding school at Groton, Massachusetts, notable for cramming boys to get into *the* Groton—the Reverend Endicott Peabody's famous character-building establishment. That year Ogden remembered as first six months of miserable homesickness, then six months of acquisition of a taste for Latin and a superior knowledge of the geography of Groton and environs, gained by frequent bicycle excursions around the territory.

At about this time, Ogden recalled, his eyes became a problem. Probably his family discovered his myopia. His mother was so seriously concerned that she had him take a course in touch-typing as a hedge against the threat of blindness, a fortuitous action that served Ogden well in the business world. She also took him out of school entirely and undertook his education in the classical mode.

Rye was a country town in those days, with dirt roads for the most part, but the Nashes lived on the main north-south thoroughfare, the Boston Post Road, which provided the Nash children with its own entertainment. Ogden and his brother Ted would sit on the wall above the Post Road by the hour and count the automobiles that moved up and down. Ten cars was a high mark.

In this bucolic atmosphere Ogden spent a good deal of his time reading. A. Conan Doyle was a favorite author, beginning with *The White Company* and ending with the adventures of fiction's greatest detective.

In 1916, when Ogden was fourteen years old, he was keeping a diary fitfully. He was going to send something to *St. Nicholas* magazine, he wrote in his diary on February 1, a poem.

The poem was of the sort of romanticism one might expect from an intense member of the teenage literati: it told of a handsome prince who had a little mockingbird that he loved dearly. One day the prince rode off hunting deer and chanced upon a castle where he saw a beautiful princess. He cast himself at her feet and proposed, but, cruel wench, she would not accept until he brought her a bloodred rose.

And so the sad prince rode home to his own castle, devastated; there was only one rose in his entire realm, and that was white.

On his return to his castle, the forlorn prince told the mockingbird his troubles and popped off to bed, to sleep like a log. The next morning he awakened early and looked out into his garden. There on the rosebush was a beautiful red rose, and draped over it was the poor old mockingbird, dead, having given his all for his lord.

What the editors of *St. Nicholas* had to say, if indeed the poem was dispatched, is not recorded in literary history. Spring came on March 25, and Ogden noted gleefully that he had seen two rabbits and played his first game of baseball. Exeunt poet and diarist for the season.

The government finally relented, World War I came to Europe, creating new demands for turpentine and resin, and Edmund Nash managed to pull the family finances together enough to educate the children. Ogden was sent to St. George's boarding school for boys in Newport, Rhode Island.

He learned to dress in a style made famous by the tailors J. Press and Brooks Brothers: button-down collar shirts, slope-shouldered jackets, and very seldom to be caught, particularly for photos, without a necktie. Even as a youth he was a very dignified fellow, and he either inherited or developed a wry sort of humor at an early age.

At St. George's Ogden distinguished himself. He played football and baseball well enough to make the first teams. He was a member of the editorial board of the literary magazine, *Dragon,* and of the school yearbook, *The Lance.* He belonged to the glee club and the choir and was president of the civics club in his senior year.

He won prizes for scholarship and particularly for languages, Latin and French, and he was on the honor roll. He acquired that veneer peculiar to his class, a manner marked by a practiced indifference to practically every-thing.

At St. George's he continued his pursuit of the classics with considerable success. In later years one teacher would stand out in memory: Arthur S. Roberts, his English instructor at St. George's. In a letter to Roberts more than half a century later, Nash expressed gratitude to the man who had given him such a basic grounding of the language that he could later suc-cessfully toy with that same language in his poems.

During Ogden's St. George's years, the family deserted Rye and took residence at 20 Fifth Avenue in New York City. In the autumn of 1920 Ogden Nash journeyed up to Cambridge and the Harvard Yard, entering the class of 1924. His Harvard career, however, lasted but a single acade-mic year. Later Nash told two stories about his reason for leaving Harvard so soon; one was that the family had suffered economic hardship. The other was that Ogden had tired of formal education. Perhaps it was a bit of both. The Western world was finally feeling the results of the Peace of Versailles and the accumulated overproductions of every sort of crop and many goods for war. The German mark collapsed, and so did the British market. The trouble spread across the Atlantic, so 1921 was a year of seri-ous recession in America, and the elder Nashes were touched by the same reverses that sent the stock market tumbling.

Ogden might have set out to work his way through college. (Advertiser-publisher William Benton worked his way through Yale as a cardshark.) But Ogden Nash did not. He faulted himself on that score: he didn't, at the time, have the necessary drive to do so.

Three pages of two hundred devoted to Ogden Nash's formative years; it seems such a slight amount. But the fact is that Ogden Nash's youth was totally unexceptionable, and he showed no sign of the genius he would begin to exhibit a few years later when he was involved in the publishing scene. Harvard left little mark on him in his attitudes or associations. He was a product of the Eastern Establishment, to be sure, but an establish-ment that was already beginning to crumble a little bit.

So after but a year of college, he set out to make himself self-supporting. Ogden was scarcely equipped for many genteel occupations, but he did learn of an opening as a master in French at St. George's, and he got the job, which spoke eloquently for his record there. The St. George's experi-ence lasted only a year. ". . . I lost my entire nervous system carving a lamb for a table of fourteen-year-olds," he said later. Through his family he found a job with Dillon, Read and Company. Later biographical sketches called him a "bond salesman." No such glory came to Ogden Nash. He worked in the mail room from four o' clock in the afternoon until mid-night, coming out onto Wall Street with no one about but the cats prowl-ing the garbage cans. "It was a lot like Don Marquis's *Mehitabel*." (Don

Marquis's famous alley cat and her sometime correspondent, Archie the cockroach, were enormously popular in the New York literary world in the early 1920s, when Ogden Nash was yearning on the edges.)

During that year of sorting mail, Nash learned what he did not want to do: work on Wall Street. He thought he wanted to write seriously, but he did not know quite what he wanted to write. Since the age of six he had been writing "verses, jingles, rhymes." He had already considered the matter many times and had produced a large number of serious poems.

"I wrote sonnets about beauty and truth, eternity, poignant pain," he said. "That was what the people I read wrote about too—Keats, Shelley, Byron, the classical English poets."

But somehow—he was not loquacious about it—he got the idea that such heroic poetry was not his style, and mostly he kept quiet about it. Later, he said, "I decided I'd better laugh at myself before anyone laughed at me."

Should he be a playwright? Should he write the Great American Novel?

What he wanted at this point was an exposure to a writing life, and he found it in the world of commerce, writing advertising copy for car cards. The company was Barron G. Collier, named for its president, who proudly called himself "the king of streetcar advertising." Collier had a franchise for the New York streetcars, and Ogden's work appeared all over New York, in those card cases above the seats of the streetcars and the elevated railways that coursed up the avenues. He spent nearly two years writing advertising copy for straphangers at $25 a week. He was miserable almost from the beginning; the hurdy-gurdy prose demanded by the trade depressed him.

In search of independence, Ogden had moved out of the family apartment on lower Fifth Avenue to a place on Nassau Street, nearer the Wall Street district. But when he got into car cards, farther uptown, he moved again, this time to move in with five other New York hopefuls in a cold-water flat in the shadow of the Third Avenue elevated railway in the East 60s. He and roommate Joseph Alger decided to write a book. Alger had been two years ahead of Ogden at St. George's and had gone on to Harvard where he made a name for himself on the comic magazine *Lampoon* and was elected to the Hasty Pudding Club, one of Harvard College's sacrosanct institutions that makes its way into grown men's *Who's Who* biographies. They wrote a children's book, called *The Cricket of Carador*, highly regarded by the authors at the time, but later to be a mild source of embarrassment to at least one of them.

However, Doubleday saw fit to publish it.

At Doubleday Ogden Nash ran into Daniel Longwell, a young Columbia University graduate who was then advertising manager of Doubleday, Page & Co., which had its headquarters at the Country Life Press in

Garden City, Long Island. Longwell and Ogden had known each other since boyhood. The Longwells lived up the street from the Nashes in Rye, and Longwell had looked on superciliously at the kid who used to play with his little sister.

In 1925 when *The Cricket of Carador* was in the publishing works, Longwell was looking for a new assistant. His advertising copywriter at the time was Frank Chapman, who then had the sort of literary imprimatur common to the gentleman's trade: he was married to the daughter of writer Irvin S. Cobb. That year Chapman decided he was not cut out for a publishing career and told Longwell he had decided to quit Doubleday to study singing.

Dan Longwell was fretting over the loss of his dogsbody when he happened to think of that young man from the past who had wandered into the present: that man with the lugubrious expression, Ogden Nash, who had just produced half of a publishable children's book, who had two years' experience in advertising copy writing, and who had expressed interest in a literary career. Longwell offered Nash the job at $90 a month, which was a cut almost to the quick, and so desperate was Ogden to get away from card advertising that he took the job, even though it meant he would have to buy a reserve-commuter's ticket, to get from Manhattan to Garden City, and spend many hours a month on the trains.

2

The Young Publisher

It was a lively literary world into which Ogden Nash stepped in 1925. He came at the most productive period of American literary history: down in Greenwich Village Eugene O'Neill was experimenting with the drama at the Provincetown Playhouse, and Paul Robeson's career was beginning there. On Broadway, Elmer Rice, Maxwell Anderson, and Sidney Howard were enjoying commercial success. F. Scott Fitzgerald's novel *The Great Gatsby* was published that year, and Edna Ferber's *So Big*. Sinclair Lewis's *Arrowsmith* won the Pulitzer prize. John Dos Passos brought out another of his social novels, *Manhattan Transfer*, and Theodore Dreiser published *An American Tragedy*, which was recognized by many, but not all, as a classic piece of literature. Ernest Hemingway, in Paris, was writing short stories and novels and this year published *In Our Time*. Several veterans of *Stars and Stripes*, the soldiers' newspaper of the American Expeditionary Force, were talking of starting a magazine, something to fit the times and titillate those who had traveled afar and could no longer be kept down on the farm, in other words, New Yorkers, and the New Yorkers who swarmed to the city after their experiences in Europe. Leader of the group was Harold Ross, a Coloradan. He was determined to operate on the premise opposite from that of *Collier's*, *The Saturday Evening Post*, the *Ladies' Home Journal*, *Woman's Home Companion*, *American*, *Country Life*, and *Country Gentleman*. Those magazines were designed to appeal to the broad spectrum of American society, still heavily rural and small-town oriented. Editor Harold Ross set out to produce a magazine "which is not edited for the old lady in Dubuque ... a magazine avowedly published for a metropolitan audience ..." It was named by John Peter Toohey, a well-known press agent. When Ross and backer Raoul Fleischmann were asking about for a name, they sought out, among others, Toohey, who at that moment was eating lunch at a restaurant near offices they had rented on West 45th Street, the Algonquin Hotel Rose Room.

"What kind of magazine?" said Toohey.

"A metropolitan magazine."

"What metropolis?"

"New York."

"Then call it *The New Yorker*," said Toohey, turning back to his soup.

Editor Ross had announced that the new magazine would encompass "gaiety, wit, and satire, but it will be more than a jester. It will not be what is commonly called sophisticated, in that it will assume a reasonable degree of enlightenment on the part of its readers . . ."

Into *The New Yorker*'s fold and around it had crept such figures as Ross's pal Alexander Woollcott, the critic and essayist who had first made his name by facing down the Shubert brothers when they tried to control the theater reviews of *The New York Times*. The reason Ross had found press agent Toohey at the Algonquin was that he had gone there seeking advice from any and all of a formidable group of litterateurs who assembled there each day at luncheon because the food was good, the prices were reasonable, and the Algonquin was located on West 44th Street in the heart of the magazine offices and on the edges of the newspaper and theatrical districts, just a stroll through the arcade from Ross's establishment. Ross was probably also seeking Woollcott, the mainstay of that informal New York club that had captured the imagination of the "sophisticated"—the Algonquin Round Table. The members assembled in the Rose Room around a big table, first come, first served, except that few had the nerve to take the chair Woollcott had chosen as his own. Woollcott was usually there, along with playwrights George S. Kaufman and Marc Connelly; novelist Edna Ferber; magazine writers Dorothy Parker, Robert Benchley, and Robert Sherwood; newspaper columnists Franklin P. Adams and Heywood Broun; and a traveling circus of stars and comets, the bright luminaries of Ogden Nash's universe.

Trade publishing—the publishing of books for the general public—was then an exciting gentleman's profession, lucrative, as one could see by the Rolls Royces and Cadillacs lined up in front of The Century Association clubrooms, or by the rolls of the Ivy League clubs. Macmillan dominated lower Fifth Avenue in its big stone building (big for those days) below 14th Street. The black front of the Charles Scribner's Sons building stood above the bookstore's show windows on the same avenue, near 48th Street, and lesser publishers built their rabbit warrens in the office buildings on the side streets off the avenue. A new man, Bennett Cerf, had just bought the

Modern Library series from Boni and Liveright and was getting ready to establish Random House, in space rented from the hard-up Roman Catholic Archdiocese of New York, a part of the cardinal's palace at 51st Street and Madison Avenue. Alfred A. Knopf was busily promoting books by European authors, and Americans, exposed to Europe by the events of 1914–18, were responding nobly. Richard Simon and Max Schuster had joined forces to establish another publishing house. Doubleday, which had been in business since 1900, was in the middle of this exciting world. Ogden Nash leaped into publishing like a trout into a stream; he was in his element, moving among the scions of wealth, those who had attended boarding school and Harvard College. The three years at St. George's and the one at Harvard had paved the way; he was eligible to join the Harvard Club of New York City, an association that would be of enormous benefit to him in years to come. He had all the right attitudes, social standing, and credentials for a successful publishing career.

This new world of publishing was a delight to Ogden Nash. Dan Longwell started by teaching his assistant how to write a letter—not a bookkeeper's "yours of 21st inst." as Nash was wont to begin in those days. None of those stuffy business letters would do. Longwell told him to write as if he were talking directly to the addressee, not "smarmy" (gaudy) letters, but straight and to the point.

Doubleday's list was eclectic, to put it mildly. Ogden was writing copy for Booth Tarkington's new novel, *Women.*

"At a thousand tea tables indigestion seethes against Mr. Tarkington's frank and malicious amusingness . . ."

And then there was *Hopalong Cassidy's Protege* by Clarence Mulford.

"'Ambushin' is goin' out of style around here! swore Mesquite Jenkins as he gazed on his pal Hopalong Cassidy, dangerously shot by sneaking rustlers . . ."

Amusingness? Dangerously shot? Those were the 1920s, when American usages were still trembling on their British bases, and adverbs were used adjectivally with impunity. Doubleday did have need of a copywriter with a command of the American, not the English, usage.

Very shortly Ogden was caught up in the excitement of controversy. Doubleday had published a book called *The Constant Nymph* by Margaret Kennedy, which the old-fashioned Doubledays of the family considered to be on a level with *Lady Chatterley's Lover*, that famous banned-in-Boston romance. These were the Doubledays who had thrown Theodore Dreiser off their list for writing obscene and immoral books, and they considered *The Constant Nymph* to be as bad or worse. Dan Longwell met the bosses head-on, fought for the book, and finally won on the argument that it would be a bestseller if they would leave him alone. They did, the advertising program was successful, and *The Constant Nymph* sold several hundred thousand copies. Writing advertising copy for it, in those columns in newspapers and magazines headed L. L. Day (Doubleday), Ogden Nash felt at that moment that he had found himself.

It was a life suitable only for a young man. Up at six and down to Pennsylvania Station to get the 7:49 train to Garden City. A day's work at the office, and then back on the train to commute in reverse home to Manhattan. The trains were slow in those days and the stops were frequent. Nash managed to read Tolstoy's *War and Peace* from cover to cover, and once, when there were difficulties on the line, he read the entire day's edition of *The New York Times.*

The routine was often broken. Sometimes he stayed after work for a few drinks and dinner on Long Island with Dan Longwell, then an avowed bachelor, and more talk in the Longwell room in a boarding house about half a mile from the office, until the last trains to Manhattan loomed. Sometimes Nash got home at midnight and was up at six again to make the circuit the next morning.

At other times he and Longwell came into Manhattan, ostensibly on business, and stopped off at the Columbia University Club on 43rd Street to enjoy the forbidden fruits of America's prohibition laws. Bourbon whiskey, the sort made in Kentucky, was illegal, and the only decent distillations of that sort seldom traveled. What was sold in the speakeasies as "bourbon" either had been stolen from a bonded warehouse or, more likely, blended in the basement of the establishment from alcohol and caramel coloring. It was the sort of liquor that made men go blind. The expert bartender of the Columbia club, sometimes in those days called a mixologist by jokers, eschewed such dangers and turned to Scotch whisky for cocktails. He knew that the Scotch had been brought safely across the sea in the original bottles, if carried illegally into the United States by fast speedboat, and so the old-fashioneds the young men drank were concocted of Scotch. For the first decade of his drinking, said Nash, he did not realize that Scotch whisky was not the normal ingredient for an old-fashioned.

Pleasant as these sessions were, they were filled with shop talk. Cornucopias of ideas spilled across the bar tables as these two publishing people plotted to sell their company's wares to the public.

The Doubledays knew how to live, certainly. Much of their time was spent on the golf courses of Long Island, and so, of course, was that of their minions. Longwell brought Ogden into the golfing fraternity, and they got on famously since both shot in the high 90s. Occasionally they golfed with one of the Doubledays, which meant more shop talk and more ideas.

In addition to his advertising copy, Ogden aspired to write "seriously." He began several short stories and a novel. He also continued to write poetry, but, as he said, he did like his joke, and he found that what was coming out was more light verse than poetry, and he had the good sense to realize very early what his poetic limitations were.

"I'd written a great deal of verse throughout my youth; I like to think of it as poetry, and it certainly was serious in conception and execution, but sometimes I was writing like Swinburne, sometimes like Browning, then like Kipling, then like Tennyson. There was a ludicrous aspect to what I was trying to do; my emotional and naked beauty stuff just didn't turn out as I intended."

It would be better, Nash decided in a burst of what had to be genius, to be a "good bad poet than to be a bad good poet." And he abandoned Swinburnism, Tennysonism, and Browningism for Nashism, to look back only occasionally later on.

Lest all that early effort be a complete loss, Ogden Nash began to turn his old poems upside down, accentuating the ludicrous. His energy was boundless. Many nights, after he got home from Garden City, he worked at his own writing. In the summer of 1926 *Country Life* gave Nash his first sale, a poem for the Christmas number, called "The Bishop's Christmas Wish."

But these efforts were so slight a bit of Ogden's career that most of his associates were not even aware of them. He really expected to continue in publishing. Writing was just something he wanted to do on the side. Advertising was the thing, but not only advertising, for Dan Longwell had the confidence of the firm and soon Ogden was given the responsibility for reading some of the manuscripts that came in over the transom and a few guidelines that enabled him to reject most of them without further consultation. On December 19, 1927, for example, he wrote a hopeful young writer named Gloria Goddard that her novel, *And Ever Shall Be*, would not do for the Doubleday list. It was Doubleday, Page's experience, said Editor Nash, from the depths of his full year of experience, that books dealing with the future did not work very well. And so author Goddard's work was rejected by Ogden.

The name of the game was to find books that would make money and new authors who would produce such books. Anywhere and everywhere was their raw material, in newspapers, of course, and above all, magazines.

One night in 1927 at Longwell's they went through the *Saturday Review of Literature* from cover to cover, as publishers did in those days when that magazine's praise could make a book commercially successful almost overnight. The issue contained the invocation to Stephen Vincent Benét's long poem, "John Brown's Body." The two young men were fascinated, and next day at Longwell's instruction, Ogden telegraphed Benét asking that Doubleday be allowed to publish the book. He had a letter back, announcing regretfully that Benét was already under contract to his college classmate, John Farrar of George Doran publishing company. But the Doubleday boys had their way, finally, because George Doran's company was swallowed by Doubleday, which was on its way to becoming the behemoth of the book trade.

At Garden City, Nash met Christopher Morley, a novelist who had promoted himself a job as "editorial advisor and consultant" to Doubleday. Morley lived with his wife in Roslyn, Long Island, and occasionally met with Longwell and Nash to address some thorny problem.

Their first encounter concerned Morley's new novel, *Thunder on the Left*, for which Ogden wrote advertising copy:

NO NEUTRALS . . .
What ringing echoes at discussion follow *Thunder on the Left!*
Those who know say "It always thunders twice in the same place."
. . . for readers of Morley's tingling novel become re-readers . . . they can't help themselves. There are no neutrals about this provocative book.

Morley's major interest at that time was The Foundry, an omnibus enterprise conducted in an abandoned factory in Hoboken, New Jersey, with any number of young hopefuls from the New York subliterary scene. The idea was to publish *The Foundry* magazine, which accepted, but did not pay for, literary contributions, and to encourage books and to stage plays. It cost Ogden $55 to "join" the club. He also believed in it enough to solicit others, among them Longwell and other Doubleday people.

Ogden's latest creation was an untitled novel, set on the Atlantic shore. The hero is a gentleman who had made a fortune at an early age manufacturing rubber pants for babies. At the beach he dives in recklessly, forgetting that he is not Johnny Weissmuller. He swims out too far, very nearly going down to the deep six, and then is hied in, beneath hissing rollers, up onto the wet and shining sand, where he lies quivering with emotions that race between annoyance at the inconvenience and gratitude at his deliverance. After quivering a while, he gets up and wanders along the beach to his destiny, which is Margaret, the wife of another man . . .

The novel did not get a great deal further, thank goodness, and reading it one wonders why it got that far, for the octane rating was extremely low from the beginning.

In spite of the novel, Christopher Morley encouraged Ogden and befriended him. And soon Ogden was talking like a man who knew his publishing, suggesting that Chris concentrate at The Foundry on books about the theater.

Morley was very much interested in the theater and was actually trying a sort of Off Broadway for the Roaring Twenties. By 1928 the hopeful Nash was writing sketches and stories for The Foundry and working on several ideas for plays to be staged there.

In 1928 Ogden Nash was living on East 84th Street. His social life consisted of dinners, usually at his parents' apartment or his brother's place on 55th Street, weekends at the house of his sister who had married and lived on Long Island, or weekends elsewhere to attend house parties and the balls that were still given by East Coast Society. One weekend in the fall of 1928 Ogden traveled to Baltimore to attend such an affair. There he met a young lady named Frances Leonard, a flower of Baltimore's very proper and very southern Society. To say that he was smitten is inadequate; he was overwhelmed. When he returned to New York after the weekend, he began writing Miss Leonard.

In his first letter he promptly asked her to come to New York so they could meet again. He put on his brightest, most self-deprecatory tone to tell her what he was doing: trying to persuade citizens to rush to the bookstores and buy Doubleday, Doran's wares. He also let her know that he was really an important executive, by telling the story of his stenographer, who had quit to get married, and how she had mixed up letters on her last day so that one of Doubleday's authors received a note thanking him for applying for the job but turning him down.

He amused her with his troubles. That day he had received a letter and twenty-eight volumes of Doubleday's edition of Rudyard Kipling's works from a furious bookbuyer who had seen a picture of Kipling *with a pipe in his mouth.*

That day, said the ardent swain, pressing to impress, he had a letter from an Oriental gentleman named Mirza Mahmoud Khan Saghappi, page to the Mad Shah of Persia and son of the royal physician, who said that Nash was threatened with death if Saghappi's book (published by Doubleday) was not better advertised.

He wrote glowingly of New York in the autumn, the chestnut vendors on the corners, the policemen in their blue overcoats, and the lights going on at four thirty.

But Frances did not come to New York; rather, in mid-December Ogden went to Baltimore again. If he had been overwhelmed before, he was now drunk with her. On his return to Manhattan he counted the minutes since he had gotten off the Congressional Limited and refrained from writing her for an hour and eighteen minutes. Again, he asked her to come to New York.

She did not. She did tell him he could write her occasionally, and he warned her that she did not know what she was bringing on herself. How true that was! For the smitten young man began deluging the young lady with letters. What it meant to Miss Leonard is hard to tell from the correspondence. He did amuse her, that much was clear. But it seems apparent that whatever interest she had was perhaps ten percent of his. But, as Ogden Nash knew only too well, Miss Leonard was one of the prime belles of Baltimore that year. Nash had been enormously lucky to have enjoyed Miss Leonard's company for most of that first evening. Her escort had been a Naval Academy midshipman, resplendent in his uniform. Under normal circumstances, a stranger from New York might manage one dance or two, but on this evening the midshipman apparently looked too long upon the wine. Ogden had been able to virtually monopolize the young lady and had escorted her home. Now, still writing from New York, he knew there were other midshipmen and dozens of young men in Baltimore and Annapolis who had the enormous advantage of propinquity.

So he set out to woo Miss Leonard with the power of his pen. Fortunately for posterity his frequent and often amusing letters described his daily activity.

He had dinner one night with an author named John R. Coulter, whose nonbook, *The Baffle Book,* had been published. Nash wrote her all about it. He also wrote about his activities in reviving an old scandal, in order to push *I Was a Bandit* by Eddie Guerin, a seventy-year-old crook who was then languishing in a British gaol after what Nash described as fifty years of failure at his profession. Guerin had once stolen the equivalent of half a million dollars, but he was caught and jailed before he could spend any of it. He had gone to France to rob, been caught, tried, sentenced to penal servitude in the French penal colony on Devil's Island in French Guiana, escaped, and then been fool enough to make love to a policeman's wife. The Guerin story was advertised as a morality play, but the fact was, said Ogden, that it was really an advertisement for the criminal life—how not to do it.

Nash reported to Baltimore on January 2, 1929, that he had gone to Hoboken to see The Foundry production of *After Dark* and had gotten a thrill from meeting the cast. It showed, he told Miss Leonard, how young he was still because that was the sensation he had enjoyed earlier at meeting authors. What he was really saying, of course, was that he was really a very important fellow, hobnobbing as he did daily with lights of the literary scene. He had to be forgiven for this, his urgency to impress.

He was a busy man. Some evenings he spent at the Harvard Club, but more were devoted to business. He saw *After Dark* eight times, for various reasons, one being a trip to present Morley with the first copy of his new book. To amuse Miss Leonard in one letter he mentioned the people he had met recently:

> An actress who liked to talk about her husband's suicide.
> A stenographer who thought Ann Arbor was an authoress.
> A subway guard who showed him a gold watch he had stolen from a German prisoner of war in 1918.

As it was with book publishers then, the line between advertising and editorial departments was almost nonexistent. Advertising Manager Longwell promoted several trips for himself to Europe and elsewhere in search of ideas and writing talents. On one of these trips he encountered in London the Crime Club, an organization of the leading mystery story writers of the British Isles. He brought home to Garden City the idea of creating a whole new division of Doubleday, called The Crime Club, Inc. The Doubleday directors agreed, and the subsidiary was born. Suddenly, in addition to his duties in advertising Ogden Nash found himself advanced to editor of the Crime Club.

Trying to find his proper metier as a writer, in 1929 Ogden spent a great deal of time with Christopher Morley at The Foundry. There were two reasons for this activity: first he was interested in trying to write for Morley's theatrical enterprise. He was also interested in writing stories and other prose. Second, he was interested in getting a new novel out of Morley for 1930. Ogden also wrote a play, for Broadway he hoped. He gave it to a producer who praised it fulsomely, but nothing happened. He got a promotion and was regarded as a serious and coming young editor. Doubleday was turning over ever more responsibility to him. He was given the author Jim Tully, the King of the Hoboes. From Tully, who had just returned from England, he garnered delicious bits of gossip, how, when the novelist Thomas Hardy died, and George Bernard Shaw and Rudyard Kipling were pallbearers at the funeral, they refused to keep step as they carried the coffin and nearly dropped what was left of Hardy.

Another tale: Charlie Chaplin was in London and when he went down to Limehouse to visit old haunts someone asked him to brighten the lives of the urchins on the street by telling them who he was. Chaplin's reply was that he hated children.

Such stories were meat and drink to the publishing trade. To young editors they served in lieu of salary raises. In Ogden's case money was definitely an object in his job, for he had to be self-supporting. He was also now thinking of marriage, and, of course, he could not marry until he could support a wife.

The object of his affection came home from Europe in July and went almost immediately to Cape Cod. Ogden was invited for a weekend, but his father was ill and his mother was not well. As the only child remaining in the nest (after the Third Avenue experiment he had returned to the family fold), Ogden felt the need to stick close to home.

But by August his parents' health had improved and he and two friends were dreaming up one of those 1920s house parties celebrated by F. Scott Fitzgerald. George Elliman and Charles Duell, two of Ogden's friends, were spending the summer alone in the Elliman house at Bayside, Long Island. It was to be a moving house party, that is it would start at dinner at Bayside on Friday night. Saturday was to be spent playing with boats on Long Island Sound. The party would move about but end on Sunday at the Ellimans. Christopher Morley and his wife would be the chaperones. Could Miss Leonard come?

Miss Leonard hemmed and hawed a bit, but in the end she came. And the house party that began on August 23, 1929, became a turning point in the life of Ogden Nash. He proposed marriage to Frances Leonard, and she accepted him.

Of all the poems Ogden Nash ever wrote, one of his shortest is the best remembered.

REFLECTIONS ON ICE-BREAKING

Candy
Is dandy
But liquor
Is quicker.

3

The Poet Begins

In the spring of 1929 Frances Leonard and her mother had done what the well-heeled often did to amuse themselves—they set off by steamer for a European holiday. The Nashes did what less well-to-do New Yorkers did; they repaired to a summer spa, theirs being Newport. Ogden went up for weekends, but his busy life centered around the city and Doubleday headquarters on Long Island. Doubleday was then beginning to shift its editorial operations to New York, and in 1929 Ogden was working at 244 Madison Avenue. His initial sale of a poem to *Country Life* had been followed by a long fallow period. He took a stab at writing short stories and sketches, to no avail. They were really quite infantile in conception and amateurish in execution. He wrote one such about two characters named Hattie Boomer Spink, a successful lady author, and her husband, Morton Spink. It did not seem funny to editors. Ogden decided he needed an agent and approached Sydney Sanders, one of the leading literary agents in New York. But Sanders was unable to place Nash's work, and it was not long before the arrangement ended.

Nash met Prosper Buranelli, a short, vigorous Italian-American gentleman from Texas, who openly admitted that he had deserted his wife and eight children to come to New York and be a writer. Buranelli walked about Manhattan in a green hat with a feather in it, singing snatches of Verdi operas whenever he felt self-conscious. In just one meeting Ogden decided that Buranelli was the greatest ghostwriter in the world. At the time he was ghosting *My Name Is Mike*, the memoirs of Michael Fiaschetti, a famous New York detective. It was Ogden's task to nurture the project to publication. He spent many hours in Moneta's restaurant on Mulberry Street, listening to Mike tell Prosper about famous unsolved murder cases.

Ogden at twenty-seven was attractive to women. One lady mystery writer, middle-aged, he said, kept asking him to parties, and he suspected her of matrimonial designs. There were others whose yearnings were simpler, as the young matron he met at a party who suggested that they go away together for a dirty weekend. When he refused, she was shocked. That had never happened to her before. But Ogden, in his letters to Miss Leonard, indicated that he was saving himself for her. He did not tell her about certain parties that he and his friends rigged up.

In the fall of 1929 Ogden Nash was walking on air. His letters to Frances were now love letters, bubbling with affection and yearning. His lady love had agreed to become Mrs. Ogden Nash, although the formal announcement of engagement was going to have to wait for a time.

There was, in fact, something rather strange about this engagement. Miss Leonard was in no hurry to get married, which was just as well considering Ogden's financial situation. But down in Baltimore she continued to carry on an extremely active social life, escorted by other young men. Ogden showed signs of misery, but there was nothing to be done. Miss Leonard was a young woman of determination. The correspondence of the period indicates that Ogden was the supplicant in all things and that Miss Leonard, in a sense, kept him dangling.

One mark of Ogden's newfound responsibility at Doubleday was the fact that he now was in a position to reject books and ideas out of hand. He rejected a proposal by a professor at Northwestern University who wanted Doubleday to publish a book on British General Howe's military campaign in Pennsylvania against the American rebels in 1777. He rejected a proposal from a Brooklyn writer who wanted to do a book, *Why We Welcome Premier Ramsay MacDonald to America's Shores.*

A lady in Indiana asked if Doubleday wouldn't like to publish her husband's book. He, she said, had the latest and only authentic revelation of God on Earth. Ogden did not know quite what to say so he took the project to the head of Doubleday's religion department, an atheist from Texas. He said no.

That fall Nash got a driver's license for the first time and began driving a Chrysler car around the countryside, particularly between Garden City and Manhattan. Sometimes he drove Dan Longwell back to Garden City after an evening in town.

That fall Nash also began to take a new interest in *The New Yorker* magazine. He had, like all in his precious and brittle world, become a reader of this brash and often irritating publication. His favorite writers were

Dorothy Parker and Robert Benchley, for they wrote the sort of poetry (Parker) and prose (Parker and Benchley) that Nash admired.

One of Miss Parker's little poems had stuck with Ogden, as it had with thousands of other New Yorkers:

> Men seldom make passes
> At girls who wear glasses

And one of her aphorisms:

> If all the girls at Vassar College were laid
> end to end . . . it wouldn't surprise me a bit.

Ogden collected the funny writings and from time to time he sent clippings (not these two) to Frances. He thought she would be particularly impressed by articles by Benchley.

And so the romance went on, at furious speed on Ogden's part, and far more majestically on the part of his lovebird.

Or was she?

That autumn the correspondence cooled. The reason was a falling out involving another man. Ogden had obviously objected, playing the role of the injured fiancé, and from the tenor of the letters he was writing it seemed that the romance might be on the rocks.

But Ogden put the best face on the situation that he could; he continued to write loving letters, even offering to give her up if she thought she wanted someone else, and he solaced himself by plunging even deeper into office life.

He conceived an idea for a book on censorship, *Banned in Boston,* which would consist almost entirely of passages from the books banned by the Boston civic authorities as too indecent to inflicted on the psyches of Bostonians. He was "reading" perhaps two manuscripts per night, which meant skimming them to see if Doubleday could make any money out of them.

Prosper Buranelli, the demon ghostwriter, showed up again on Ogden's schedule, this time with a Dr. Jack and Charles Hedlund, all in a clutch. Dr. Jack was an osteopathic physician from Trenton. One day a broad-shouldered, double-chinned Swede with a thick accent, bottle-bottomed spectacles, a heavy mustache, and blue eyes had appeared in his Trenton office complaining of a sore shoulder. This was Charles Hedlund, a Trenton carpenter of considerable skill. As the osteopath was treating him, Hedlund remarked that he must have hurt himself the second time he was shipwrecked.

Like many an osteopath in these days when the dark suspicions of the medical fraternity fell their way, Dr. Jack had a lot of time on his hands, and he was a voracious reader. One of his favorite books was *Trader Horn*, the story of a down-at-the-heels jungle merchant in Darkest Africa who had parlayed a tale of a trading post, ivory, wild animals, native wives, and black magic into a fortune.

To Dr. Jack, Charles Hedlund suddenly appeared clad in dollar signs. Did he have another *Trader Horn* here?

"Shipwrecked?" asked the osteopath. "Tell me more."

So, Charles Hedlund told the tale of his second shipwreck and his first shipwreck and all his other shipwrecks and many other adventures, some of them in Darkest Africa, too. He told Dr. Jack how he had run away from home as a boy, sailed before the mast, jumped ship in South Africa, hidden under a pile of fish to escape the police, worked in the diamond mines, served in the bodyguard of Cecil Rhodes (the founder of Rhodesia), fought against the British during the Boer War, hidden in the jungle from the British after the war, been captured by natives in Madagascar, and spent some time removing snakes from a gold mine. How he got to Madagascar from South Africa he did not say. Probably he swam.

Dr. Jack could scarcely restrain himself. He signed up immediately as Charles Hedlund's business manager and wrote to Doubleday, proposing a book and asking what there was in it for him.

Doubleday's response was to call this meeting in Ogden Nash's office and to bring in the trusty Prosper Buranelli, superghostwriter. So it was arranged; Charles Hedlund would tell Prosper his story, and Prosper would write it.

The meeting was a grand success.

"What's in it for me?" Dr. Jack asked.

"Did you ever have any native wives?" Prosper asked Charles Hedlund. When Hedlund shyly demurred, saying he had a family in Trenton, the ghostwriter grew cross.

They had to have something about native wives. That was what the reading public wanted, and they must give it to them.

While Ogden and Charles Hedlund were digesting that revelation, Dr. Jack was scenting the wind.

"What's in it for me?"

Finally, Charles Hedlund admitted that when he was a young fellow in Africa, he did have all the normal impulses and yearnings, and he guessed that a few native wives had been brought forth. Prosper was satisfied, prepared to continue detailed questioning elsewhere, and they went away. As Ogden shooed them out his door he could hear Dr. Jack still muttering his question.

"Where do I come in?"

A few days later Prosper called Ogden to ask him to lunch so they could discuss the results of his questioning of Charles Hedlund. But Ogden knew his man too well: Prosper, the amazing Prosper, who maintained three separate households that Ogden knew about, who recited D'Annunzio as well as singing Verdi to cover any pauses in conversation, who knew every bartender of every Italian speakeasy in town and never bought a drink. No, said Ogden. He had an unbreakable date uptown at the Barclay for luncheon. But to make sure that nothing went awry with his favorite ghost, Ogden looked about the office for a substitute, and the sales manager admitted that he did not have a luncheon date. Off he went to meet Prosper and bring back a report on the book's progress.

Next day the sales manager showed up late at the office and looked at Ogden as Daniel must have looked at his persecutors after they sent him to the lions, through sad, red eyes. The luncheon, he said, had lasted until four in the morning.

That fall, Ogden's letters showed that Frances had many thoughts about the impetuous engagement into which she had been thrust. She seemed anything but a girl who was ecstatic about the prospect of getting married to this particular man. Ogden was the soul of patience. His letters even more reflected his work at Doubleday. He wrote how he had been photographed for the press, handing a book over to an author, and how he had been summoned to the house of Mrs. Frank N. Doubleday, wife of the company chairman, for tea, and how he promptly won favor by being beaten soundly at deck tennis, and how he made a dreadful gaffe when making small talk.

He had admired the Doubleday dog, an English sheepdog. Mrs. Doubleday had accepted his compliments graciously. Yes, he was a nice dog, but they still missed their St. Bernard, who had died a few months earlier.

Yes, said Ogden, he could understand. The second really could not be like the first.

Only later did he learn that this was the *second* Mrs. F. N. Doubleday.

But Ogden did not fall from grace. A few days later he was again honored by a call from on high, this time from the chairman of the board himself. Mr. Doubleday no longer came to the office. When he wanted information about the company he summoned the lackeys involved. The procedure was for the employees called to make their way to a roadhouse called Rothman's in East Norwich, Long Island. Then Mr. Doubleday would arrive in his enormous yellow Packard limousine, and the chauffeur would drive them around the Long Island countryside while the old man asked his questions. On this occasion Ogden was already in the country. For some time he had been working at the Long Island offices and staying alternately with his brother Ted and his sister Eleanor, both of whom had married and lived on the island. So Ogden drove over to the roadhouse with another Doubleday employee, Harry Maul, and, sure enough, along came the yellow Packard. They got in and the drive began. First there were questions. Then old Mr. Doubleday began to talk. He told them he had just come back from England, and while there he had taken Doubleday author T. E. Lawrence (Lawrence of Arabia) down country to visit Doubleday author Rudyard Kipling. The two had chattered away in Arabic and Hindi, he said, so he really hadn't known what was going on. But what a revelation for a couple of wage slaves!

Long Island social life seemed to be everything F. Scott Fitzgerald had claimed. Ogden was then staying with his sister and brother-in-law, Mr. and Mrs. Culver McWilliams, in Hewlett. One evening they took him along to a dinner-dance attended by a crowd of their friends, mostly "young marrieds." Ogden sat next to a handsome redheaded girl with green eyes, who began the evening by setting him straight: she was just celebrating her third wedding anniversary, she said. But then she began holding his hand under the tablecloth, and when he did not make suitable responses she turned her attention to the man on her other side. Late in the evening Ogden saw them leave the party together. As the evening became night, he, his brother-in-law, and sister decided it was time for working folk to go home and went out into the parking lot to get their car. There in the back seat, they interrupted the redhead in an extremely intimate undertaking.

Such social notes undoubtedly were transcribed at least partially in the hope that they would make Miss Leonard realize that she had an option on a valuable commodity in the marriage mart. But, if so, they had no visible effect, for down in Baltimore Miss Leonard was carrying on like any unattached female of her set. She went to balls with other young men. Likewise to teas. She went driving. She went to Illinois. She showed no indication of wanting to settle down to wedded bliss. His Lancelot's anguish was apparent in his letters, but mildly stated, for he was afraid of losing her altogether if he complained too much, and his love for her seemed to flourish on neglect. She grew fretful at his many letters and importuned him not to write so often. He tried to comply, but his natural ebullience broke through, and soon he was writing as much as ever.

Not even family or business complications kept this self-appointed postman from his almost daily rounds. His father had been ill all summer, staying in Roslyn with Ogden's sister Gwen. The family had given up their apartment in New York, and part of the fall was spent finding them another while Ogden alternated among his siblings. Part of the summer he spent with Gwen, who raised racehorses. Part of it was spent with elder brother Ted, and part with sister Eleanor. Younger brother Aubrey was off in Europe on his honeymoon; he came home just before the first of October. That was moving day in New York, where the denizens of the great apartment buildings had the quaint custom of switching caves each autumn. The month of September was a furious round of activity with thousands of New Yorkers crowding one another to view other habitations which, theoretically at least, would bring them greater joy in the twelve months to come. Ogden and Aubrey found an apartment that would do on East 73rd Street, and the weaning writer and his parents moved in.

Ogden, unlike Charlie Chaplin, was enormously amused by children, his nieces and nephews being the specimens examined most frequently. Brother Ted's children came home from a summer at a western dude ranch, dropping "hell"s and "damn"s like cowboys on the trail. They were taken to Mineola to the county fair and auto races and returned to regale their uncle with a gleeful report on the outing: three bad accidents had occurred during the afternoon, and sixteen people had been carted off to the hospital. All this intelligence and more was imparted to Baltimore.

Ogden also wrote more about his friends. He went to the Yates Satterlees for dinner, and they played the gramophone: "Moanin' Low" and "I've Got a Feeling I'm Falling," both tunes of the day that he associated with Frances.

One lovely October day Nash took the Baltimore & Ohio line down to Baltimore for a weekend, to settle his relationship with Miss Leonard, but three days later he was back in New York. Nothing was settled. He was writing his letters again, trying to be bright and witty, yet trying, too, to impress her with his worth. He mooned around the Garden City office that first morning back, getting nothing done, until finally Christopher Morley showed up at noon and expansively declared a picnic. Morley, Ogden, and Charles Duell, who had joined Doubleday, all went over to the delicatessen of a gentleman named Lloyd B. Kleinfelder and purchased apples and cheese and sardines. They then drove in Morley's automobile to a spot on the drive of the Garden City Cathedral, to hold their picnic. From the inner precincts they were observed as they frolicked in the sunshine on the grassy sward, and soon along came a cop. He had, he announced, been summoned by someone from within, probably the bishop, to eject these vagabonds from the sacred grounds.

Driven from the temple, they went peacefully from the quiet of God's vineyard to a house of the devil: they drove ten miles to a speakeasy roadhouse, where they finished their lunch and quaffed illegal beer and ate pretzels to make them thirstier. After a suitable interval, they started back for the literary clime of Garden City. But Morley's automobile's gasoline gauge had broken some time earlier, and he had dismissed the need for it with a sneer; now, two miles from the nearest service station the car ran out of gas. Charles Duell and Ogden got out and walked to a station, where the owner lent them an old gallon cider jug and filled it up with green gasoline. They got back to the office at four o'clock.

Did these tales of Ogden's adventures, related day after day to his lady love in Baltimore, and accompanied by averments of the greatest devotion, did they soften the heart of the lady?

No one knew, least of all Ogden, who that fall alternated between ecstasy and despair, dependent on the whim of the object of his love.

Perhaps only semirequited love was good for a poet. Anyhow, that fall Ogden began something new. He wrote a poem in praise of John J. Hessian, a faithful Doubleday executive at Garden City, in which Ogden rhymed brink with Inc., much to Longwell's surprise and delight. Longwell never said "Oggie Nash" was a good poet—quite to the contrary, he regarded Nash's poetry as inspired idiocy—but he liked it. One day in November 1929, Commander Richard Evelyn Byrd made history. The year before, Byrd had gone down to Antarctica, bent on duplicating in the south his feat of flying over the North Pole, and established a base camp on the Bay of Whales in the Ross Sea. He called it Little America. Byrd was a good showman; he had taken an Eagle Scout along with him to Antarctica; that was the sort of dramatic publicity stroke that he managed well. All during the winter of 1928–29 and the spring and summer the Byrd Expedition's exploits had been front-page news in America. On November 29, 1929, Byrd announced that he and a crew of three did fly their Fokker trimotor aircraft over the pole. America went wild with the news.

News of that thrilling nature was needed just then to take people's minds off their very real troubles. The stock market had shown some tremors in the spring of that year, the first indications that the marvelous long-lived boom might be faltering. But the bulls ignored the signs, and scarcely a bear dared walk down Wall Street, so great was national euphoria. It was the same in publishing; nearly anything Doubleday could bring out, Ogden could sell to a well-heeled public that was floating happily along on margin. Then came "Black Friday," October 29, and stocks suddenly dropped like rocks; in short order the market lost 26 *billion* dollars, at a time when most people did not even know what a billion was.

It was too early to tell what effect the financial panic would have on publishing, but the auguries were not good, and on this November 29, a Saturday afternoon, Russell Doubleday, one of the older members of the family, had asked Dan Longwell and his assistant, young Mr. Nash, to play golf with him at the Piping Rock club and talk a little shop. The game over, the threesome repaired to the nineteenth hole, where they heard over the radio the news of Byrd's remarkable feat. Inspired by the quality of the gin at this rich man's playground, Ogden scribbled a bit of verse on a scorecard. Dan Longwell and Mr. Doubleday read it and laughed. When they left the bar, Dan Longwell had possession of the doggerel, but that was not important; the verse was just a bit of Ogden's jokery.

The next morning Ogden picked up the *New York World*, then the city's leading newspaper. The left-handed column of the front page was always devoted to "The Conning Tower," Franklin P. Adams's daily column about life in the big city, easily the most popular column of its sort in the country.

There in the middle of F.P.A.'s daily stint was Ogden's poem about Admiral Byrd.

And right along with the poem was the name of the author, Ogden Nash.

4

O Underrequited Love!

The poem about Admiral Byrd's exploits at the South Pole was not the last of Ogden Nash's contributions to Adams's column.

After Dorothy Parker wrote "Men seldom make passes . . ." Ogden thought of a further note and wrote a response about a girl, rhyming spectacled and neckticled, bassinets and fascinets.

Not very good, not very funny, but a new sort of rhyming that once again hit F.P.A.'s column.

There was more like this, quite a bit more at the end of 1929. Some of it appeared in "The Conning Tower." Much of it was distributed within Doubleday by what Ogden referred to as The Dan Longwell Benevolent and Protective Association.

"Spring Comes to Murray Hill" was one of these verses, and it did have charm; much later Archibald MacLeish would choose this poem to buttress his contention that Ogden was a real poet and not just a versifier.

SPRING COMES TO MURRAY HILL

I sit in an office at 244 Madison Avenue,
And say to myself You have a responsible job, havenue?
Why then do you fritter away your time on this doggerel?
If you have a sore throat you can cure it by using a good goggeral,
If you have a sore foot you can get it fixed by a chiropodist,
And you can get your original sin removed by St. John the Bopodist,
Why then should this flocculent lassitude be incurable?

Kansas City, Kansas, proves that even Kansas City needn't always be
  Missourible.
Up up my soul! This inaction is abominable.
Perhaps it is the result of disturbances abdominable.
The pilgrims settled Massachusetts in 1620 when they landed on a stone
  hummock.
Maybe if they were here now they would settle my stomach.
Oh, if I only had the wings of a bird
Instead of being confined on Madison Avenue I could soar in a jiffy to Second
  or Third.

Mr. MacLeish wrote that the poem gave him a glimpse of the city in the background with all its sex and stimuli.

What made the poem, once again, was the ridiculousness of the rhymes, and yet they were totally comprehensible: doggerel and goggeral, chiropodist and St. John the Bopodist, incurable and Missourible, abominable and abdominable.

The simple fact was that a lot of people did not think the rhymes were poetry, but a lot of people thought they were very funny.

So, whatever they were, the lines were creeping through New York, about to launch Ogden Nash on a new career, a fact of which he was blissfully unaware in the last days of 1929.

Late in October 1929, Ogden's love affair with Miss Leonard, if you could then call it that, reached a serious stage. They quarreled again, and he suggested that it might be best if he removed himself from her life for a month or so. Then she could make up her mind about him. Nothing came of that suggestion; perhaps Miss Leonard was warned that even the most ardent lover cools down if immersed in enough cold water.

Although Ogden's personal life at the end of 1929 was uncertain and upsetting, he did his work at Doubleday with flair, and his enormous good humor kept him afloat in his sea of yearning.

In the 1920s the relationship between publisher and author was close and personal. Publishers published authors, not books, in those days. Later the trade would seem to move to focus on selling subsidiary rights, not books; the success of hardcover books would then hinge on hit-and-run tactics, with the backlist consigned to the shredding machine, and the devil take the author whose last book did not make a profit large enough to please the accounting department.

A publisher had to wear many hats to please the public and comfort authors, the latter a notoriously paranoid and difficult subrace, some given to bouts with the bottle, some needing handholding, and the ladies often demanding escorts when adrift in New York. One of Dan Longwell's hats was an opera topper, one of those folding ingeniousities of the haut monde. He wore it while escorting Doubleday authoress Edna Ferber to the first night of the musical *June Moon*. When the show had ended and Miss Ferber and Mr. Longwell stood up to go, he snapped open his hat with a flourish. The resulting POP so unnerved Miss Ferber that she fell into the lap of former governor Al Smith.

Ogden was not yet slated for such rarified atmospheres, but he did have his own sphere. Late in October he was a speaker at an association of booksellers dinner. Mrs. Doubleday snagged him and Dan Longwell as extra men for a party given in honor of authoress Ellen Glasgow's sister-in-law—that's how complete the author-publisher relationship could be. The party was held at the very fashionable Park Lane Hotel on Park Avenue.

A parade of people as variegated as an anthropological chart passed through Ogden's business life. He was called upon to entertain an enfant terrible, Bayard Schindel, who, at twenty-one, had published his first novel with Doubleday. *Golden Pilgrimage*, it was. Herr Schindel wore spats and carried a cane, and his object, Ogden discerned, was to get drunk. Ogden's objective was to get home as soon as possible in as dry a condition as possible. Herr Schindel arrived for the appointment a little late and a little blowsy. He then told Ogden that he had just returned from Washington where he was doing research on his next novel, and that there he had met the Minister of Siam, a gentleman who owed his job to his close association with the Queen of Siam, so close that the King of Siam had decided the best place for the gent was Washington.

What tales, what gossip that young author did have! He told how Blanche Knopf had gone to London seeking the American rights to Radclyffe Hall's *The Well of Loneliness*, the then shocking expose of Ms. Hall's lesbianism. The book's publication in England had unleased a flurry of editorial excitement that circled the world. The author gave Mrs. Knopf tea, and as they were sipping, Ms. Hall said they might as well talk about the book contract Mrs. Knopf wanted.

Mrs. Knopf was a grande dame, no less. She looked around the room, caught sight of a dowdy woman typing in the corner and demurred. She never, she said, never talked business where the servants could overhear. The dowdy person in the corner smiled, stopped typing, got up, curtsied, and left the room. The negotiations then became a little cloudy, for the dowd Blanche Knopf had sent away was Lady Trowbridge, Mrs. Hall's girlfriend.

Such tales as these occupied most of the talk between bites, and, in Herr Schindel's case, sips. Then Herr Schindel insisted that Ogden accompany him to a Spanish speakeasy. There he began ordering cocktails, and it was only when Herr Schindel had achieved his aim that Ogden was able to disentangle himself and achieve his own.

In between business duties, Ogden was not above a certain low humor in addressing his difficulties with Miss Leonard. One day he sent her a clipping from one of the New York dailies:

JEALOUS FIANCE KILLS GIRL
WHO DELAYS WEDDING

Shoots as She Pleads
In Jersey Home;
Tries to End Own Life,
But Pistol Fails.

Ogden was doing very well with Doubleday. Through a young woman named Natalie Peters he made a real splash. Natalie's father was the foremost collector of Currier and Ives prints in America, and while lavishing a certain attention on Miss Peters, a matter he brought to Miss Leonard's attention, Nash persuaded Mr. Peters to write a book illustrated by the prints. It was a very limited edition, only 350 copies, at $40 a copy. Within a few days it was totally subscribed, and Doubleday had a nice little profit before publication, which any publisher would say was just the way to do it. Even before the book was published other collectors were offering $150 a copy.

Nelson Doubleday sent Ogden up to Canada to see Rufus King, a Doubleday author who was just then being wooed by several other New York publishers. Ogden and King got on famously, the fire was put out, Rufus King remained in the Doubleday fold, and Ogden emerged a minor hero.

He was promoted away from The Crime Club to edit general books and gave his old job to Malcolm Johnson, handing over the authors, one after another, at luncheons given in speakeasies and roadhouses.

Out of the picnic luncheon that began on the lawn of the Garden City Cathedral emerged a more formal association of merrymakers. Christopher Morley was the progenitor of the "club," sometimes named the Nassau and Suffolk County Devilled Ham and Lake Ronkonkoma Club. It had two rules: one must never go to Lake Ronkonkoma, and one must do all merrymaking on Doubleday, Doran & Co.'s time. The members were President Morley, Dan Longwell, Charles Duell, and Ogden Nash, permanent secretary pro tem, whose task it was to keep the notes. That year and the next the club held several meetings, usually in roadhouses or with the liquid refreshment purchased in roadhouses.

In line of duty, Ogden dined with playwright Dubose Heyward, who was just finishing a new play. Doubleday was talking about bringing out some of his books in presentation copies, those elegantly bound leather and gilt editions that commanded large sums of money for publishers. Heyward balked; he didn't want any such for at least twenty years, and then only if people were still reading his books, a future which he doubted very much. (How right he was.)

A day or so later, Prosper Buranelli showed up at Ogden's New York office again. Prosper was tired of being the great unseen spook and wanted to write something on his own. He proposed a book on the backstage doings of the Metropolitan Opera. To sell his project, he told Ogden a tale.

The great tenor Enrico Caruso and Giovanni Martinelli, the baritone, were appearing that season. One night in a poker game Caruso played Martinelli what the latter thought was a dirty trick. The next night they appeared together in *Il Trovatore*. At one point just before a Caruso aria, the staging called for the two to clasp hands. They did, and then Martinelli withdrew, leaving the stage to Caruso for his usual triumph. He also left a raw egg in the tenor's hand. Tights. No pockets. No statuary or cornices or any place to deposit the gift. Caruso had to sing through his great number, egg in hand, something of an obstacle to his usual grandiloquent gestures.

Ogden thought the story amusing but after four years in publishing, he had acquired his share of caution. Buranelli was a fine ghost, but as an author in his own right . . . ? Ogden changed the subject. Why didn't Buranelli do a book on their friend Moneta, who had made so much money in his restaurant on Mulberry Street that he had built a mansion on Long Island, which he filled with parrots and monkeys? Buranelli then began to tell stories about Moneta, and he finally went away to think about the matter.

Christmas came in 1929, and Ogden was in New York, Miss Leonard in Baltimore. That was true of New Year's Eve, too. Ogden spent the evening of the 31st in Malcolm Johnson's apartment working out ideas for another publishing venture and he got home to Manhattan just in time to ring the old year out.

But two days later he had good news. Just as Ogden Nash had discovered *The New Yorker*, *The New Yorker* discovered Ogden Nash. Harold Ross knew something unique when he saw it, and Nash's irreverent, but never sloppy, use of the English language was something to behold.

What struck Harold Ross and the others on *The New Yorker* staff was a poem Ogden then called "Smoot."

The poem stemmed from a news item declaring that Senator Smoot of Utah was declaring war on improper books.

Senator Smoot was the Republican Senator from Ut.

Ogden told Smoot to lay on, to smite smut.

INVOCATION
("Smoot Plans Tariff Ban on Improper Books"—NEWS ITEM)

Senator Smoot (Republican, Ut.)
Is planning a ban on smut.
Oh root-ti-toot for Smoot of Ut.
And his reverent occiput.

Smite, Smoot, smite for Ut.,
Grit your molars and do your dut.,
Gird up your l—ns,
Smite h-p and th-gh,
We'll all be Kansas
By and by.

Smite, Smoot, for the Watch and Ward,
For Hiram Johnson and Henry Ford,
For Bishop Cannon and John D., Junior,
For Governor Pinchot of Pennsylvunia,
For John S. Sumner and Elder Hays
And possibly Edward L. Bernays,
For Orville Poland and Ella Boole,
For Mother Machree and the Shelton pool.
When smut's to be smitten
Smoot will smite
For G-d, for country,
And Fahrenheit.

Senator Smoot is an institute
Not to be bribed with pelf;
He guards our homes from erotic tomes
By reading them all himself.
Smite, Smoot, smite for Ut.,
They're smuggling smut from Balt. to Butte!
Strongest and sternest
Of your s-x
Scatter the scoundrels
From Can. to Mex.!

Smite, Smoot, for Smedley Butler,
For any good man by the name of Cutler,
Smite for the W.C.T.U.,
For Rockne's team and for Leader's crew,
For Florence Coolidge and Admiral Byrd,
For Billy Sunday and John D., Third,
For Grantland Rice and for Albie Booth,
For the Woman's Auxiliary of Duluth,
Smite, Smoot,
Be rugged and rough,
Smut if smitten
Is front-page stuff.

Smoot's smiting of smut had been sent to *The New Yorker* in December and had made its way to the editor's desk and had been accepted. The magazine editors informed the hopeful poet that the verse had been accepted, would run in an early issue, and they sent him $22. It was his first sale since 1926, largely, as he noted in a very satisfied letter to Frances, because he had not written anything for sale except four morbid short stories ("The Spinks," for one) which had gone nowhere.

Now, in 1930, the world of authorship beckoned again, for the Smoot poem suggested that this young man had the makings of a satirist, which was right down *The New Yorker*'s alley.

Ogden Nash still yearned to write deathless prose, even though he had not changed his mind about publishing as a career. Even as he banked the check, he was writing a sketch that he thought very amusing and was counting the money *The New Yorker* would pay.

Miss Leonard had again asked him to stop writing her so much, and a hurt young man had agreed. He had tried to hold his emotions, but his love and yearning were so great, and his desire to share with her his successes, that he had succumbed. She did not seem to be favorably impressed.

Now Ogden tried his best not to annoy her, and it was easier because he had just received a new promotion at Doubleday and was extremely busy. The company had created a New Books division. Malcolm Johnson was to be publisher of the books of new authors, and Ogden Nash was to be editor in charge of all new authors coming into Doubleday. The challenge was to bring in the comers, those who would line the coffers with gold. There was no pay increase, but a promise that if the new project worked, after three months there would be more money.

But there was another emolument. As Nash put it, he was to get three hours a day more for his life by working only in New York and going to Garden City perhaps once a month for meetings.

The promotion seemed to bring a new confidence to Ogden. He showed a new spunk in his relations with Miss Leonard. He was not going to write her any more letters unless he got letters, he announced. When he did write, there was less mooning and more talk of poker games at the Harvard Club with Dan Longwell and Malcolm Johnson and of a much busier social life. One day he was off to a tea given by George Doran for Hugh Walpole, and then he was taking a countess out to dinner. The next day he lunched with Thorne Smith, just then one of America's most popular humorous novelists.

Ogden was gaining weight for the first time in his adult life. He knew what was wrong, and he sought a counter for it; he took a very attractive girl out to see how it would go, a girl he had once seen quite often. It didn't work. He tried again a week later, taking another girl to Hoboken to Christopher Morley's theater and to dinner. It was no go, he wrote Frances a little sadly, as if he wished it had worked. But he had been bored with the latest attractive girl. The encounter had proved to him that he was stuck. He did suggest that Frances might like him better if he had given her reason to doubt him.

At this point, enjoying a growing professional success, Nash became more than a little annoyed with Miss Leonard, and it showed. He had learned, he said, how to have romance without marriage. He was, he said, on the top of the world of men, and that was something Frances would · know nothing about. And he told her she was decorative but not nearly so useful as a Mergenthaler linotype machine or a Fordson tractor, or even a pocket compass.

The annoyance continued, and so did his reports of an ever growing self-importance. Miss Leonard was writing once a week, which she considered to be quite enough. His disagreement with that contention was brought out in a sarcastic remark that he hoped she was not overdoing. Perhaps, he said, some placid workman might be more her sort.

The romance had reached a crisis stage.

5

The Golden Trashery
of Ogden Nashery

INTROSPECTIVE REFLECTION

I would live all my life in nonchalance and insouciance
Were it not for making a living, which is rather a nouciance.

To a reader in the 1990s, the $22 that Ogden Nash received from *The New Yorker* for his first accepted contribution may seem a pittance, but in 1930 the sum would buy half a dozen Brooks Brothers button-down collar shirts of the famous oxford-cloth Egyptian long staple cotton night-shirt variety. Small wonder then that he walked a little above the New York pavements.

He was now very definitely in the swim of publishing, having achieved the full-fledged grade that would later be known as senior editor. He was invited to the Dutch Treat Club, an organization of publishers and publicists for the most part, a Manhattan luncheon club of such prestige that it could command an Admiral Byrd or yearning politico Al Smith to address the lunchers without charge. This week Smith's campaign manager, Muriel Draper, was the speaker, and it just happened that she was under contract to do a book for Doubleday. In a few months, all being equal, Ogden might aspire to an invitation to membership in this organization of shooting stars.

He was constantly broadening his acquaintance: Mignon G. Eberhart, the mystery writer, came his way. So did Doc Shores, an old gunfighter from the West, who arrived in New York with white mustache and goatee, blue eyes sparkling above black frock coat, string tie, and carrying a Pullman bag full of stories about his days as sheriff in various Western communities. There he had captured more than his share of desperados, including Alfred Packer, the gent who started across the High Sierra with friends and then used them as antipasto before the journey was out.

He met a lady who insisted that Doubleday should publish her book, which advocated the abolition of America and marriage. Considering Miss Leonard, that latter thesis gave Ogden something to think about.

Doubleday in 1930 was growing fast. The world depression that followed the 1929 stock market crash was just getting under way, but instead of hurting the sale of hardcover books, the economic doldrums seemed to help. Perhaps more people were giving up expensive outside entertainments and staying home to read. At Doubleday one new idea followed another, and not all of them were equally accepted by the growing corps of executives. Ogden sensed that Doubleday was becoming polarized into two camps, and he could see that eventually he—and Dan Longwell and Malcolm Johnson—would have to cast his lot with Nelson Doubleday, the aggressive young leader of the family and of the Garden City group, or with the New York faction.

The dangers Ogden faced were apparent to him, and he began thinking a little about an escape hatch. Just then, February 1930, he had an offer from his friend and schoolmate John Farrar, to join the new publishing firm of Farrar & Rinehart. But he was not to be stampeded. The Nash position at Doubleday was still secure, if not as comfortable as it had been, and it would take good prospects and cold hard cash to stir him.

That Farrar life ring suspended for the moment, Ogden again concentrated his attention on his main job, acquiring books for Doubleday. This "new book" division of Doubleday involved the sort of publishing that made old conservative bookmen shudder. Much of what was coming out of it was "made books," as opposed to "natural books." The latter meant novels; the works of philosophers, professionals, and politicians; histories; biographies; and the lengthened exposés of magazine writers.

Ogden was guilty of adding his share to this new potpourri, which he termed "commercial lines." In March he was struck by an idea involving author Milt Gross, whom he termed the champion Jewish dialectician. Gross had published *Nize Baby*, an exhibition of his Jewish-American English rhetorical craft, and illustrated it himself with outrageous drawings. Nash wanted to sign the author to do a parody of the new genre of "picture novels" that were then popular, and he suggested that Doubleday could sell 50,000 copies in hardcover. That was a lot of copies, but hardcover books in those days *did* sell a lot of copies. Christopher Morley's *Thunder on the Left* had sold 75,000 copies. Of course, that was a real book, but Doubleday had high hopes that the "made book" could be sold as well as the real one.

As editor of the new books division, it was Ogden's responsibility to push his line to the booksellers, and this meant making appearances before various groups to tout the works. It also meant luncheons, such as the two and a half hours spent with Russell Davenport, later of *Fortune*, trying to find a name for Davenport's new book, and it meant lunches with agents. One day he took a lady agent named Baumgarten to lunch and came away with the hope that he had snagged five new authors for Doubleday. That was the name of the game.

Then it was back to the office to write copy for a Doubleday biography of Hetty Green, the tough and wealthy wolf bitch of Wall Street, which Doubleday was going to offer at the high price of $5 a copy.

The world was Ogden's raw material. One day he was lunching with Thorne Smith, the comic novelist. The next he was out for a malted milkshake with Helen Hokinson, the artist who drew for *The New Yorker* hilarious cartoons of New York suburban *Frauen* descending on the city on matinee Wednesdays to huddle over glutinous concoctions at such spas as Chock-full-o'-Nuts. He got a cartoon book out of her.

He was being quoted more and more by the columnists as he peddled Doubleday's wares, handed out first copies in the presence of photographers, and revealed new nuggets of Doubleday's mining of the literary marketplace.

He submitted more to *The New Yorker*, three prose pieces and a poem. They bought the poem but sent back the prose, much to Ogden's disappointment. But his sunny nature could not be held down. A day or two later he had new success. He met once more with Thorne Smith, and this time he signed up the author, who was being pursued also by Little, Brown, Harper Brothers, Cape and Smith, Brewer and Warren, and Farrar & Rinehart. It had taken him two months of wooing to do the job, but he had conquered, and Doubleday would publish the next Thorne Smith book.

That spring Christopher Morley suggested that Ogden really ought to write a book himself. As it so often was, publishers were of faint heart about their own kind and had evolved what was more or less of an ethic: a book by a publisher was offered to a different publisher. In that way if it was a flop, the publisher could still live in his own house without hearing the guffaws. Morley wrote a letter to Richard Simon, one of the partners in the new, very aggressive house of Simon & Schuster, suggesting that Nash's poesy deserved a wider audience than it was getting in Doubleday, in "The Conning Tower," and even in the exposure in *The New Yorker*, which was, after all, very much an "in" magazine for the cognoscenti of the

city and just beginning to spread its wings west of the Hudson, via the college crowd.

The successes of winter and early spring got Ogden's writing juices
stirred up, and he was now producing more. Early in May he wrote four
new poems. The writing process was painstaking. Despite the mechanical
advantage he regained from that touch-typing course pressed on him in
his mother's gloom over his myopia, Ogden wrote on the yellow legal-size
sheets of foolscap that graced all publishing meetings and usually he wrote
in pencil in a legible, ninety degree hand. He would start out with a concept or a word, usually scribbled in the margin, and add more thought
germs in the margin as he went along. He would then move off to the page
proper and put down a line. If that worked, he would write another and if
they fit together well he would go on. Sometimes they did not work, in
which case he stumbled and struggled with the rhyme and the versifica-
tion and the sense until he solved the problem. If he could not resolve the
matter he would abandon the sheet and start a new one.

Ogden produced in batches and then sent them off. Two of the four
poems he sent to *The New Yorker* this time were accepted.

One was "Ethnological Reflection," four lines considering the sort of
breakfast the British liked, kippers and marmalade. The other was "Introspective Reflection," which noted that having to work to make a living was
a great nuisance. The charm of this poem was his rhyming of insouciance
with nouciance.

With those appearances in *The New Yorker*, Ogden came to the attention
of a number of magazine editors. The Hearst magazines wrote, asking for
material. A few weeks after his May submission *The New Yorker* asked why
he wasn't sending more. He sent them the poems "Bernarr MacFadden"
and "Philo Vance." The former was about a physical fitness expert of the
sort whose advertisements in the pulp magazines (like those of Charles
Atlas) usually featured a handsome hunk of manhood in trunks with
bulging biceps and the waistline of a ballet dancer showing off for some
lissome creature in a bathing suit on the beach. And sometimes, nearby
was a scrawny, pimpled youth. The biceps might even be shown throwing
sand into the face of the scrawny youth. And the copy suggested that any
ninety-seven-pound weakling could become a beach star by following Mr.
MacFadden's course of physical fitness. Mr. MacFadden's particular
advertising was noteworthy because the machismo figure in the ads was
he, himself, a man with a torso that had to be a weightlifter's dream.

The Philo Vance of the second bit of verse was the wealthy, almost insuf-
ferably urbane fictional detective hero of a whole series of stories by S. S.
Van Dine that had captured the American mystery readers' imagination.
Ogden thought these stories were pretentious and said so by suggesting
that Philo Vance needed a kick in the behind.

And that more or less summed up Ogden Nash's feelings for the genre of books through which he had broken into editing at Doubleday.

Ogden yearned to write straight prose. Perhaps prompted by his memories of Dr. Jack, he wrote that he thought was a very funny prose sketch about a quack doctor and sent it off to *The New Yorker*, which was now buying his poems in batches. But the quack came back with a note from the editors telling Ogden that he was their favorite poet. There was a message there.

As the depression deepened, the Doubleday executives sought ways to assure their continued profitability. Nelson Doubleday came up with a new scheme: they had been selling their general line of books for two dollars and two dollars and a half a copy. Now they would cut the price to a dollar. The idea was revolutionary, and it stirred up the whole New York office, since it meant changing every aspect of their publishing, from the quality of the paper to the cost of the advertising.

There were ups and there were downs. Thorne Smith came through beautifully with his new manuscript. But somehow Doubleday managed to lose P. G. Wodehouse's confidence to the extent that his next book went elsewhere, and Ogden was closely enough connected with the disaster to feel a personal sense of responsibility.

By midsummer it was apparent that Ogden had cast his lot with the Nelson Doubleday faction of the firm. He went to Nelson's summer place on Long Island Sound for relaxation, which included dashing about in a speedboat. When George Doran returned on the *Olympic* from Europe, Nelson sent Ogden down to meet him. Ogden was also growing much closer to *The New Yorker* crowd and was being courted by them. The poetry editor of the magazine was Raymond Holden, and Ogden dined at the Holden apartment frequently in the spring and summer of 1930. Wolcott Gibbs, one of the magazine's brightest young stars, invited him to lunch. A few more sessions, and he was offered either of two jobs at the magazine: to become their book reviewer, or to join the staff in the fall. As part of his courtship by *The New Yorker*, Ogden attended a party at which he met one of his heroes, Robert Benchley. Nash went up to Benchley and introduced himself. He had been waiting a long time to meet the famous author, he said. Benchley replied hello, smiled that guilty smile of his, and then announced that he had to be going—whereupon he got his hat and went off into the night.

Ogden's appearances in the weekly issues of *The New Yorker* now became almost regular. Two of the long poems he sold that summer reflected his life and his yearnings. The first was obviously prompted by his half-humorous, half-fretful look at his own romantic situation.

The bits and pieces of Nashiana continued to appear in "The Conning Tower." In one day he had two. They were labelled

From the Golden Trashery
of
Ogden Nashery.

One result of this new spate of exposure of Nash's poesy was a book contract with Simon & Schuster for a collection of *The Golden Trashery*. So he began to work at sorting out those verses that he believed would stand the test of time from those that would not. Despite the topicality of Smoot, which had appeared in *The New Yorker* under the title "Invocation," Ogden included that poem, and he was right to do so. Smoot was really a generic comment on politicians. Certainly some of the names in the verse—Orville Poland and Ella Boole, John S. Sumner, and Elder Hays—soon went the way of all flesh, but it was apparent that Ogden might have chosen any names at all. He might even have selected names from the telephone book, which was one of his major sources of inspiration. Ogden's purpose was to show that Senator Smoot was smiting smut because it was front-page "news." As long as politicians remained the same, Ogden's verse would still be topical.

In midsummer 1930, *The New Yorker* editors reported to Ogden that they were receiving works imitating his style at the rate of three and four submissions each day, but they were turning them all down and wanted a steadier supply of the real thing. Ogden was hard put to deliver just then. In answer to Miss Leonard's standoffishness, he was carrying on a furious summer social life, which involved long weekends in the country, going from one house party to another, trips across Long Island Sound in motorboats, Japanese-lanterned garden evenings that lasted until 4:30 A.M., and brunches and teas and dinners.

He was asked to meet the editors of *Vanity Fair* and did. He got invited to lunch and stayed. They asked for poems and prose pieces, and he promised to produce.

It was nice to be wanted.

As if realizing that their favorite poet was about to expand his circle of customers, the editors of *The New Yorker* raised his rate from 75 cents to $1.00 a line. And a day or so later, Donald Friede said he had been following Ogden's poems in *The New Yorker* and asked Ogden to produce a book of poems for his own publishing house, Covici Friede. There was also a letter from Burtin Rascoe, of Robert McBride Publishers, suggesting a similar project. Those letters showed clearly the influence of *The New Yorker* on the tight little society of arts and letters in New York.

But with Ogden, it was no go. He had already signed with Simon & Schuster, and the book was in the works.

It was, indeed, nice to be wanted, in New York if not in Baltimore, and

Ogden let Miss Leonard know just that. For now it was a year since the famous house party at George Elliman's family's place on the island, and Ogden's romance with Miss Leonard seemed to be deteriorating by the month.

He had been a very patient man. Now he was beginning to show real signs of independence. The letters to Baltimore had a certain stony underlay that ought to have an effect, unless Miss Leonard either was under a negative influence, or did not give a damn.

SEDATIVE REFLECTION

Let the love-lorn lover cure insomnia
By muttering AMOR VINCIT OMNIA.

6

Poet or Publisher?

In September 1930 there were, in effect, two Ogdens. One was the ebullient young editor, doing his job with real enthusiasm. Just after the first of the month Lowell Thomas, one of Doubleday's most successful authors, called up. He had written *Von Luckner: The Sea Devil*, a book about one of Germany's famous raider captains of World War I. He previously had done a book about Lawrence of Arabia and books about other adventurers which had earned him and Doubleday a small fortune. This day Lowell Thomas was all in a swivet. He had just been offered a radio tryout by CBS for a job as a news commentator.

That was good news, said Ogden.

But the tryout was *tonight!* What did Ogden know about radio, and what was Lowell Thomas to do?

Ogden knew nothing about radio except that he listened to it, mostly to the Harvard football games. But an author in need was not to be ignored, and so he met Thomas at the Princeton Club, they took over the boardroom, and Thomas practiced a radio presence all day long with Ogden's assistance. That evening, around five o'clock, Ogden escorted Lowell to the CBS building and stayed with him through the ordeal. There was, of course, no immediate answer from William Paley, scion of a Philadelphia tobacco family whose daddy had bought him CBS. So Ogden went off to dine with Dan Longwell and take in the premiere of Stephen Vincent Benét's movie *Abraham Lincoln,* because Benét was coming in the next day, and they thought they had best be informed.

The next night he had a 700-page manuscript by T. S. Stribling to approve and start through the publishing processes. So there was no chance for any writing of his own.

That deprivation was a problem for Ogden number two, who was eager to get on with his own work as writer. Because of the busy fall publishing schedule, and his inability to produce, publication of the Simon & Schuster book had to be delayed until January. At least that was part of the reason. The other part was that *The New Yorker* had bought from Ogden that summer more material than it could immediately digest. One issue a week is only fifty-two times a year, and the poems had piled up. *The New Yorker* still had eight unpublished, and Simon & Schuster wanted those for the book, rather than any new, untried verse that their author might produce. Success, they knew, begat success, and the publication of the poems by *The New Yorker* would only whet the appetite of the sophisticated public to whom this book was going to appeal.

September 8 was to be a turning point in Ogden's life.

He woke up bright and vigorous as was his habit these days, and he was in the office at the appointed hour, before ten o'clock when the wheels of publishing really began to grind. He had a visit from the agent of the French aviator Diendonne Coste that morning. The great man was about to begin a goodwill tour of the United States, which meant traveling to the most important metropolitan centers, accepting keys to various cities, making speeches, getting his name and photo into the papers and plenty of hoopla from every source of publicity. The author's tour, as such, had not yet been invented, but it was obvious to any right-thinking publisher that here was an opportunity to cash in on what was not yet then known as a media event, or a series of them. What was needed was a book. Without a flinch, Ogden lined up Coste's agent for a book. By two o'clock in the afternoon they had a ghostwriter who promised to deliver the manuscript in six days. Doubleday could actually get it printed and bound within another week or two—those were the days!—and books could then be shipped and would be available along the trail as M. Coste made his triumphant journey.

But maybe someone in Doubleday's circle of authority came in with a hangover that day. Maybe Ogden was the victim of the crosscurrents he had sensed earlier. Maybe someone thought young Mr. Nash was growing a little large for his britches, for at three o'clock that afternoon, the executive publishing committee hurriedly assembled, heard Editor Nash's proposition, and fell to argument. No agreement could be reached, and that meant the book was rejected. It left Nash to pick up the pieces with agent, author, and celebrity.

It seemed to Nash a complete betrayal.

Ogden was still in shock when the telephone rang. It was Harold Ross, editor of *The New Yorker*, and he wanted Ogden to come over and see him immediately, if possible.

So Ogden announced that he was going for a walk. He left his office, went down the six flights in the elevator, and wandered across town to *The New Yorker*'s building on West 43rd Street. As he walked and reviewed the events of the day, fury replaced the shock, and by the time he reached Editor Ross's office, he was ready to listen to any proposition at all.

Ross offered him a job as managing editor of *The New Yorker*. He was to get a thousand dollars a year more than Doubleday was paying him. He would be in charge of all departments of the magazine: books, theater, movies, sports, reports, music, shopping. He would be sure that the right people did the work and that they did it the right way. He would rewrite when that was needed, and he was to contribute writing of his own and be paid extra for it.

What aspiring young writer who had experience as an editor would not find *that* a challenge?

Ogden was canny enough to ask a few questions. Why him? Didn't Ross have a dozen aspirants for such a responsible post?

Ah, said Ross, that was the rub. He had really had another man in mind, until he discovered that the other fellow was an optimist. That news had changed Ross's mind; times were too hard for *The New Yorker* to afford an optimist in the office. And he had been thinking about Ogden. In fact, he said, one of Ogden's recent verses had passed across his desk, and he had thought it was very funny. He had showed it to Marc Connelly, the playwright, and Connelly had said no, he didn't think it was funny. And so Ross had to admit that he'd looked at it again and didn't think it was funny either. But that didn't make any difference for he had gotten hold of another Nash verse that he was sure was very funny, and nobody had talked him out of it. He was about to send that to Connelly with a warning that he had better think it was funny.

Angry as Ogden was with Nelson Doubleday and the Doubleday publishing committee for letting him down, he knew that this was the most important career decision that he had ever faced. He temporized. He needed time to think it over, he said. And that is how it was left for the next few days.

Ogden departed from *The New Yorker* offices perplexed. He went back to his own office and thought about things for an hour. He went home and wrote a letter to Frances, setting down the events of the day and the problem.

The next day, Ogden went out to Garden City to talk to Nelson Doubleday. But Nelson was about to leave for Europe for two months, and this was no time to begin what might develop into a battle. So Ogden talked to others, in a guarded sort of way. They all told him he would be a fool to forsake publishing and his six years of experience and knowledge and contacts for the magazine world about which he knew nothing.

That argument was persuasive, although not quite in the manner that the Doubleday people might have hoped. The short shrift over M. Coste had ripped asunder the bonds of loyalty, and Ogden was now thinking of Doubleday in the past tense. Yet he knew inside that *The New Yorker* was not the place for him. What he really wanted was to go into publishing on his own, and he began to discuss this idea with Dan Longwell and Malcolm Johnson, his closest friends at Doubleday. The three of them assessed their own strength, which was the authors they could take with them. It looked good; they could bring people whose records indicated that the income they'd generate in a year would be half a million dollars.

But . . .

There was the small problem of capital. None of the three had any money other than their earnings.

Ogden had many friends and acquaintances in the Newport set, people who did not have to consider how much it cost to operate their yachts. So he took a long weekend to go to Newport, and he renewed acquaintance with the moneyed. He came back satisfied that when the time came he would be able to raise the backing.

The absence of Nelson Doubleday removed the pressure for the moment, so Nash settled down again to publishing and writing. Theodore Morrison, editor of *The Atlantic Monthly*, asked him for an occasional poem. He particularly liked the Smoot piece.

Vanity Fair had published a story of his. Finally, he thought, he was coming into his own as a writer of prose. Publisher Friede wrote him again, congratulatory and wistful because Covici Friede was not Ogden's publisher. Richard Simon wrote, congratulatory and delighted, because Simon & Schuster was. He wondered if Ogden had any more stories like that up his sleeve, and, if so, offered to bring them out under Simon & Schuster's Inner Sanctum imprint as a book.

In behalf of Doubleday, Nash opened negotiations with George S. Kaufman to publish in book form his successful new play *Once in a Lifetime*. Kaufman was not enthusiastic, but he did not say no.

The romance with Miss Leonard was on dead center, a place where romances do not survive for long. Everyone concerned knew it; something had to be resolved. Perhaps it was Miss Leonard's mother who suggested that the solution was a trip to Europe where the young woman would be freed from all the usual influences and could consider the merits of her beaus and what the future ought to bring her.

It was Ogden's understanding that the wedding was definitely to be staged in June.

THAT REMINDS ME

Just imagine yourself seated on a shadowy terrace,
And beside you is a girl who stirs you more strangely than an heiress.
It is a summer evening at its most superb,
And the moonlight reminds you that To Love is an active verb,
And your hand clasps hers, which rests there without shrinking.
And after a silence fraught with romance you ask her what she is thinking,
And she starts and returns from the moon-washed distances to the shadowy
*   veranda,*
And says, Oh I was wondering how many bamboo shoots a day it takes to
*   feed a baby Giant Panda.*
Or you stand with her on a hilltop and gaze on a winter sunset,
And everything is as starkly beautiful as a page from Sigrid Undset,
And your arm goes round her waist and you make an avowal which for
*   masterfully marshaled emotional content might have been a page of*
*   Ouida's or Thackeray's,*
And after a silence fraught with romance she says, I forgot to order the limes
*   for the Daiquiris.*
Or in a twilight drawing room you have just asked the most momentous of
*   questions,*
And after a silence fraught with romance she says, I think this little table
*   would look better where that little table is, but then where would that little*
*   table go, have you any suggestions?*
And that's the way they go around hitting below our belts;
It isn't that nothing is sacred to them, it's just that at the Sacred Moment
*   they are always thinking of something else.*

Early in October Miss Leonard announced that she and her mother were going for six months. If she expected a complaint from Ogden, she was surprised for he wrote her that he thought it was a good idea, particularly since the winter promised to be pivotal to his career. The note he struck was indeed a new one for the previously prostrate swain, an indication of a stronger Ogden than perhaps Miss Leonard had seen: no protestations of undying love, no pleas for affection, just information about his dealings with George S. Kaufman (they lost the play to another publisher), and about his letters to Robert Benchley and Alexander Woollcott suggesting that they give him a book for Doubleday.

Christopher Morley was just back from Europe that October, having gone there for three months upon the collapse of his Hoboken enterprise. They celebrated his return with what must have been the final meeting of the Nassau and Suffolk Devilled Ham Society and Lake Ronkonkoma Club. At the meeting Morley told Ogden that just before he had gone to

Europe scouting for Doubleday, he had suggested that the company also send Ogden along. The contacts would be invaluable for the future. Everyone had agreed that it was a good idea, and the treasurer had been approached to supply the cash. But at the last minute Nelson Doubleday had stepped in, announced that Nash was needed in New York, and scuttled the plan.

Here, then, was another count in Ogden's indictment of Nelson Doubleday.

With Frances out of reach Ogden found his amusement with family and friends. The Roaring Twenties were over, but the American syndrome of high, wide, and handsome entertainments was not. Ogden's brother Aubrey suggested that they go to New Haven to witness the Yale–Georgia football contest in the second week of October, and they did. It was a thrilling contest with much scoring, and Albie Booth, *the* football hero of the season, played about half the game, which added to Ogden's enjoyment. He had not seen a football game in 1929. Having spent that autumn in close pursuit of Miss Leonard, he had taken his football by radio.

The high amusement of the day, however, was not on the field but in the stands. Ogden thought he saw thousands of drunken Georgians that day, waving Confederate flags and shouting rebel yells. To complicate matters, the American Legion was holding its national convention in these parts, and the Yalies had invited 12,000 Legionnaires and their Auxiliaries to the game. A group sat near the Nash party, and two of the Auxiliaries got so smashed they had to be carried out of the Yale Bowl.

Actually, as Ogden learned on the following Monday from a sober Legionnaire who wandered into Doubleday's offices with a manuscript, the veterans had been convening in Boston and were on their way home. The Yale Bowl fracas had been nothing compared to the Boston experience. For Boston had seen thousands of drunks in blue overseas caps rushing through the streets for nearly a week, turning over cars for "fun" and building fires on the steps of the public library. They drove a cow into the lobby of the Copley Plaza hotel and milked her there. Someone drove a small Austin automobile into the hotel, took it upstairs in an elevator, and drove the car around the halls. They rode fiery steeds through the halls of the Statler Hotel.

Apparently, it was the most alcoholic revel ever staged by the Legion; before it ended five hundred Legionnaires were carted off to Boston hospitals to be treated for alcohol poisoning, and a bootlegger Legionnaire was arrested with more than five hundred bottles of whiskey in his room.

Based on annual performances elsewhere during the 1920s, the Boston hoteliers thought they knew what to expect, and before the horde arrived the Statler had insisted that the Legion post a bond of $50,000 to cover possible damage to property. But when the last Legionnaire had left town, and the insurance adjusters came, they discovered that the veterans had out-done themselves this year. They had virtually wrecked the public rooms of the hotel, and the cost was put at $175,000.

The next weekend, Ogden took off and went to Long Island for one of those typical country weekends at which the American upper crust seemed to be becoming almost as adept as the British.

His friends the Gawtrys lived at Cold Spring Harbor, a posh community on the North Shore of Long Island. The Gawtrys were very much Society. He was a country squirish sort of man, with weathered face and pipe. She was a Van Rensselaer. Their daughters were attractive and marriageable if one wanted a horsey family. One other man and one woman were also at the house that weekend. Ogden had known the girl for years around New-port; she had been a dear pal of his ex-sister-in-law, Ted's first wife. The extra man was an architect in his thirties whose wife was at the moment confined to a loony bin.

Ogden took the train from Pennsylvania Station and arrived at Cold Spring Harbor at about noon. He was picked up and taken off to the West Hills Country Club for lunch. An enormous entertainment was being held there, and apparently anyone who was anyone on Long Island was in attendance. He saw old Mrs. Doubleday and made an impression by find-ing her a table and five chairs when the males of her own party failed. One of the Gawtry daughters was in charge of selling programs, so Ogden car-ried programs around the hall for most of the afternoon.

After lunch the races began. From the top of the hill one could see the races start and finish and look at the lovely yellow and brown and green countryside in between. There were five races and they were most satis-factory to the horsey crowd: five ambulances arrived and carted off the casualties.

The gladiation ended at about 5 P.M. They all drove through the chill evening to the Gawtry house, which was on Huntington Harbor, a big rambling Long Island country house, surrounded by trees and populated by dogs. The Gawtrys were fresh air fiends and they scorned closed autos, so the trip was made in cabriolets with the tops down. When the company arrived, city boys Nash and Shepherd were blue and trembling with the cold. Their host took note and dosed them with copious drafts of old Irish whiskey. Then they all sat down to a splendid high tea with jams and scones and whipped cream. They then all drove to the house of another friend for dinner in an expensive, renovated seventeenth-century Dutch farmhouse. Since the host was a Doubleday executive, Ogden was on familiar ground. There were thirty-five at dinner.

Ogden sat next to a horsey girl, with a horsey old lady on the other side of him, and tried to keep up with the conversation, all spasms and fetlocks.

Ogden listened helplessly for an hour and then tried to make his mark with a story about Adolf Menjou, the actor. But since nobody in this crowed had ever heard of Adolf Menjou, the story fell flat as a saddle blanket, and the talk went back to withers and the blind staggers, and then turned to the minor difficulties of horsiness. He met a very pretty girl named Louise Bedford who admitted that at different times she had broken her hip, leg, ribs, and collarbone.

Ogden could not compete, so he sat silent and listened, drank champagne and tried to fake along as the crowd roared out the song "John Peel."

After dinner they drove another twenty miles to the ball, which was held in the mansion of a gentleman named Robbins. Ogden saw many old friends and acquaintances and had a very good time. They did not get back to the Gawtrys and to bed until 4:45.

On Sunday they got up late and spent the middle of the day in recuperation. Then they drove twenty miles to the house of Reggie Townsend, the editor of *Country Life* magazine. Mrs. Townsend spent part of the evening telling Ogden about her indigestion. Mrs. Townsend's mother had a harp, which she played, and the crowd did some choral singing. Ogden got the train back to Manhattan, where he arrived full of horsey thoughts, mingled with song and harp chords and indigestion.

That next week he went with friends to a speakeasy and there ran into an old girlfriend and her new husband of one month. The husband was blotto, completely passed out. Ogden played the part of Good Samaritan, spent half an hour sobering up the husband so that he could walk, and took them home in a cab. The next night, Ogden took Allen Lane of London's Bodley Head publishing house out to dinner and to see the play *Girl Crazy*. After the show they went to another speakeasy, and there he saw his old girlfriend again, this time *sans mari*.

Such, of course, was all grist for Ogden Nash's poesy mill, and in time these bits and pieces would find their way into his writings. But just now writing was very difficult. Donald Friede took him to lunch and virtually pleaded for a series of stories to make into a book. There was no chance, said Ogden. He had no time. Anomalous as it was, even as he had decided that he must leave Doubleday, his star there had resumed its rise, and he was getting more authors, more success than ever before. He lunched with his new author Sarah Haardt, who was Mrs. H. L. Mencken. He lunched next day with Barry Fleming, a Doubleday novelist who was feeling low. Ogden bucked him up by calling him America's Anatole France.

Down the street, so to speak, Simon & Schuster was pulling out the stops on the publicity organ to give Ogden's book a good ride. Some of the elements were already in place. Edna Ferber, Oliver La Farge, and Dorothy

Parker had all read Ogden's work in *The New Yorker,* and the moment they said they liked it, he had made them promise to reduce that to writing when the time came.

Now, as publication day loomed, the problem was to get a proper title, a matter of enormous importance, and over which Ogden had struggled with a dozen authors in behalf of their own books. Ogden liked *Rancor to Windward.* S & S did not. The publishers liked *The Golden Trashery of Ogden Nashery.* Ogden did not. Dan Longwell suggested *Love among the Republicans.* S & S said that sounded like a political tome.

Finally, Ogden lunched with George Blake, of Faber and Faber, Ltd., of London. Blake said that his house wanted to publish the Simon & Schuster book in Britain and suggested the title *Hard Lines.* By this time all concerned were exhausted, and no one could find any fault with that title. So *Hard Lines* would be it.

November ended. Nelson Doubleday came back from Europe with many tales of publishing derring-do and the doings of Kipling and S. P. Herbert and Edgar Wallace. Ogden had several cautious conversations with his newly returned boss but found nothing in them that would renew the confidence he had lost on September 8.

Meanwhile *The New Yorker* was wooing Ogden in a fast and intensive courtship. Several years earlier, Editor Harold Ross had hired a young socialite named Ralph Ingersoll as a general orderly, or dogsbody as the staff called him. Ingersoll's major asset then was his relationship to High Society, the circulation area that Ross wanted to dominate. Ingersoll was the grandnephew of Ward McAllister, a newspaperman who had become Mrs. Astor's dogsbody, the man who invented the concept of New York's Four Hundred—the only people worth knowing in Society—and who later became the arbiter of that Society.

Ross was always under the impression that if he could only find a proper managing editor to keep the varied talents in line and manage deadlines and the paperwork of publishing, all would be serene. Ralph Ingersoll had not succeeded, but he had made himself so valuable as Ross's flunky that he was not fired. With Ross, the dream remained and a succession of people had come through the doors to be told that the proferred job would be the "hub" of *The New Yorker*'s editorial operation. The job would put the man in charge of sports, The Talk of the Town, Profile, theater, movies, books, fashions, and all else, everything that Ross had now told Ogden he would have.

No one of the staff, of course, told Ogden the truth, that Ross's "hub" men were called geniuses by Ross and Jesuses by the staff, and that each of them lasted just a few weeks before Ross lost his temper and decided that this particular genius was not a genius after all and went on to the next. James Thurber served a term as the "hub," never even told that one of the documents he signed each week was *The New Yorker* payroll, before he escaped to a safer world within the magazine. Ross tried to suborn Wolcott Gibbs and failed, E. B. White was cajoled. Hobart Weekes was enlisted. Arthur Samuels, Bernard Bergman, and Raymond Holden came into the "hub," one after the other. The latter was in office in the fall of 1930. Holden had a fine sense of self-preservation, and he knew that if something did not happen, he might soon be looking at the offices from the outside. Ross had made the offer to Ogden in October, and Holden had been in touch several times to renew it. The more Ogden wriggled and delayed, the more attractive he became to Ross, particularly since Nash's poems were just then being bought by the dozen and were creating a fine stir for the magazine, *and* because Ralph Ingersoll had just told Ross that he was going to quit at the end of the year and go to work for Henry Luce.

Ross pushed the panic button, and Holden then offered Ogden $2,500 a year more than he was making at Doubleday, plus extra payment for everything the magazine bought of his own. At the end of a year he would get a large raise and a stock bonus. He was invited to a party by Wolcott Gibbs. The Holdens had him to dinner again. Ross called him to the office and put on his best manners and most persuasive arguments.

There was still the independent publishing house dreamed of by Ogden, Dan Longwell, and Malcolm Johnson. But the depression was growing markedly worse as winter drew near, and there was no sign of all that big money from Newport. Dan Longwell, too, was growing more restless under the heavy hand of Nelson Doubleday, but without the money the publishing dream could be no more than that. *The New Yorker* offer was real and immediate.

The first of December came and went. Ogden made his decision. He signed up with Harold Ross.

7

Life among the Cognoscenti

December 1930 found Ogden Nash living in the fast lane with very little time to think about his inamorata, who was just then doing museums and churches in Dresden. Dorothy Parker invited the new Ross victim to a party, and he mingled with all his heroes: Benchley, Woollcott, Franklin P. Adams, Marc Connelly, George S. Kaufman, Edna Ferber, and Donald Ogden Stewart. Mrs. Parker called him a hero, which perhaps just then he did not quite understand.

He had a long talk with Adams, who began by announcing that he was receiving scores of poor imitations of Nashery and ended by suggesting that Nash send him some more poems from his trashery.

Not on his tintype, said the life of the party, now quite full of himself, or, perhaps, of Mrs. Parker's gin. F.P.A. didn't pay!

O, fickle poet! Six months earlier the budding author would have given his eye tooth for a mention in "The Conning Tower." Fortunately, Adams laughed, and a difficult moment was past.

Edna Ferber invited Ogden for a weekend in the country.

Simon (Richard) and Schuster (Max) took Ogden to lunch. They cited the encomiums of prepublication praise that were arriving from the world of publicists in New York (most of whom Ogden had buttonholed for favorable comment) and spoke expansively of the advertising campaign they could base on these endorsements. Simon predicted that *Hard Lines* would be a runaway bestseller. They offered him a three-book contract with a $1,000 advance. He said maybe.

The poetry editor of *Vanity Fair* called to ask wistfully why Ogden had never submitted any verse to them. What a delicious moment for an author! He replied that he had submitted two verses several months earlier, and they had been rejected. The crestfallen editor apologized and said "please."

Nelson Doubleday gave a dinner to speed the parting employee. All Ogden's friends from the company were there. They dined on caviar and terrapin and drank champagne. Nelson made a fulsome speech, and the applause came in all the right places. He presented Ogden with the company's parting token, a green-gold cigarette case that had cost more than a month's salary for that particular editor. He also said he wanted Ogden back at Doubleday within five years.

To thank Miss Ferber for the country weekend, Ogden sent her a jar of Beluga caviar, and she sent him a note:

For gents who send me flowers and gin
I have but pleasant looks
I feel no girlish tremors over
Lads who give me books.
But when caviar is sent me by Frederic Ogden Nash
I am swept by wild emotion
Which is nothing short of Pash.*

Three days before Christmas Ogden began his new career as the "hub" of *The New Yorker's* editorial staff. He started with very high hopes. He liked the atmosphere and the people he met and the idea of having a single boss instead of a board of directors who could shoot him down for reasons he considered puerile.

He did admit that his boss, the *genius loci*, was a very strange fellow. Reportedly Harold Ross had been the worst ship's news reporter in San Francisco and the best card shark in the press corps. His hair stuck straight up in a long-neglected brush cut, and his teeth stuck out. His eyes slanted like those of an Oriental, and his shirt collars flapped in a very unBrooks-Brothersy way. Every time Ogden saw Ross, he looked as though he had just swallowed something unpleasant. It was nothing personal, Ross always looked that way. Virtually every conversation would open with Ross's comment, "This magazine is going to hell," and the reason given, of course, was lack of organization. Since Ogden was the squire just knighted to bring organization to the precincts, that was a gentle reminder.

But as everyone said, Ross was a *genius* and that accounted for much. It might have counted for more if the editorial staff had not been heavily populated with geniuses, of which Ogden Nash was just the mostly recently

*© Copyright 1985 by Harriet F. Pilpel as Trustee.

arrived. He was sure he was going to be happy and successful on 43rd Street, although he told Frances he still did not know what he was supposed to do and expected to be just a babe in the woods for the next three months. But the future loomed gloriously behind the fog, and he spoke of buying a pink house with angels on it, and bills to be paid at Bergdorf Goodman, which was *the* female department store for the rich, and, naturally, Miss Leonard's favorite. The bills would be paid from the raises Ogden would get and the stock options and the bonuses and the sale of his writing.

Max Schuster took him to lunch on December 23, and Richard Simon cornered him for dinner. They wanted a new book right away.

Dorothy Parker asked him to take her to a tea that Alexander Woollcott was giving on Christmas eve, and he did, and then took her out to dinner and spent the evening with her.

He had stern orders from Simon & Schuster to go to a studio photographer for suitable promotional pictures, and December 26 found him fretting in the chair of Sherrill Schell for an hour.

At the office Ogden was still confused. Whatever organization there was seemed to stem from his friend Raymond Holden, who appeared to be editor of the special sections, and Mrs. Katherine Angell, a steady and sensible force within this zoo of geniuses, who seemed to be more or less managing everything else. But Ogden reported directly to Editor Ross when he could find him, for Ross hated being bearded in the office, and when he was not wandering about, speaking casually to his geniuses, he spent much of his time in speakeasies carrying on conversations.

"Nobody can ever say I'm not incoherent," Ross once told Robert Benchley, who was then to be seen for several days wandering from speakeasy to speakeasy, chuckling.

But that was actually anything but the case. Ross was, as Janet Flanner put it, an autodidact, which means to one less familiar with *Webster's Second International Dictionary* than Ross or Miss Flanner, someone who is self-taught. His self-teaching had made him one of the sharpest critics of American English usage then going, H. L. Mencken on center stage, notwithstanding. Underneath his rude exterior beat the heart of a professor of linguistics; he was happiest when someone was reading aloud to him from *Roget's Thesaurus of Words and Phrases*. And how he could talk . . .

He was unhappiest when trying to get a new idea across to someone, for he began with the feeling that his attempt to convey it would be a failure; when it was, Ross lapsed into a soliloquy of pain punctuated by four and five letter words. He was, without doubt, the saltiest editor ashore on Manhattan Isle, blasphemous but so chaste that he permitted no overt references to sexual didoes to stain the pages of *The New Yorker*, and one of Ogden's tasks was to expunge from the prose of Mrs. Parker and Mr. Benchley all the double entendres they loved to fabricate.

If Ross was somehow trapped in the office by an outsider and could not hide in the closet, he was likely to be found tinkering with some new invention, such as the electric door lock with buzzer. The idea of the buzzer was to give him protection, even from his workers; he liked to have advance knowledge of his problems and to steel himself to meet them. Unfortunately, none of his inventions worked, and the staff kept popping in to ask questions. This habit, Editor Ross held, precluded Efficiency, and Efficiency must be attained. Efficiency was the watchword of this great shambling concoction of mixed emotions. Ogden did not know it, but he, Ogden Nash, was supposed to be one of those Efficiency Machines, to bring order out of the usual dustbin chaos and especially to bring Mrs. Parker's weekly contribution in on time. She was notorious for dillying and dallying until the very last moment. One of her early excuses for tardiness had been that she had been ready to sit down and do her bit, but at the moment someone else was using the office pencil so she had gone to a speakeasy to wait, and one thing had led to another. That excuse would no longer suffice, for *The New Yorker* had survived the shock its untidy birth dealt the New York community and had wriggled through its growing pains and was making money. Ross, who was continually pessimistic about the future, kept trying to bring in Efficiency.

He gave Ogden some articles to rewrite, and he encouraged Ogden to write some of his own. As the New Year approached, Ogden was bent to these tasks.

But Ogden soon developed half an idea that Ross had hired him because the editor felt he needed a "man about town" and that Ogden's collection of speakeasy admission cards so, but wrongly, identified him. This feeling was intensified as Ogden learned more about the "late" Ralph Ingersoll, who had departed for Time, Inc.'s greener pastures. Ingersoll was indeed a Man About Town. If there was any truth in Nash's contention, and there probably was, for Ross was fascinated by inherited wealth and the people who wore it, then the editor must be forgiven. For Ogden Nash did, indeed, have all the characteristics of the Eastern Seaboard Upper Class: a traceable and impressive lineage, proper boarding school, the right accent, Harvard, and entree to the best clubs, watering holes, and house parties. He was so much the proper New Yorker that when a photographer insisted that he take off his coat for some of the poses in conjunction with the promotion of his book, Ogden objected. Even if they were good, he said, he would never allow them to be used. Photographer Schell artfully assured his unhappy subject that the informal poses were only for his own satisfaction. But when the proofs came back, the shirt-sleeves photos proved to be far the best, and Ogden knew it. He fretted. He did not know what to do, so far removed from gentility was the idea of being caught in dishabille.

Ogden's reverie on that subject was interrupted by the arrival of his first *New Yorker* paycheck, which he mentally compared with glee against what he had been getting from Doubleday just two weeks earlier. He was, he told Frances in that day's letter, growing unutterably greedy.

A belated recognition, that. For several years, at least since he had been contemplating marriage, Ogden had been considering the gap between the rich and everybody else. In his book he had included two poems that addressed the subject. One was called "More About People."

MORE ABOUT PEOPLE

When people aren't asking questions
They're making suggestions
And when they're not doing one of those
They're either looking over your shoulder or stepping on your toes
And then as if that weren't enough to annoy you
They employ you.
Anybody at leisure
Incurs everybody's displeasure.
It seems to be very irking
To people at work to see other people not working,
So they tell you that work is wonderful medicine,
Just look at Firestone and Ford and Edison,
And they lecture you till they're out of breath or something
And then if you don't succumb they starve you to death or something.
All of which results in a nasty quirk:
That if you don't want to work you have to work to earn enough money so
*   that you won't have to work.*

The second, called "Lines Indited with All the Depravity of Poverty" dealt more directly with the author's yearnings: One way to be very happy, said the author, was to be extremely wealthy. Then you could break all the laws you wanted and spend money like water, and undertip and buy horses and get a divorce, and not get up in the morning until nearly noon, and ride on the trains in bedrooms instead of upper berths.

Through word of mouth, advertising, and publicity artfully planted with the various columnists of New York's dozen newspapers (the *World* alone boasted four major columnists), Simon & Schuster had done its best to create an air of excitement in the literary community to greet *Hard Lines.* Just before publication Simon & Schuster informed Ogden that the advance sale was over 2,000 copies, which they considered an excellent start. After that, it was going to be up to the public, who would be guided by the enthusiasm generated by the soothsayers.

On January 8, 1931, Simon & Schuster ran one of its full-column advertisements on the book page of the *New York World* (and other papers). It was a chatty ad, and most of it was devoted to *Hard Lines*, and specifically to a letter from Dorothy Parker to Ogden Nash, written early that fall when she had been in Switzerland.

> I trust you will pardon this intrusion of an old subscriber who used to
> dabble for a living in rhyme as well as vers libre, but has now got
> away from it all owing to a plethora of intellectuals, racquet club
> members, players on two pianos, raconteurs, and homosectuals.
> I want very much to tell you that
> Were you upon an Alp as I am
> You would get Ogden Nash's verses
> Though you had to commit arson or mayham.
> I little thought at my time of life
> To be anxiously awaiting the New Yorker,
> Although I do not buy it but borrow it from my friends,
> Thus contributing nothing to the stockholders' exchorquer.
> But now it is my latest hope for I think you are considerably greater
> Than Walter Savage Landor, Walter de la Mare, and Walter Pater.
> I wish you all success in life as in literature and I remain your
> respectful admirer,
>
>   Sincerely,
>   Dorothy Parker

Since that time, of course, Ogden had replied to the letter in kind and had seen Dorothy Parker at the party she had given in New York. But New York did not know that, and almost all New York knew Dorothy Parker, the sometimes savage book reviewer of that magazine.

The book, just ready to come out, was already doing better and better. Every day Ogden called up Simon & Schuster, and every day he was encouraged by the word. Macy's bought two hundred and fifty copies, which was a very big order, and said they would take another hundred if the author would come down and autograph them.

Baker and Taylor, the jobbers, were buying heavily, Brentanos and Scribner's, too. Two of the New York City Doubleday shops took a hundred copies each. All was aflutter in Ogden's world.

The flutter threatened a downward swoop a few days later. Ogden had been told by Dan Longwell that Edna Ferber thought the book was very good, and he had passed that information along to Max Schuster. On the weekend Max Schuster had retired to his country house and written a blockbuster advertisement, citing names and comments from various important people. He had forgotten to bring the notes he had made at the office about people and statements, and he made them up from memory. He quoted Edna Ferber.

When Ogden saw the advertisement in the papers that next week, he shuddered. Miss Ferber had a violent temper and had been in the past stirred to suing rage by the misapplication of her name. Only too well did Ogden recall several uncomfortable scrapes in which he had been peripherally involved during his Doubleday days. So he sat down and dashed off a letter telling Miss Ferber it had all been a horrible mistake, it would not occur again, and pleaded for her forgiveness.

He did not hear back. But Richard Simon did. He called Ogden to tell him he had a letter from Miss Ferber calling him a racketeer and threatening to put the matter into the hands of her attorney.

What to do?

Ogden counseled Simon to telephone Miss Ferber and put on his best manner. Simon did. He no sooner had her on the phone than she was cooing at him, as sweetly as if eating a bonbon, asking *his* forgiveness for her outburst of bad temper. At first, she said, she had been annoyed at the misuse of her name, but with Ogden's note she had realized it was all a mistake, and she forgave all. She wished she had not mailed the angry letter to Simon. Then she said she thought the book was very good, and she offered to lend her name in any way.

Ogden had also been busy peddling in his own way. Logrolling, he called it. He had sent a copy to Oliver La Farge and got back a letter of praise. He had sent copies to Robert Benchley, Marc Connelly, Milt Gross, Frank Sullivan, Stephen Vincent Benét, Nelson Doubleday, and Sarah Haardt, who, he had not forgotten, was Mrs. H. L. Mencken. Sullivan wrote back that he thought Ogden's book "would do more to improve the condition of the slaves than any book since Harriet Beecher Stowe's Tom."

Alone among Ogden's acquaintances, Benét commented on the single serious poem in the book, the last, "Old Men," a eulogy in effect.

OLD MEN

People expect old men to die,
They do not really mourn old men.
Old men are different. People look
At them with eyes that wonder when . . .
People watch with unshocked eyes;
But the old men know when an old man dies.

Many other important publicists and New York celebrities of the day began to add their names to the lists of the endorsers that Simon & Schuster was publishing in the advertisements.

Nelson Doubleday replied and signed his note "affectionately." That, said Escaped Underling Nash, was a miracle.

Finally, Ogden did hear from Edna Ferber and her letter was all a man who sent her caviar could have wished. She gushed over the book.

Sarah Haardt responded with an enthusiastic letter, and more, evidence that she had not forgotten either that she was Mrs. H. L. Mencken. Henry, she said, had also liked *Hard Lines* and was gearing up to give it a good review in *The American Mercury*.

The previews kept coming in, good, good, and better. The *New York Daily News,* not always fond of the rarified atmosphere in which Ogden Nash floated, also decided that this book was worthy of the proletariat as well as the worlds of the literati and Café Society.

The best news of all, from Ogden's point of view, was that Alexander Woollcott would review the book on January 27 on his national radio show. Woollcott was the one reviewer in America who could make a book overnight, and he had done so several times with works that took his fancy.

Then came January 14, the day before publication. That night Ogden sat up late figuratively chewing the blanket in anxiety. He could not hold a pencil in hand, and he paced the floor for hours with the feeling that disaster was about to strike. The daily book reviewers were even then putting their columns to bed, and on the morrow the results would appear. What if they all unleashed their claws against him? Worse, what if they all ignored the book?

But January 15 dawned, and after Ogden had collected the *Times* and the *Herald Tribune* and *World* and the *News* and the *Mirror* he could sit down with a second cup of coffee and relax, for the reviews were there—he had only half-doubted that they would be after Simon & Schuster's buildup. And they were uniformly good reviews. The review by the distinctly lowbrow *Daily News,* in particular, was proof of his triumph of matter over mind.

He checked Simon & Schuster that day. The bookstores were reporting good sales. S & S had already printed more, the first printing of 4,000 copies virtually exhausted. The advance sale had hit 3,200, 1,000 copies more than expected.

On January 16 Ogden continued probing. He stopped off at the Grand Central book shop on his way home from the office, and a clerk told him that they had sold a hundred copies in two days.

The reviews continued to be excellent. He was interviewed and reviewed and re-reviewed. One radio reviewer, who said he liked the book, did point out that part of the success had to be attributed to the fact that Ogden Nash knew so many famous writers and could command their attention. Ogden thought that rather beastly, coming when it did, but he also knew that it was true. There was an enormous advantage to being a member of The Club.

Ogden's new fame expanded his horizons. The book editor of the *New York Herald Tribune* telephoned to ask him to review the newest P. G. Wodehouse book about Bertie Wooster, Jeeves, and the buzzing members of the Drones Club, *Big Money*.

It was the third week of Ogden's employment at *The New Yorker,* and Ross already showed signs of expecting Ogden to have learned all about magazine publishing that any "man about town" ought to know. Once a day Ross would call his new "hub" man into the sanctum and fix him momentarily with an eye that then moved the room guiltily while its owner gulped down a glass of water from the carafe on his desk and then lit a cigarette.

"The magazine is going to hell," he would say. "No organization. Too many geniuses and nobody to take any responsibility. I'm licked."

Ross had been saying these same words, or a reasonable facsimile, steadily for five years, and the others of the staff heard the litany with the deadened ear that some Roman Catholics bestowed on the Rosary.

Ross would then look guiltily away and fiddle with something on his desk, all the while lighting one cigarette from the butt of the last. If he could remember what he wanted to talk about, they talked. If he did not, Ogden went away, back to his rewriting and his own writing. Stubbornly he was turning out prose pieces. Without comments, Mrs. Angell and Mr. Holden were returning them. He did not know who had turned thumbs down. All he knew was that no piece of copy ever went to the printer without the big "R" on it, the handwritten initial that signified Harold Ross's absolute control of his magazine.

And here, already, Ross was looking for clay on the shoes of his latest genius. Every day there was a blowup in which the editor lost his temper and went charging out of the office like a bull to take refuge in a speakeasy. These were signs that the old hands could read, but not Ogden. He was still so new to the job that he did not even know what was going wrong.

8

Man about Town

In the last half of January 1931 Ogden thought of little but "the book." Two days after publication Macy's called Simon & Schuster to tell them *Hard Lines* was the best seller in the store. The *New York Evening Post* called to arrange for a Nash interview. The next day Ogden went to the Simon & Schuster offices and saw orders come in for two hundred more copies. On January 23 S & S announced that they had sold three thousand copies in one week.

Four days later S & S put the next weekly figure at four thousand copies. Ogden was on top of the world. He pulled a batch of short stories out of the bottom drawer and set out to find an agent to peddle them, based on present success. He started thinking about a play.

His friends were entertaining him, day and night. He lunched with Joseph Alger, old New York roommate and coauthor of *The Cricket of Carodor*. He lunched with Christopher Morley, who announced that he was working on a new novel. He lunched with Dan Longwell. Oliver La Farge took him to dinner. By the end of the month, the book was still moving nicely in the stores, and Ogden had permitted himself to grow very cocky.

Via letter, Frances asked him if he knew yet what he was suppose to be doing on *The New Yorker*. He now had a glimmer of the truth: his job was to hold Harold Ross's hand. But, in addition, he had real managerial responsibilities: to see that all the departments came in on schedule so they could be edited, approved by Ross, and the type set in order; handle Profiles, which meant assign them and edit them; read manuscripts, which meant accept or reject, subject to Ross's approval; remain late on Saturday, arranging the Talk of the Town. And he also had to chase around the city to find Dorothy Parker to cozen, pull, or wrench from her the weekly article.

He had some ideas of what he would like to do: harness the spare energy of the editorial department. There were, said the managing editor, far too many people doing far too little. What this would lead to, Ogden did not know. He suspected he might get so efficient that he would end up eliminating his own job.

After three weeks, the book was still selling at the rate of four thousand copies a week. Simon & Schuster said it looked like a real bestseller.

He had other indications of impending stardom: all sorts of offers aimed to take advantage of this notoriety. The Hannan Shoe Company asked him to write a series of six verses to use in their advertising. He could name his own price.

Oh! said the dedicated artiste. To sell out for mere mammon would be to cheapen himself. He refused. But not all the advertising fraternity were so crass as that. Another young man came to ask Ogden if he would not write a poem in praise of the new Empire State Building, then the tallest in the world and the pride of New York.

Not likely, said Ogden, for he had just turned down one offer to work for mere money.

This was different, said the adman. The Empire State Building represented "class."

Not likely, said Ogden. But if he changed his mind, how much would they pay?

Pay? asked the astonished adman. Would he, an artist, expect to be paid?

The phone continued to ring, and the letters continued to arrive, and in February the book went into another printing of five thousand copies, and later that month Simon & Schuster boasted in an ad in *The New York Times Book Review* that they had just gone back to reprint another ten thousand copies. A lady agent came to see Ogden to say she thought she could get him a movie contract. Go ahead, he said.

All this heady success was reported, inch by inch, to Miss Leonard far away, and she obviously was impressed and turned a little humble in the face of his success. She was proud of him, she said. He reveled in her good opinion, but he was just a little more standoffish than he had been, no longer much sign of the imploring swain here, but a self-confident young man who had asked this woman to marry him and was awaiting her return to perform.

Still there was no absence of affection. One day he wandered by E. B. White's office. As usual he was prepared to pass without comment even though the door was open, for if anyone disturbed Mr. White at his cerebrations a memo was likely to be circulated by Ross to the effect that people were bothering White and interfering with production. But on this day the door was open and E. B. White stopped Ogden to tell him he had written a little poem about him and then to read it:

If I were Ogden Nash I would marry a girl in black taffeta
And sit around the house all day and laffeta.

What was staggering about this to Nash, he said, was that he had been promising himself for a long time that after he married Frances he would buy her a Bergdorf Goodman's dress of black taffeta.

The end of February brought new pressure. In addition to his own duties he had to take on the job of Raymond Holden temporarily while the latter went on vacation. In obedience to Murphy's Law (If anything dreadful can happen it will), the sky above Ogden's desk at *The New Yorker* began falling. Dorothy Parker was at her most elusive, hastening from soiree to speakeasy to hideout to avoid the long arm of her editor and then admitting that she had not done her weekly stint.

Since Dorothy Parker was supposed to write either about the theater or about books, but in any event to write one page per week, her reluctance created many a delay, as Ogden telephoned, chased, and cajoled until the copy got into the hands of the irritated printers, who let their feelings be known in ex post facto telephone calls, fielded by Editor Ross, and penalty charges paid by business manager Raoul Fleischmann. Ross quite naturally (for Ross) took the position that Mrs. Parker was a necessary genius and that the responsibility for her failures lay with the editor in charge of her.

At the end of the first week of Holden's absence, Ogden waited patiently on Saturday morning, watching the clock. Mrs. Parker's column was due at noon. At eleven he had a presentiment and telephoned to ask her how it was coming.

This week she was not going to do it, she announced.

So, Editor Nash then had to scurry about among the holdovers and possibles of other contributors to find a page he could substitute and get it over to the fretting printers.

The magazine went to bed on Sunday night, and Ogden alone was the nursemaid. All others were out listening to Gladys Swarthout at the Metropolitan Opera, chortling at the Marx Brothers' pranks in the movie houses, laughing at Marc Connelly's jokes in *The Green Pastures* on Broadway, basking before log fires in Connecticut, or drawing on the walls and wreaking mayhem in the speakeasies.

Fielding two telephones was only the mechanical part of it. What was to be done about the commas, or absence thereof, in the new piece? Ross was an absolute bearcat about commas, and everyone knew it.

The achievement of the magazine in the past five years was indicated by the telephone calls from the newspapers, asking silly questions about the content of the coming issue.

At one o'clock Ogden's ordeal was not yet finished. It was well after two before he could turn off the lights, close the doors, and go home.

But, of course, when Editor Ross saw the magazine on Monday, there was no excuse, no excuse at all. Mrs. Parker's column ought to have been in there, even if it had to come by immaculate conception.

Early the next week, Ogden lunched with Dorothy Parker and learned that she had really been ill on the previous Saturday, a combination of too much gin and pleurisy. As usual, she charmed him and promised to try to repent.

The book continued to do well. Sales fell off in the first week of March, but the second week opened with a thousand new orders, which was most satisfactory. Ogden continued to reap the harvest of success: *College Humor* had asked him for a piece, and he dug deep into the drawer for something he had once thought was funny but now thought was pretty dreadful. He sent it anyhow, and virtually by return mail he received a check for $100 and demands for more, more, more.

The only thing that bothered him was that in recent weeks the materials he submitted to *The New Yorker* had been coming back to him, without comment.

Then, one morning toward the end of the March Ogden walked into his office and sat down. He had passed a stranger who was sitting in the bullpen. After a while the stranger was called into Ross's office, and as he passed the open door of Ogden Nash and looked in, Ogden couldn't repress a smile. For suddenly he had a vision of the future. The following morning when Ogden arrived he found the young man sitting in his office, at his desk. That is how Ogden Nash learned that he had been fired. In such matters Ross was a total coward, and he would go to any length to avoid firing a man personally. In this case Holden was still away, and no one else had really been responsible enough for Ogden's coming to push the unpleasant task onto him. So Ogden learned from his replacement, James M. Cain, that Ross had decided Ogden's genius was not sufficient to bring Efficiency to *The New Yorker*. (Cain lasted a few months, "the 26th Jesus," as he called himself, then came in one day to find a stranger at his desk . . .)

Whether or not Ogden could have stayed on the staff of *The New Yorker* in another capacity is not quite clear. Thurber had "failed" as managing editor and had remained. Ross certainly did not feel that he could afford a

resident poet, and Ogden's rewriting of manuscripts had not been eminently successful, nor had many of his prose pieces passed muster.

Being fired was a shock to Ogden, but not a disaster. Money was piling
up from the sales of *Hard Lines*, and other magazines were requesting his
work. But Ogden did not think of turning to a freelance career. His immediate reaction was to return to publishing. And that is what he did; but not
to Doubleday, for he had little faith in Nelson Doubleday's honeyed final
words. John Farrar had been after him to join the new publishing house of
Farrar & Rinehart, and this is where he went in April.

It was a busy and confused month for Ogden. Moving downtown to a
new office was no great task, and he knew the work involved, but it was a
question of new ideas and new people as well as the old. One of his first
efforts was to try to get a book out of E. B. White. He also began sharpen-
ing his old contacts.

Then his father, who had been ill off and on for years, suddenly took a
turn for the worse, and on April 27 Edmund Nash died.

Frances Leonard and her mother came back to America in May and there
were no more questions in Miss Leonard's mind. She had left an ardent but
more or less mundane book publisher and sometime poet behind her
when she went to Europe. She had returned to a national celebrity, whose
picture appeared on the pages of newspapers and magazines.

They were married June 6, 1931, in Baltimore, and most of Ogden's family came down for the ceremony. So did his friend Charles Duell. Then
Ogden had to hasten back to his job in New York, and Frances had to prepare to move from the gracious house on Baltimore's Rugby Road to a
New York apartment.

Or so one might think. But she didn't. She stayed at home, Ogden went
back to New York, and he came down when he could, which was at least
often enough to start a family. For it was not many months before Frances
declared she was pregnant.

Ogden spent his evenings as a publishing man about town, dining with
authors sometimes. He spent many evenings at the Yale Club with John
Farrar and days searching for more authors.

He went up to Connecticut to visit the Richard Simons for a weekend
and to talk about his second book of verse, which would come out in October. Again they were having title trouble. This time Simon & Schuster
offered a $25 reward through *Publishers Weekly*, the book trade magazine,
to anyone who would come up with a suitable title.

Ogden was already known around New York as a pithy philosopher as
well as a poet, from just two of the sixty verses in *Hard Lines*, one noting
that alcohol was more effective in eliminating inhibition than sweets, the
other suggesting that many marriages were the shotgun variety.

NUPTIAL REFLECTION

The reason for much matrimony
Is Patrimony.

Such verse, of course, made little money at his *New Yorker* rate of a dollar a line. But it had already established his reputation in New York, and the word was spreading.

Simon & Schuster did a good job of continuing to spread the word. In their *PW* ad for a title they inserted a small teasing sample of the new work, "The Oyster."

The oyster, said Ogden, was a confusing animal, bisexual but very happy, sitting on the bottom, basking. The author would not mind being an oyster, but only in months that did not have an "R."

Farrar & Rinehart seemed to be fairly well financed for a new, young house, and that summer Ogden helped the principals in an agonizing decision; they had a chance to buy *Cosmopolitan* magazine. After a number of discussions, they did not make the purchase, although Ogden argued for it. Perhaps they should have for in the 1980s *Cosmopolitan* was still going strong, and what was left of Farrar & Rinehart had gone through several transitions and become the distinguished but none-too-large Farrar, Straus, and Giroux.

Hard Lines was still selling a hundred copies a week as the summer wore along, when the author and publishers found a title for the new book, *Free Wheeling*. Simon & Schuster predicted big sales once more.

Ogden's horizons had expanded considerably since his Doubleday years. He now declared that he was interested in doing a revue for the theater, and Richard Simon obligingly produced a producer, Billy Rose, who had done *Sweet and Low* and *Crazy Quilt*. When Simon mentioned the matter to Billy Rose, the producer said yes, he definitely wanted to meet the author of *Hard Lines*. But it was like so many of the ideas that flitted about New York, with no more staying power than the summer's fireflies.

The autumn found the new book publishing house flourishing. But, instead of times improving, as the newspapers kept predicting they would, when 1932 slipped in, the depression was growing much worse, and by June Ogden and Farrar & Rinehart were checking the account books day by day. They were on a monthly budget, watching pennies. Everyone took pay cuts, and Ogden's salary began climbing back down the ladder. Their accountant, who watched the books for half a dozen small publishers, informed them that they were doing better than any other publisher he worked for. But that was small solace, considering the state of business and of bookbuying. When people did not have any money, they did not buy books, and publishers were beginning to believe that books were the first discretionary purchase people gave up.

Frances spent much time in Baltimore, having her babies there. Daughter Linell was born in March 1932. Then, in the spring of 1933, daughter Isabel was on her way into the world.

Ogden wrote many poems about wedded bliss and about babies in these years. Some were published in *The New Yorker*, but most in other publications, and some not at all until they appeared in book form.

Ogden was indeed a busy man, and although doing well enough with his writing, he had not achieved a level of income that would let him establish a spacious Park Avenue apartment, and that sort of style was the way Frances had been brought up to live.

The books of verse continued to pay off in a small way. A year and a half after publication of *Hard Lines*, he got a royalty check for $200 for the six months ending June 30, 1932. He also got $450 in royalties on *Free Wheeling*. A new book was in the works, and to produce it Ogden was selling to a number of magazines; *The New Yorker* was not really anything like his major market.

In May 1931 he had begun selling to *The Literary Digest*, then the foremost magazine of literary criticism and public affairs in America.

Ever hopeful, he and Farrar were talking about a prosperous October. He was looking for an apartment.

The big hope for Farrar & Rinehart in the spring of 1933 was *Anthony Adverse*, and before publication they had an advance sale of ten thousand copies. They had signed up another book that promised to do well, *The Life and Letters of William Howard Taft* by Henry Pringle, who had won a Pulitzer prize for biography the previous year.

At the end of May 1933 Ogden's third book was in the works. He was extremely busy for he did the advertising and the publicity for the Farrar & Rinehart list, and he was what would later be called "acquisitions editor" as well, which meant he scouted for books and signed them up, subject, of course, to the judgments and whims of the partners. By August 1933 business seemed to be picking up a little. Ogden was hard at it, producing advertising, finding new authors, editing manuscripts, appearing on the radio on behalf of his own work and his company's books, and making speeches at dinners. He was living at the Harvard Club.

His major concern that summer was *Anthony Adverse*, which he and his colleagues hoped would erase for the firm the strictures of the depression. But although the novel was enormously successful for author Hervey Allen and Farrar, it did not work magic. The executives examined their debits and credits again and decided that they all had to take further pay cuts. This cut put Ogden back from the $150 per week at which he had joined the firm to $25 a week, slightly more than he had earned as a beginner at Doubleday in 1925. His room rent at the Harvard Club was $2.75 a day, or $19.25 a week. If he decided to eat . . .

What kept Ogden going, of course, was the steady income from writing he sold to magazines and the semiannual boosts he received by way of royalties from his books. *Happy Days,* his third, was published by Simon & Schuster in October 1933, and it too was a success. He did not have to worry about his wife, who was living happily with her family in Baltimore in the luxury to which she had been born. But if they were ever to get together on more than a weekend basis, something was going to have to change.

Finally Frances and the children did come to live in New York. But by that time the depression had grown so much more severe that it seemed unlikely Farrar & Rinehart would survive.

To Ogden the past year had meant moving steadily backward financially, at least in the publishing aspect of his career. It seemed futile to keep on going backward, no matter how hard he worked in publishing. He had secured the services of a very good agent, Curtis Brown Associates, and they had enlarged his markets. He was selling to *The Saturday Evening Post, Harper's Bazaar,* and *Redbook,* as well as *The New Yorker.* That summer he did another of his Christmas poems, written in the heat of midsummer for the year-end issue of a magazine. This year the magazine was *Redbook,* and they paid him $225 for the verse, or nearly ten weeks' publishing pay. *The Saturday Evening Post* became his best market; he got $450 for "The First Thousand Miles."

Since he was earning more money as a freelance than as a publisher, his thoughts turned to making the full break and becoming an independent writer. He consulted with the agency, and they said he could do it. Further, Curtis Brown secured a contract with *The Saturday Evening Post* that guaranteed him at least $100 each for twenty-six verses during the next year. That was twice as much as his Farrar & Rinehart income.

He made the break. He said a reluctant good-bye to his friend John Farrar, packed up the family, left New York, and went south to Baltimore.

9

The Compleat Poet

Late in 1933 Ogden Nash moved in for a little while in uxorious elegance with his in-laws on Baltimore's Rugby Road.

He had not severed his connections with Farrar & Rinehart completely; technically, he was on a year's leave of absence from the publishing firm. The idea was to see if he could make a living as a writer.

For a poet and philosopher, which Nash certainly already was, there could hardly be a better existence. He was freed from the workaday world that had demanded ten to twelve hours a day of frenetic effort from him, usually six days a week, for eight years. The success of his books caused the magazine editors to take notice, and the enormous number of hopeful imitators only whetted the editors' desire for the real Nash. His work continued to appear regularly in *The New Yorker*, which was working hard in the 1930s to be *the* magazine of the tastemakers of the Eastern Seaboard. All the publicist crowd read the magazine. That didn't hurt Ogden's salability to other magazine editors a bit.

His background and long experience in New York had produced a wisdom and gentle cynicism far beyond his years. His own curiosity and his enormous energy led him to examine all sorts of phenomena, particularly the human race and most particularly the American branch, and to arrive at conclusions not noticed by others. He was, of course, the consummate gentle WASP, writing in a period when the WASP and the values of the Anglo-Saxon forebears were still dominant in America, or at least, as Ogden might have said, when no apologies were necessary.

Work was now two hours a day in the morning and two hours in the afternoon. Raising children took a good share of the rest of his day. Baltimore meant a new life in many ways for Ogden Nash. He and Frances began looking for a house, and the process gave him a poem: "Apartment to Sublet—Unfurnished." This poem dealt with a family tired of living in apartments. They wanted a house, so they could have dogs and cats and even mice. A rabbit? Perhaps. A garden? Definitely.

Soon, the Nashes, father, mother, and two daughters, were living in a leased house at 4205 Underwood Road, and Ogden discovered that the far lesser pressures of life in Baltimore agreed very nicely with him. He knew already that New York was not even four hours away via the B. & O., and the Harvard Club was there for those business trips that could not be avoided.

Otherwise he was his own man, and if he wanted to stay up until midnight or longer and sleep until nine or longer, as he had suggested in that wistful poem about being rich, then he could. The only catch was that money had to be produced to support all this. But for Ogden in 1933 and 1934 money was really no problem. He was brimming over with ideas and so energetic that he was sometimes producing several poems a day, many of them on this new subject of domestic life.

He wrote about cats, and dogs, and much, much more about the children.

The Nashes moved into the new house in November. Almost immediately they began to learn the realities of life in a house, with no superintendent to fix the plumbing or the electric wiring or the furnace.

One minor disaster then followed another. The plumbing went berserk. The electrical system decided to eat fuses. The furnace complained about its diet.

All this experience was common ground with millions of Americans, but they, of course, could not see it with the eye of the philosophical poet, as could Ogden. He had to pay the plumbing bills and the electrician, but he got it back by writing about the disasters. And America loved it all.

Ogden was also writing prose, and some of it was selling. *The Saturday Evening Post* bought some of it. He had played enough golf in his Long Island days to be able to write about golf intelligently, and now he wrote "Home Is the Gaffer," a light piece about bad golf, and the *Post* bought it. Next came "Your Friends Are My Friends." In all, in 1934, he sold 106 poems and articles to various magazines, bringing an income from magazine writing of more than $11,500. This was a third more than he had earned in his best year as a wage slave, and since prices were dropping along with wages, it was a very handsome income for 1934. In addition, the books kept popping out; *Happy Days* in October 1933 had been the latest.

To celebrate its coming and to help promote the book, Ogden had made a journey to New York, and an appearance as an entertainer before the Dutch Treat Club. He had been asked to read some of his humorous poetry. So he chose from the book a poem called "The Four Woods Colts." For Ogden this was an unusual poem. It dealt with the fortunes of four illegitimate children. Each verse told the story of one of these men, how he rose to be a lawyer, politician or a banker, or a captain of industry, despite his unfortunate parentage as the child of a lady of the evening or lady of easy virtue or of rape. When read to the Dutch Treat Club at the Park Lane Hotel the poem brought down the house, and sage editors, lawyers, and captains of industry went back to their offices chuckling. Someone had made a recording, and Rupert Hughes, one of the California crowd, carried off a record with him to Los Angeles. Hughes was invited to a stag dinner at Charlie Chaplin's in Beverly Hills along with Emil Ludwig, the German writer, Will Rogers, the humorist, and several executives of the film industry. He played the record, and it brought cheers. Charlie Chaplin suggested that it ought to be printed. Rob Wagner, the editor of a little Hollywood magazine called *Script,* asked Ogden for permission to do so and, as soon as he had disengaged himself from the welter of leaking pipes, balky furnaces, and dead electrical circuits of the new house, Ogden granted it gladly. But he had to tell Wagner that the poem had already been printed in his new book. Secretly, the interchange convinced him that Hollywood people never read *anything* but scripts, but even so it *was* flattering to be lionized by someone such as Charlie Chaplin.

The poem was published by itself in April 1934, as "For Prominent So-and-Sos," but has seldom been seen since. It was hardly of a piece with the vast opus of Ogden's, which was much more in the vein of refinement, eschewing the Rabelaisian touch.

Closest were a few of his earliest poems about chorus girls and the like and the celebrated four-liner about candy and liquor.

Nash's work was so extensive that soon he was commanding much of the attention of one of the Curtis Brown senior agents, Mrs. Sewell Haggard. She found him new markets, *Good Housekeeping* and *Life.*

In 1935 he was hard at work, producing about ten poems each week, most of which Edith Haggard managed to place in magazines. He was working on an idea for a Broadway show in which the Shubert Brothers had shown some interest and on a radio script.

His work was done at a long table—later he had a special table built. He still used, and always would, the lined yellow pads of the conference room for his scribbling. He still started with ideas, putting down words and perhaps a few doodles.

One page began with the name of Mr. and Mrs. Daingerfield Cabot Cadwalader Stuyvesant and trailed off to nothing. It was going to be a play or a sketch or something, but it turned out to be a piece of lined yellow paper that was put away in a drawer.

He would read the newspapers and make notes of names and odd situations. He would read the dictionary and make notes of words and etymology. He would write notes to himself, reminding himself that he really didn't have any worries, or suggesting that what men needed was a pair of suspenders for every pair of trousers. He would ask questions: why didn't someone invent some more rhymes for wife than strife and knife and rife? One random thought that amused him a great deal was the idea that he might buy up all his own books as they came off press and live off the royalties.

He was always inventing remarkable names, such as Pauncefoot Bloodcatcher, and most of these found their way into poems. He would try out rhymes:

frivolous
lascivolus

promiscuity
assiduity

countenance
mountenance

Always he was capable of the joke at his own expense. It was (and is) the habit of book publishers to seek an introduction to a book by some prominent person, in the hope that this will help drag the book into prominence and profit. When Nash's fifth book, *The Primrose Path*, was published by Simon & Schuster in the winter of 1935, Ogden wrote his own introduction, disguised as George Bernard Stein. It was, of course, a burlesque of George Bernard Shaw, and prominent names dropped like termites out of a sprayed foundation.

"G.B.S." could remember asking Ernest Hemingway what he thought of Ogden Nash's work. Hemingway replied: "Whose work?"

The introducer had repeated this remark around town and gotten agreement with it. He invoked the names of artists Pablo Picasso, Diego Rivera, Lupe Velez, and Orozco. They all agreed that Ogden Nash was not an artist they knew.

He brought up John D. Rockefeller and James Joyce and James A. Farley, then the U.S. postmaster general and chairman of the Democratic party, and President Franklin D. Roosevelt. He spoke to one of the Van Renssaelaers—this one from Queens—a very important figure, he said, because he had nearly won the Irish Sweepstakes, and he asked Mr. Van Renssaelaer what he thought of Ogden Nash.

Mr. Van Renssaelaer spoke with tones of authority. Nash, he said, was the greatest secretary of the treasury since Andrew Mellon, who had presided over the nonenforcement of the prohibition laws. Then came the names of Ogden Reid, the editor of the *New York Herald Tribune*, and Ogden Goelet, a New York socialite. No one knew anything about his man Ogden Nash.

No one, but several million people in the United Sates who had made of Ogden Nash in five years one of the nation's leading humorists.

10

The Primrose Path
of Ogden Nash

The Primrose Path was Ogden's first real book since he had left New York and the so-called security of a full-time job. Ted Robinson, writing in the *Saturday Review of Literature,* wrote his review in verse. It turned out to be a perspicacious review, although the verse was abominable.

I have heard people say, "It is a clever idea.
But he will be unable to keep it up indefinitely I feah.
And of course, once you see how it's done, anybody can do it easily."
They say that very confidently and breezily—
But I remember that people first said it
When Ogden Nash had only one book (*Hard Lines*) to his credit,
And here is the fifth book, and even better than his first one.
As for anyone doing it, a lot of imitators have gone to it,
And they just can't do it.

Every poem, said the critic, had a point to it, a really meaningful point, which is one of the key elements of poetry. Was Ogden a true "lyric artist"? Robinson called attention to "The Secret Town."

This serious verse was a panegyric by Ogden to his wife. Mystical and adoring, it was a paean about the woman he loved more than anyone else, who lived in a secret castle of her own within the city he had built around her.

It was, of course, another gift to Ogden's beloved Frances. Over the years there had been many such. They did not dim in ardor.

To critic Robinson this poem was proof that had Ogden wished, he could indeed have returned to his first yearning and become a lyric poet of renown. But like most of the American public, Robinson saw in Ogden's satirical verse something far more important, something needed. Here was something that warned the politician, the greedy capitalist, and the overbearing that the people were out there, watching, and that truth would out. The truth need not be nearly so baldly stated as his poem about the "Four Prominent So-and-Sos," which had been put to music by Robert Armbruster, and, as noted, had become something of a ribald classic out in the hustings of California. The critic also made note that Ogden's writing was never really sexual, perhaps a lesson the poet had learned from Harold Ross, although even in his years at Doubleday Ogden had lamented the excesses of the Flapper Generation. In those days he had been in charge of Doubleday's "College Novel Contest," and he remarked once in annoyance that all the college novelists seemed to try to outdo one another in crass sexuality, and that the girls were much more randy about it than the boys.

No, gentility had now become Ogden Nash's hallmark, and so it would be. He was one of the most genial and easy going people in the world, an aspect of his character that never failed to impress those who learned to know him.

Robinson also pointed out Ogden's remarkable ability to capsulize philosophy. The review was one that Ogden had to appreciate. He lived at publication time in real tension; he was so sensitive to criticism that a single harsh word could ruin a day. Well, he had nothing to fear from Robinson.

C. G. Poore, in *The New York Times Book Review*, was not quite so complimentary to Nash's *The Primrose Path*. Poore wrote: "There's junk in it . . . It could certainly do with some plowing under." But the thrust of his review was that Nash was still Nash, "fundamentally and magnificently unsound . . . He is—as each volume inches him along toward a five foot shelf—more and more authentically himself."

The philosopher received much such praise, but like philosophers almost everywhere, if one were to read Nash's poems about domestic life, the male had honor almost everywhere save in his own household. As the verses indicate, there are often clashes between husband and wife, with a great deal of exposure of the male's delinquencies and shortcomings.

In a poem about husbands, written from a wife's point of view, Nash outlined the faults with which the male was taxed at home: "he" interfered with discipline in the nursery. "He" had forgotten an anniversary, and, when reminded, "he" had solved the problem, "he" thought, by giving his wife a great big kiss.

Nash, as a husband who worked at home and was thus underfoot all day long, was able to pierce the he-she scene with a rapier because he lived it. Poem after poem chronicled domestic situations with a clarity of one who knew what he was talking about. A wife might find that there was one thing more annoying than having a husband underfoot, and that was having him not underfoot, out of town, and this meant staying at the Harvard Club, or a hotel, and *that* to a wife's mind meant carousing with disreputable friends, drinking too much, and staying out till all hours. And, if a young wife had a fertile imagination, there was always the suspicion that her husband might be looking at another woman.

A wife in one of Ogden's poems worried about getting fat, and when the poetic wife would indicate "she" might be putting on a bit of weight, the poem's husband did not say "Absolutely not!" or "Don't be ridiculous," or all the things a husband should say to reassure a wife.

And there were many domestic situations, poetically explained. "He" wanted to stay home by the fire on those evenings that "she" wanted to go out, and "he" wanted to go out on those evenings that "she" wanted to stay home.

"He" wanted to stay up when "she" wanted to go to bed and "he" wanted to sleep in when "she" wanted to get up, or vice versa.

One of Ogden's poetic husbands drank too much at cocktail parties, and if his wife stabbed him with a look, "he" was inclined to be annoyed. At home "he" was always too tired to hang a picture or clean out the garage, but "he" would walk five miles playing eighteen holes of golf without a whimper.

When family argument reached the crisis stage, the male of Ogden's poems would retreat to the chauvinist attitude that women were by nature unreasonable and had no concept of logic.

If "she" served hamburger for dinner, "he" complained that they never had steak any more. If "she" went to the butcher's and bought a whole raft of steaks and served them every night, then when the bill came in "he" whooped like a brave at Wounded Knee.

When "he" changed his clothes, everything seemed to fall to the floor or rest on the bed, or hang on a chair, and if offered a clothes hanger, "he" did not seem to know what it was.

The great compliment to Nash was that he was able to translate into poems that readers could understand and appreciate all the little domestic differences that must occur in any marriage.

In the fall of 1935 Frances and her mother went to Europe again, leaving Ogden to baby-sit for the two Nash daughters. It was not quite as hard as it sounds; he gave up his own house and moved with the children to his in-laws's house on Rugby Road, where there were servants to ease the pain and let him work.

Immediately, friends began taking pity on the bachelor father and invited him out. He gave a dinner party of his own after the Navy–Notre Dame football game of 1935, and it provided him with material for a poem. One pair of invited guests had houseguests from New York that weekend, and, in his usual geniality, Ogden said to bring them along, the more the merrier. So they did, and Ogden, being the polite host, seated the stranger lady on his right. During the dinner she made small talk: did he know *The New Yorker?*

Yes, said Ogden.

She just loved it. She read it every week from cover to cover. He was a writer, wasn't he? Why didn't he send something to *The New Yorker?*

Having taken care of her dinner host, the lady then turned her attention to her house hosts and first criticized the lady for being too bossy, and then criticized her hostess's husband for not doing what his wife told him to do.

Here in the center of Maryland society, Ogden had so much material passing before his door that he need not go outside.

As the poet Ogden was entertaining and taking stock of his entertainees in poems, the real life Frances and his mother-in-law ensconced themselves in Almond's Hotel on Clifford Street in London, having a whale of a time, the left-behind baby-sitter Ogden gathered.

After several weeks of work, baby-sitting, and entertainments in and entertainments out, Ogden was pining for his love, and so, announcing that he had just finished the outline and draft of the first act of the play he was going to sell to the Shuberts, he got on a B. & O. train and went up to New York.

He then went to the Curtis Brown agency for a talk. Yearning to join Frances in London he had rationalized a two-part magazine article, part one written on an outbound steamer, telling what he expected to find on his first voyage to Europe, and part two, on a home-bound ship, telling what he had actually found. If the agent could get $750 for each of these, then the trip was paid for. Also, just to show that a poet could have a refined sense of double-entry bookkeeping, Ogden got hold of the publicity agent of the French Line and secured a promise of first-class passage at tourist rates in exchange for giving the French Line a good bit of publicity.

Ah, *tempore,* ah, *mores!* What had become of the serious young artist who told Hannan Shoes to take a walk when they offered him money for a poetical endorsement so short a time before?

Ogden sent for his birth certificate and prepared to get a passport. But on the way home to Baltimore conscience struck, and Ogden called off the whole trip. He had too many responsibilities at home, he said.

And when he got to the house on Rugby Road, there they were, both of them, playing on the floor of the nursery.

They gave him trouble but they also gave him pleasure and inspiration.

For the poet there was always plenty to consider, courtesy of the children. Children? Little girls? Dear small female tots? A pair of more bloodthirsty monsters this innocent father had never before seen.

For years before fatherhood he had been reading poets who spoke of children as in praise of angels, of meekness and gaiety and cuddles. And certainly Ogden had found all this to be true of his own daughters.

But they had another side or two, facets the poet discovered when he began telling them fairy stories and tales that had delighted his generation when they were tiny tots. Here he had a pair of baby Borgias, who wanted nothing less than to see the three little pigs eaten up by the wolf. His idea of good reading for children was *Winnie-the-Pooh*. But when the girls learned that Winnie-the-Pooh ate nothing but honey and that Piglet ate nothing but haycorns, they lost all interest in the adventures of Pooh and friends.

DON'T CRY, DARLING, IT'S BLOOD ALL RIGHT

Whenever poets want to give you the idea that something is particularly meek and mild,
They compare it to a child,
Thereby proving that though poets with poetry may be rife
They don't know the facts of life.
If of compassion you desire either a title or a jot,
Don't try to get it from a tot.
Hard-boiled, sophisticated adults like me and you
May enjoy ourselves thoroughly with Little Women and Winnie-the-Pooh,
But innocent infants these titles from their reading course eliminate
As soon as they discover that it was honey and nuts and mashed potatoes instead of human flesh that Winnie-the-Pooh and Little Women ate.
Innocent infants have no use for fables about rabbits or donkeys or tortoises or porpoises,
What they want is something with plenty of well-mutilated corpoises.
Not on legends of how the rose came to be a rose instead of a petunia is their fancy fed,
But on the inside story of how somebody's bones got ground up to make somebody else's bread.
They'll go to sleep listening to the story of the little beggarmaid who got to be queen by being kind to the bees and the birds,
But they're all eyes and ears the minute they suspect a wolf or a giant is going to tear some poor woodcutter into quarters or thirds.

It really dosen't take much to fill their cup;
All they want is for somebody to be eaten up.
Therefore I say unto you, all you poets who are so crazy about meek and mild
*   little children and their angelic air,*
If you are sincere and really want to please them, why just go out and get
*   yourselves devoured by a bear.*

Jack and the Beanstalk, thought Ogden, might be more in their line. So the poet read how the heroic lad had climbed the beanstalk to beard the giant. It was not long before this poet was shocked to learn that the hero of his progeny was the giant, who had discovered that the additive of a few ground-up people bones added immeasurably to the flavor of his whole wheat rolls.

The poet's audience sneered at *Peter Rabbit.* In *Little Red Riding Hood* they cheered for the wolf. *Snow White* was only interesting when the Wicked Stepmother was on scene. Much better were the tales of witches who turned princes into frogs. What the girls wanted was gore and plenty of it. As a boy Ogden had written that poem about how a little bird had made a white rose red to please a princess by staining it with his own life's blood. The Nash daughters liked the blood all right, but poof to roses.

They could also be cuddly little bears. The poet decided there was some magic quality in milk that affected children the way gin affected adults. It must be the milk that made their little toddles across the floor so much like the meanderings of a drunk trying to find the way to the door of the saloon. Ogden wrote a poem about those meanderings. There was a birthday and a birthday party, and the poet watched the father as "he" welcomed the little guests at three o'clock in the afternoon and prepared to entertain them. The father provided bubble pipes and bubbly water, "he" told them tales and wiped their noses and stopped their quarrels. But when they went outside and began turning the hose on one another, and when the ice cream developed into an ice-cream ball throwing contest, and when the guests began complaining about the quality of the favors, Daddy headed for the great outdoors and hid behind the doghouse. The poet, Daddy's friend, chronicled the event.

Observing life in a suburban setting, the poet wrote often about animals. There was, he discovered, an awful risk in accepting the gift of a nice, cuddly little kitten. Did the reader know what it was?

Predictably, the difficulty was that ultimately the cuddly little kitten grew up to become a C * T.

Ogden did not confine his efforts just to poems of domestic bliss and discord. One day he went to Pimlico to get background for some racing

The infant poet, 1902. Courtesy of the Photography Collection, Harry Ransom Humanities Research Center, the University of Texas at Austin.

Ogden Nash (left) and friends, circa 1920. Courtesy of the Photography Collection, Harry Ransom Humanities Research Center, the University of Texas at Austin.

Ogden Nash (right) and friend, circa 1920. Courtesy of the Photography Collection, Harry Ransom Humanities Research Center, the University of Texas at Austin.

Ogden Nash (left) and Bill, spring 1920. Courtesy of the Photography Collection, Harry Ransom Humanities Research Center, the University of Texas at Austin.

Ogden Nash (center) and two friends, circa 1920. Courtesy of the Photography Collection, Harry Ransom Humanities Research Center, the University of Texas at Austin.

Ogden Nash, 1921. Courtesy of the Photography Collection, Harry Ransom Humanities Research Center, the University of Texas at Austin.

Ogden Nash at Sunnybrook, December 1930. Courtesy of the Photography Collection, Harry Ransom Humanities Research Center, the University of Texas at Austin.

Nash and wife Frances, circa 1938. Courtesy of the Photography Collection, Harry Ransom Humanities Research Center, the University of Texas at Austin.

Frances, Linell, and Isabel, circa 1940. Courtesy of the Photography Collection, Harry Ransom Humanities Research Center, the University of Texas at Austin.

S. J. Perelman, Ogden Nash, Vernon Duke, and Al Hirschfield celebrating "Sweet Bye and Bye," 1946. Courtesy of the Photography Collection, Harry Ransom Humanities Research Center, the University of Texas at Austin.

poems, because his agent said that would be a good idea. He arrived in a driving rain. But he must have had a prescience about the mudders: he won $52. This victory could be attributed only in part to luck. Ogden had grown up at least halfway in a south where fast horses and pretty women went together, and some of his friends suspected that if he had not chosen to be a poet he might have made a handsome living as a handicapper. One of the allures of Baltimore for Ogden was always that he had three fine racetracks within striking distance. Another might have been that the racetrack seemed to be one attraction of Ogden's life that Frances did not share. Her taste was much more for foreign travel.

Off in London early in November, Mrs. Ogden Nash seemed to wonder what her husband was up to.

Ogden did like a drink, a drink of liquor that is. He wrote a poem celebrating martinis, coming to the conclusion that the gin had something to do with the effect. He noted the same phenomenon attendant to an old-fashioned. The rye whiskey lent it a certain *on ne sait quoi.* And take a mint julep, yes, the bourbon did something for it that nothing else could do.

From Europe, Frances wrote that she suspected he was drinking too much. This complaint brought Ogden very near to showing outright indignation. He cabled Frances that her perception was awry and reminded her that he had written twenty-two letters to her since she left in October, penned twelve poems, paid $1,500 in bills, and worked on his play. He then demanded that she cable an answer. But then Ogden's uxoriousness asserted itself once again, and he fell all over himself in the last few lines of the cable, sacrificing all the impact of his righteous indignation by telling her he missed her and asking her to come home soon.

Professionally, life was going along very nicely. *Redbook* wanted a year's contract with him. His verses, which at first had been dismissed in London as an aberration of the English language, had now begun to catch on over there. *Nash's Magazine* in London bought a dozen of his old poems for $900. A solid London publisher, Dent and Co., Ltd., had contracted to publish his next book.

In the middle of the month, Ogden had a call from Hervey Allen, over whose *Anthony Adverse* publication he had presided in those last days at Farrar, and he went down to the Belvedere Plaza Hotel to meet the Allens for a talk. Allen had always been grateful for the many extra services Ogden had performed as editor, and now he offered the Nashes the use of Bonfield Manor, his Baltimore house, for the winter. Allen and his wife were going to Florida. All Ogden would have to do was pay the heating bill.

Ogden cabled his wife. She apparently did not reply. At the end of November he cabled her again. She seemed not to come to grips with the problem. Then he began getting scolding letters, more complaining about his drinking, and this time he did reply angrily.

He was having some difficulty working at home with the children around all the time, and no wife to fend them off. He was very happy in this new existence, but with his unerring sense of time and place, he knew precisely what was happening to him.

He was being overwhelmed by little feet. One of the poems of *The Primrose Path* said just that and indicated that if he had a little more privacy and a little less responsibility, he might soar as a poet.

Occasionally, even in Frances's absence, Ogden had to go to New York on business, to see the agent and to meet with the editor of *Nash's Magazine* who was then in the city.

He lunched with his old friend Charles Duell, who brought along James Hilton, the new literary wonder of New York, whose *Lost Horizon* was then making a splash, cooed over by Alexander Woollcott and praised by lesser critics. He saw Malcolm Johnson and other old friends. He talked to *Cosmopolitan*, and they offered him a retainer of $400 a month, which was a very nice way to look into 1936.

When Ogden got back to Baltimore he found a letter from Frances that renewed the long-distance quarrel. She accused him of yearning for some other woman. He cabled her that he was angry, but he assured her that she was the only girl for him. Ultimately, she came home and the quarrel was resolved.

As with so much else in life, such quarrels taught Ogden new truths.

One of his poems in the new collection spotlighted the difficulties of the married state felt by many men. Ogden's poetic "he" was, the verse indicated, a peaceful sort of man who did not like quarreling, and who would, like most husbands, go a long way to avoid a spat. "He" was conciliatory. All "he" wanted was a quiet, peaceable existence with very little nagging.

"He" tried to keep his mouth shut on issues that "he" knew would raise red flags like those before a female bull. "He" would agree to almost any ridiculous proposition to avoid a fight.

And yet, how often did "he" find himself being castigated, catechized, and correlated with a number of pleasant sorts who happened to be his friends, but who had aroused the ire of "her" by keeping him out late or taking him to play golf or to the races when "he" should be doing what "she" wanted him to do.

When such talk began to fly, Ogden had learned, the only possible solution was to get out of the house and wait for things to cool off. A poem on the subject addressed the misguided among the masculine contingent, those fellows who thought it takes two to make a quarrel. Obviously, they had not yet been married.

The poet had news for them. It never took more than one, female gender.

The year 1935 had begun well enough, but with Frances's trip abroad and all the confusion of the household, it had not turned out very satisfactorily as a work year. The poet had managed only about a hundred verses and short prose pieces.

The winter of 1936 was also not very productive. One reason was illness. Ogden was admittedly a hypochondriac, given to dosing himself with various nostrums. When he could not sleep, he took luminal. When he had colds, he took various remedies. And colds came often in the bitter winters of northern Maryland.

Thus illness became a regular part of Nash's life. One of his poems was a celebration of the grippe, and then there was bronchitis, and there were other diseases common to mankind, all of which caused Ogden Nash to sympathize with poor humanity and mostly himself when he was sick.

Yes, as Ogden noted, Maryland has been a great place for germs since the first Englishmen established the first settlement on Kent Island in Chesapeake Bay some three hundred years before his time. Chief among them all, since the eradication of malaria, was the flu bug, which laid hundreds of thousands of Marylanders low each winter. The poet's "he" was often one of them.

The poet wrote many poems about "his" illnesses, and they concerned the reactions of "his" family as much as the problems of the invalid. The poetic invalid got many bleak looks and remarks such as "You're just trying to get out of going to the Parkhursts on Saturday night," etc. But of sympathy, there seemed very little. Temperatures were taken, and according to the gospel of the poetic household, temperatures were what counted. A sniffle without temperature was given no credence whatsoever, save by the poet's invalid, to whom a temperature of 99.1 was as good as one of 100. Particularly on Monday mornings. If "he" was sick, "he" spent hours and days and maybe even weeks in bed, complaining, but somehow, miraculously, recovering for weekends.

The grippe came and went, and so did colds. One cold prompted a poetic study of "The Germ." Another prompted consideration of colds in general. The poet reported that "he" consulted his doctor, "he" did himself up in mufflers and mittens, and drank diluted bicarbonate of soda and took aspirin, and kissed no one, and sneezed out the window, and coughed up the chimney. "He" kept to his bedroom and out of the way. "He" might as well, because family and friends regarded the poet's invalid as a carrier and shunned him. Whereas "he," from his lonely bedroom, ruminated on others "he" had seen with colds. Those other fellows drank cocktails by the barrelful, did not gargle or take aspirin, and went to parties, and kissed all the ladies, and said loud hellos, spewing millions of germs, and sneezed in the bus stops, and coughed on the dance floor, and were enormously popular with everyone. There was, as the poet observed over his bitter cup of herbal tea in his bedroom, no justice.

Of course, the well poet could see another side of life, too. If "she" was sick, "he" told her to grin and bear it, and it wasn't really so bad after all, probably mostly in her imagination, and why didn't "she" take some Vitamin C and a couple of aspirins?

If 1935 had been an iffy sort of year for the poet, the early months of 1936 were worst of all. What with the continued difficulties of marital adjustment, the wintry weather, the grippe, and the dear little babies underfoot, the winter of 1935–36 was a very long one indeed.

But then, in April, finally in came spring. And with spring came a whole new challenge to Poet Ogden Nash. Hollywood called.

11

There's Gold in Them Thar Beverly Hills

Ogden Nash went to Hollywood in the summer of 1936, hired by Metro-Goldwyn-Mayer to write a motion picture based on the operetta *The Firefly*, written by Otto Harbach for the stage. Operettas were much in vogue. The successes of Nelson Eddy and Jeanette MacDonald in a whole series of operettas caused all the studios to try to follow suit. That was certainly in the tradition of the motion picture industry.

In the 1920s the moguls of the motion picture industry moved themselves and their production enterprises to California on the announced precept that the weather was better out there. Cheap real estate was the underlying reason. The heart of the enterprise, the distribution system, was maintained in New York where the money was to be found.

From Hollywood and its environs the producers began beckoning writers from the East, in the logic that a great writer ought to be able to write anything, and even if he couldn't they could put his name on the credits and get a certain value from that. It was easy enough for these men who thought in terms of hundreds of thousands of dollars to offer big pay and bigger promises. To them, the pay was peanuts, and in that they were more knowing than their victims. The big money turned out to be what would later come to be known as "Mickey Mouse" money. A writer was brought out on a six-month contract with options and was paid in multiples of $500 bills by the week.

Ogden had achieved a certain fame among the Hollywood crowd

through his ribald poem, "The Four Prominent So-and Sos." More important, of course, was the excellent reception of his poems in national magazines and the good sales of his books. So MGM offered him a six-month
contract, with options, and he accepted. He always claimed it had been
done with mirrors and that MGM's Eastern story executives had thought
they were signing the novelist Donald Ogden Stewart. But that was
Ogden's little joke.

For a writer like Ogden, who considered a 1935 Christmas bonus of $280
from *The New Yorker* a splendid sum, a weekly salary of $750 seemed phe-
nomenal. It was only later that he and the others discovered the "Mickey
Mouse" part—a writer who earned a thousand dollars a week felt com-
pelled to live like his peers, which meant a nice big house with a swimming pool, perhaps in Beverly Hills or perhaps in Brentwood. One did not
buy real estate on a six-month writing contract or on the strength of an
option, and one did not buy furniture either. So one rented a house, perhaps at 348 Canyon View Drive, Brentwood Heights, with actor Peter
Lorre as a neighbor, as Ogden did, and one paid through the nose for the
house, for the help and the booze and cars and clothes and entertainment
and recreation. A few niggardly types managed to save up enough money
to spend a little elsewhere, but most Eastern writers fell willingly into the
big spending habits of the new owners of Hollywood and spent to the hilt.
They did not realize it, but having worked hard to become professionally
independent, as had Ogden Nash, the Hollywood writers found themselves back on the assembly line, showing up for work at a studio every
day and awaiting the orders of their masters.

At Ogden's movie factory, Metro-Goldwyn-Mayer, there was a great
deal of motion at the studio and very little work. Mostly the writers waited
for story conferences, which were called by the producer when he was not
(A) Interviewing actresses, (B) Calling his broker, (C) Looking for the
director, (D) Worrying about the budget, (E) Impressing other producers
by lunching at the Brown Derby (later at Chasen's), (F) Explaining to his
wife why he had not come home last night, (G) Consulting with his ana-
lyst, (H) Visiting his barber, or if sufficiently high on the scale, having his
barber visit him. Whatever, the last and least important item on his schedule was the calling of a story conference. When a conference was called,
the writers all assembled eagerly, pencils and pads in hand, and waited.
The producer usually made a speech, explaining what he was trying to do
in adapting the novel or the biography. (Virtually all motion pictures of the
period were adaptations of successful works in other fields, only the small
cheap studios and United Artists were doing much with original works.)

That explanation probably occupied the whole first conference, and the
writers ended up with a few words and a handful of doodles on their pads,
and the advice from on high that they repair to their lairs and think. The

second conference might introduce the director, who would explain his point of view, with many looks at the producer and a few asides from that quarter. That meeting might end with demand for "treatments," which would mean a few hours work. From an endless number of "treatments" came outlines and scenarios and a dialogue and finally, if the whole project did not get stuck somewhere, a shooting script, probably engineered by the director. For the most part, the writers played cards, or drank, or chased girls, or sat looking out the window at the studio lot. Ogden once said he spent two and a half years in Hollywood and did no more than four weeks real work in the whole time.

What impressed him most that first year was the pecking order and the paranoia.

"The actors are afraid of the directors," he told a *Baltimore Sun* reporter when he returned to visit his wife's parents. "The directors and the managers are afraid of the actors. Some people are afraid of the communists, some are afraid of the capitalists. Some are afraid of labor. Some are afraid of censorship in Spain . . . I don't know why, but I could see it all the time. Of course, there's no reason for it at all. If someone would just get up and say 'boo' the bugaboos would collapse."

"Why don't you say 'boo'?" the reporter asked.

"I wouldn't dare," said Ogden.

The reason, of course, was those big salaries. Hollywood was the one place where the liberal writer could be earning $2,500 a week, said Ogden. That had to be considered.

They gave him an office with a typewriter desk, a big sofa, an enormous California-style ashtray, and a telephone. He sat at the desk at first and then on the sofa and waited for the telephone to ring. It didn't.

They invited him to see rushes, and they invited him to previews, sneak previews, premieres, breakfasts, teas, lunches, soirees, musicales, receptions, motor trips, beach parties, yachting excursions, cocktail parties, and once in a while to a story conference.

After Ogden went to Hollywood in 1936 his output of poems and prose stopped almost cold. There was a clause in his contract that prohibited him from publishing new material while he was writing for the movies, and this meant his verse. He wrote a little, but it didn't work.

"It's just funny," he said, "what a deadening effect a regular check coming in each month has on your ambition. I can work only under pressure. And I don't like to write unless I can use it right away. I don't enjoy it when I have to salt the verses away."

So that year he wrote only ten poems. After he had found the house, Frances and the children came and then they settled down to the life of the film colony.

Ogden's first film assignment was to refashion that old operetta, *Otto*

Herbach's *The Firefly* into something more modern. Someone had bought the film rights, and then the moguls had decided that *The Firefly* was not motion picture material as it stood. Yes, said the studio wizards, with Ogden Nash's genius he should have no difficulty at all in taking *The Firefly* high into the stratosphere. What was wanted, they explained, was a melodrama, about international espionage. Plenty of poems, of course.

Ogden, being new at the game, took it very seriously and turned out a melodrama plot for *The Firefly*. He gave it to the producer and never heard another word.

Weeks went by. The only way he knew he was still on the payroll was to call his agent and discover that the check had been received again, that the agent had taken his cut and put the rest in Ogden's bank account. That was reassurance of a sort.

So what did Ogden do to while away the time between assignments?

He took up badminton, very popular with film writers that year. There were some writers at his studio who had been playing badminton uninterruptedly for three years.

But Ogden was not allowed to break any records. One day late in 1936 his telephone rang, and he happened to be in the office. On the telephone was a producer, who wanted him for a writing task. The name of the movie would be *The Shining Hour*. Ogden's work on the movie consisted largely of a "treatment." Other writers were called in, and eventually *The Shining Hour* was completed and distributed. It did not shine at the box office.

The Leonards came to visit for a month at Christmastime 1936. The next summer Frances went back to Baltimore to visit the Leonards, leaving Ogden in charge of the children again. He had plenty of time to take them to the beach and to play games with them. One of their games was "dinner." The girls would dress up and eat with their father. Linell, the eldest, would play her mother's role, and Isabel would play another, perhaps Mrs. Leonard's. The conversations, Ogden reported to Baltimore, were remarkable imitations of grown-up small talk.

When Frances returned to California, the Nashes embarked on an active, if restrained, social life. Most of their friends were not of the motion picture industry.

In 1937 Ogden worked on *The Feminine Touch*, with writers George Oppenheimer and Edward L. Hartmann. It was produced by Loew's finally in 1941.

One day in the fall of 1937 Ogden went down to the MGM commissary and at the table sequestered for writers he encountered a slender gentlemen of morose and foreboding appearance. This person, he discovered, was Sidney J. Perelman, better known as S. J. to his readers or Sid to his friends. Perelman and Ogden had shared Ross, and they still shared the pages of *The New Yorker*, or had until purloined by lucre to toil in what Perelman called "the dream factories."

They compared notes on the various penances that had been inflicted on them in the name of motion picture projects, for in the magnificence of MGM their paths had not crossed before. Then, lo and behold, a few days later they met again, in the office of a producer by the name of Fleet Mousejoy, a name so improbable that Perelman is still suspected of having invented him. They nodded in surprise, and, when his esquireship introduced them to one another, they said they had met. This seemed palpably impossible to Producer Mousejoy, for one of the unwritten laws at MGM was that no lesser figures ever existed until introduced by a producer, so he catalogued for each the other's attainments and watched approvingly as they shook hands like a pair of wrestlers preparing to hit the mat.

Having done the honors, the impatient Mister Mousejoy then got down to business. Sam Goldwyn or maybe Louis B. Mayer had recently been East again, perhaps. Anyhow, someone who had to be in a state of catalepsy had spent a sum in the upper reaches of five figures to acquire that super bestseller of the year, Dale Carnegie's *How to Win Friends and Influence People*. It was the greatest self-help book of a whole era. Just the name HOW TO WIN FRIENDS AND INFLUENCE PEOPLE, when displayed on a theater marquee, would be worth a minimum of a million dollars to MGM, announced Mr. Mousejoy.

The movie had already been cast, the producer said, employing Joan Crawford, Fannie Brice, and Mickey Rooney, and with those stars it was guaranteed to run the gamut of emotion from A to B.

Perelman struggled with his knife-like profile to wedge a line into the soliloquy.

"But look, Mr. Mousejoy . . ."

"We're going to write a new chapter in motion picture history, my friends."

"Fabulous," Writer Nash agreed, "but there's one little hitch, Mr. Mousejoy. There's no actual story. It's a book of inspirational essays—psychology for the layman sort of thing."

The producer was unimpressed by roadblocks. Who cared? MGM had hired them. "Two brilliant minds," he called them fondly, and he did not see how they could miss coming up with the sensation of the year. Now, he said, he had a few ideas that might help out . . .

So Ogden and S. J. Perelman sat spellbound for half an hour as the producer went on. "Maunderings," Perelman termed the Mousejoy monologue.

Then, the "two brilliant minds" were dismissed by the producer to retire to a cubbyhole in writers' alley, and they tried to make some sense of what the producer had been saying. They looked at the book. The picture of Dale

Carnegie on the dust jacket was very impressive, but not sexy. Nor did it look anything like the teen-age Mickey Rooney, who just then was starring in a series of motion pictures about an irrepressible freckled kid called Andy Hardy. They looked inside. Not only was that brief observation Ogden had managed to squeeze into the meeting fully justified, but they saw that the book had no story, no plot, no characters, no tone, and no continuity of any kind.

Somehow, perhaps at the commissary over tankards of gin disguised as lemonade, they fabricated part of a plot line. Miss Crawford and Miss Brice were to play the roles of striptease danseuses down on their luck and holed up the YWCA. There, they stopped. And gin though they might quaff, even switching in afternoon to Scotch, they could find no excuse to bring Mickey Rooney into the tale. So they said to hell with it and quit trying. They would wait for their mentor, Fleet Mousejoy, to come up with the solution to the Rooney equation. Meanwhile, for five weeks they worked at perfecting a quiz game based on the Sherlock Holmes tales, which they hoped to market if time did not run out. The producer telephoned a few times, but only to check in and assure them that he was giving fullest play to their creative talents, and then hang up before one of them could pose the Rooney problem.

They had nearly brought the Sherlock Holmes quiz to the stage where marketing experts are called in, when suddenly they were summoned to the Mousejoy lair. Fearfully, the guilty pair assembled, without a line on paper, prepared to be chastised, perhaps even booted out of never-never land into the world of work. But the producer had other matters on his mind and did not even look at their yellow pads for evidence of graffiti.

Mr. Mousejoy was sorry but he had a big shock for them. He had been summoned by the high and mighty to New York and must leave immediately. *How to Win Friends and Influence People* was going to have to go on the shelf for the moment, and the pair of them were being transferred to other projects. It was, he said a little shakily, adieu for the moment.

So, in 1938, Ogden went to work on a picture called *Hold That Kiss*. Even in March he was talking about being home in Baltimore for Christmas, and that meant home for good. He knew what was happening to him. In 1937 and 1938 he produced only six poems. But the paycheck came every week and every six months it became a bigger paycheck. The beach was pleasant, the sun was warm, and the breezes soothed. It was hard to get away.

Despite his current poetic inactivity, Ogden was still very much a force on the publishing scene. His reviews were generally very good, and now he had five major books under his belt. Some reviewers called him the first new writer of light verse to have come along in twenty years. This was not very kind to some of the standbys, such as Samuel Hoffenstein, who had been doing more or less what Ogden was doing early in the 1920s, and for *The New Yorker*, too. He succumbed to Hollywood, and went out to become a very successful screenwriter, until he died in the mid-1930s. Ogden, when he thought about such things, gave full credit to Hoffenstein as a major influence in his work. More, he admitted that he had adopted Hoffenstein's approach and viewpoint to a large extent.

But other critics considered Ogden to be "an original." William Rose Benét said just that. William Soskin called his verses a compendium of "bitter insanity, wry foolishments and considerably inspired lunacy." Burton Rascoe declared that Nash was "engagingly original." *Harper's* magazine liked his unexpected originality of rhyming. *The Atlantic Monthly* said kind words even about his prose pieces and that his poems were "fresh and joyful caricatures."

This was, indeed, a very good press, and it showed no signs of growing less enthusiastic.

Ogden had changed publishers, moving from Simon & Schuster in New York to Little, Brown and Company in Boston. Little, Brown brought out *I'm a Stranger Here Myself* in 1938, mopping up the poems he had written since 1935. There was a difference in this book; the poems were mostly longer and more complex. There was little about New York and Park Avenue and Broadway and infinitely more about such matters as dieting, gossiping, the new "hunt crowd" who had invaded Maryland and Virginia from New Jersey and New York, about banks, money, the common cold, and other afflictions. Thomas Sugrue, reviewing the collection in the *New York Herald Tribune*, caught immediately the difference.

". . . Mr. Nash is about halfway on his journey from Park Avenue to Main Street. He is getting closer and closer to the fundamental stuff of middle-class American life and farther away from the artificialities which prompted his first work."

Nash would never be another Edgar Guest, the great unwashed poet of the people, but he had cast his lot with suburbia, said Sugrue, and the result was salutary. He compared Ogden to the eighteenth-century essayists who took as their study humanity. Nash, said the critic, had the field to himself, because all the others with the souls of eighteenth-century essayists seemed to have become psychologists and psychoanalysts. There was a good deal of truth to what Mr. Sugrue had to say. Ogden had discovered back in the 1920s when he was writing bad copies of the style of great poets that he did not have the stuff in him to face the exigencies of life head-on, but needed to slip around and take a sidelong view of the subject, sneaking up on it, as it were, and then assaulting it with his poetic rapier.

Sugrue suggested that at this stage of his life, Ogden had captured the essence of the "suburban snob." If Ogden's Baltimore friends happened to see that review, they could not have liked it much, for a great deal of his raw material was right around him. His wife and children, it seemed obvious, appeared frequently in other guises in his pages. Who else was the lady who discovered one day on the scale that she weighed precisely what the charts said she ought to weigh, and then worried that she had to go on a diet so she would not gain any weight and get up above that figure?

Or the lady who wanted to send her absent husband a telegram to inform him of some momentous fact, and because she wanted also to save money she compressed the wire to ten words to get the cheap night rate. Her husband then could not make any sense of the telegram and had to call up long distance from some far place, thus spending ten times as much as she would have spent in the first place if she had added another five or ten words to the message. This was the sort of thing that happened to Ogden when he was in Los Angeles and Frances was in Baltimore.

He wrote a poem introducing dogs. What was his raw material? A dog named Spangle who allowed the Nashes to provide bed and board.

Ogden wrote a poem on the habits of one men's shop that sounded like it ought to be either J. Press or Brooks Brothers, the haberdashers to the Ivy League. It had to come from the bittersweet experience of Frederic Ogden Nash. He had bought some shirts from the store. He had walked in and charged them to his account. They were fine shirts and they lasted a long time. At about the time that the shirts were ready for the ragbag he had paid the last bill. He needed more shirts, but his favorite store was too expensive for his means, now that he had wife and children to support. So he had manfully stayed away from his favorite store and bought his shirts cheaper elsewhere, knowing that they were inferior.

Then, one day he got a letter from that haberdashery saying they had been examining their list of customers and that he had not bought anything from them for several years. Had they offended him?

This friendly letter was followed by other letters, each more insistent than the last that he tell them why he was annoyed, and if he was not annoyed, would he please, please come to the store and show them he still cared by buying something on his account?

Finally, he had given in and gone down and bought some more shirts, which he charged.

Being a writer, and thus notoriously "slow-pay," time had passed, and the bill had remained constant. The depression had also caused the store officials to tighten their credit strings, too, and it was not long before the friendly store, which had only a short time before been importuning him to buy, now became downright unpleasant about collecting, and finally turned the account over to their lawyers. So he had paid, and as quickly as possible had forgotten the unpleasant incident. Then, behold, a year later, from the store came another obsequious letter noting that it had been over a year since he had bought anything and wondering if they had offended him. And it had all started over again.

The soothsayers, the pundits, the columnists, and commentators of America addressed themselves to the weighty issues of the day: if they were Republicans, to the excesses of the second Democratic administration of Franklin Delano Roosevelt, which continued, as far as they were concerned, to carry the country toward hell in a hot canoe. Were they Democrats, they concerned themselves with the plight of the poor and the state of nations. Ogden addressed more weighty matters: his two new suits, and how important they made him feel, the problems of living through Monday, the difficulties of getting coffee *with* your meal. Oh, occasionally he allowed himself a sidelong look at the political world, but that is just what it was—a sidelong look. One day he wrote a poem about James A. Farley, the postmaster general, still; the chairman of the Democratic party, still. The holding of both offices distresses this citizen, at least a little bit, and he wanted to see the day when a cabinet office was created for the chairman of the party so the postmaster general could worry about delivering the mail. For, among other things, the cost of first-class mail had gone up from the two cents a letter that seemed almost to have been the price from time immemorial, to three cents a letter, which was regarded as scandalous, and the cost of airmail from a nickel to a dime. Ogden Nash's verse about the post office may have been sidelong, but it was a chord that sounded good to millions of Americans.

He wrote about spring, and about hats. He wrote about the difficulty of getting up in the morning. He explored the philosophy of plumbers. He wrote about racing, which he liked, and about parsley, which he did not like. He wrote a great deal about his wife, on whom he continued to dote with the wistfulness of a lamb chasing its mother. One subject he did not write about in his book: his daughters. They, with their mother, had dominated his last two books. But not *I'm a Stranger Here Myself*. In suburbia wives might rule, but daughters did not dominate. Or perhaps part of the reason was that when he went to Hollywood and again became a wage slave, he was not around the house, underfoot, and observing the little dears all day. "Interoffice Memorandum," "Let Me Buy This One," and "Barmaids Are Diviner than Mermaids" were much more to the point of his existence than couplets about little children.

BARMAIDS ARE DIVINER THAN MERMAIDS

Fish are very good at swimming,
And the ocean with them is brimming.
They stay under water all year round,
And they never get drowned,
And they have a gift more precious than gold,
Which is that they never get cold.
No, they may not be as tasty as venison or mooseflesh,
But they never get gooseflesh.
They have been in the ocean since they were roe,
So they don't have to creep into it toe by toe,
And also they stay in it permanently, which must be a source of great
*   satisfaction,*
Because they don't have to run dripping and shivering up and down the
*   beach waiting vainly for a healthy reaction.*
Indeed when I think how uncomplicated the ocean is for fish my thoughts
*   grow jealous and scathing,*
Because when fish bump into another fish it doesn't wring from them a cry of
*   Faugh! and ruin their day's bathing.*
No, if it's a bigger fish than they are, they turn around and beat it,
And if it's littler, they eat it.
Some fish are striped and some are speckled,
But none of them ever heard of ultra-violet rays and felt it necessary to lie
*   around getting sand in their eyes and freckled.*
Oh, would it not be wonderous to be a fish? No, it would not be wondrous,
Because we unmarine humans are at the top of the animal kingdom and it
*   would be very undignified to change places with anything under us.*

He had promised himself that he would get the hell out of Hollywood, and later he wrote that toward the end of this stint he used to wake up nights and then wake his wife and ask her who he was. He was suffering from an advanced case of "immaculate conception," the process by which movie producers and directors took a perfectly good script and so changed it that the writer would never recognize it (and often wished he could withdraw his credit from the screen).

Finally, Ogden did wrench himself free of Hollywood for a time, and Christmas did find him in Baltimore. In January 1938 he and Frances went to Europe to spend some of that easy money. It was Ogden's first trip abroad. They visited Paris, and they visited London. Dan Longwell, the friend and old boss from Doubleday days, had gone in 1934 to join Henry Luce and plan Luce's new magazine *Life*, which began publication in 1936. Longwell had been to London many times and knew many people. He put the Nashes onto Winston Churchill, who had been amused by Nash's verses. Churchill was a very busy politician, active in various committees and warning against Hitler's preparations for war, which were so much more obvious to him than to many of his colleagues. Winston put the Nashes onto his son Randolph, who took them to dinner. Longwell had also written A. P. Herbert, who took them boating on the Thames and then on tours of the House of Commons and the House of Lords. They visited Heinemann publishers and were given tea. Ogden accounted the trip a great success, and he attributed much of the reason to Dan Longwell's waypaving.

In March the Nashes came home to Baltimore, to bad news. In the spring of 1939 Ogden's mother became seriously ill. It seemed advisable to remain in the East for a time, and that, too, helped him break the spell of Hollywood. But in the summer Ogden had to return to Hollywood to fulfill his contract; Frances remained in Maryland with the children. He took a bungalow at the Garden of Allah that summer, as was fashionable. Robert Benchley had stayed there, and so had Dorothy Parker and dozens, scores, of refugees from the East before them and hundreds after.

He had now become involved in another medium, radio. The J. Walter Thompson advertising agency had brought him onto the Chase and Sanborn hour. He appeared with Rudy Vallee to read his poetry.

He amused himself in the absence of his family by dining out. One night Ogden dined with F. Scott Fitzgerald and his current love, Sheila Graham, a onetime actress who became a Hollywood columnist. Ogden was the only person in Hollywood who had dined with Fitzgerald who was *not* writing a book about him, Fitzgerald said.

He ate with producer Wolf Mankiewicz, who told him he was tired of the crap of Hollywood and wanted to make nothing but good pictures. He would be using Ogden's talents, he said.

On the radio shows Ogden met Ginger Rogers, whom he found overly made up and coarse; Charles Coburn, whom he found charming; Dorothy Lamour, who was very pleasant but dumb enough to fall in love with Bob Hope; Don Ameche, who was very kind to Ogden; and Edgar Bergen, who reminded him of an old friend.

He was divesting himself of the Hollywood glamour as quickly as he could, but he was not creating any poetry. The money had piled up. There was no need, and therefore there was no poetry. In 1939 and 1940 Ogden did not sell any poems. He was trying to get back into the swing of writing, but Hollywood again held out its golden lure. MGM offered him a six-week contract. That, he swore, would be the last.

Ogden's old books were still doing well. But Little, Brown had a problem. They wanted a new book to follow *I'm a Stranger Here Myself* and maintain the continuity, but Ogden's output was virtually nil. So in 1940 they brought out *The Face Is Familiar*, a selection of Ogden's previous works.

In California, at least he was reading his poetry on radio. His last appearance under the advertising agency contract was on the Bing Crosby program on Thanksgiving day, reading his poem "Mr. Artesian" to an enormous radio audience.

Ogden went home to Maryland and believed he had left Hollywood forever. He had been signed up to do a sustaining program later in the year. But by the end of November Hollywood beckoned again, and the Nashes closed up their Baltimore house and sent the children to stay with the grandparents in their summer place on the Eastern Shore of Maryland, and they went to California again. This time they found a furnished house on South Peck Drive in Beverly Hills. The promise was that it was to be only six weeks and certainly no more than ten. It was a promise Ogden had doubly promised himself to keep.

12

And Now, May I Present That Wealthy Poet, Ogden Nash

In 1941 Little, Brown published *The Face Is Familiar*, and Ogden began a new career—one which he detested from the first moment.

The Face Is Familiar dredged back into the dim, distant past, as early as 1931, for some of the verses to make up the bulk of the book, because of the shortage of new Nash compositions.

There were several reasons that Ogden did not produce much during the Hollywood years. First, he was forbidden to publish new materials as long as he held a screenwriter's contract. Second, as he had noted, the regular paycheck was so comforting that he did not feel the impetus to earn more money. And third, at the end of his Hollywood years he was very busy.

When Ogden returned to Hollywood in the fall of 1940 he found it much changed. Earlier he had worked in an abandoned motion picture studio, which had been turned into cubicles for writers. But now the writers had been moved to a modern air-conditioned building.

There was also a difference in the way the studios behaved. Ogden discovered that the producers now cared where he was all day long. He was expected to check in at the gate at 9 A.M. and check out at 6 P.M. and a guard was there to write down his name and the time. Once he went away for three days in midweek, and when he returned, that very day he received a memorandum reminding him of the hours of the five-day week.

On this final contract Ogden was employed to write a script based on an original story, "The Female of the Species." It was one of a number of scripts being prepared for the new glamour girl of 1940, Hedy Lamarr. Ogden came for six weeks and stayed three months, working all the time. He finished the script and turned it in, and the script promptly disappeared into the maw of the MGM lion. Ogden's contract ran out, and so he returned to Baltimore in the middle of February 1941.

No longer did Ogden sneer at Hollywood.

He did not like Hollywood. He objected particularly to the false glamour of the film capital, but he also knew that no one had dragged him there. He had succumbed to the attraction of big money. This did not make him eager to dwell on Hollywood or its style of life, but he was not to burn his bridges, which he could have done in short order with a series of satires addressing "Tinseltown" the way he addressed politics and politicians. But he did not. He wrote a wicked verse about "Zanuckville" and Louella Parsons, the Hearst Hollywood columnist, and Alice Faye and Orson Welles and Garson Kanin, and a hero named Ogden Gravel, who wanted most of all to travel far, far away from Hollywood. But it was a thank-you note to some friends. This verse did not grace the pages of *The Face Is Familiar*.

No, Ogden was very careful about what he said in public about the gilded world of Darryl Zanuck. After he had seen his old friend Dan Longwell and given him an earful of his opinions of the motion picture industry, he cautioned Dan against quoting him because he might one day wish to return to Hollywood.

"I would like to return to the West Coast in a year or eighteen months," he told a reporter from the *Baltimore Sun*, "but right now I would like to stay here."

As to his literary career, he was not quite certain what he would do. "I'm not writing a novel and I've never even tried to write a play," he said. "Screen work is very good training for playwriting," and he suggested that one day he might well write a play.

Ogden was reorganizing his literary life, getting back to writing his poems. When he returned from Hollywood, he was not quite sure what sort of reception he would receive from the magazines he had abandoned four years earlier. New York, where most magazines are produced, has always been merciless in its demands for continuity as long as a writer succeeds with the public. Let the writer drop out for even a year, and he might as well be dead.

What saved Ogden was that the old work still drew attention, and now he was in that odd position of the celebrity who gets credit for work he has never done. For years he and Dorothy Parker were mixed up by anthologists and journalists and professors. He was often given credit for some of Mrs. Parker's pithy verses ("Men seldom make passes . . .") and Mrs. Parker often got credit for his ("Candy is . . ."). On one occasion a professor from New York's City College wrote him asking questions about how he had come to write "I never saw a Purple Cow, I never hope to see one . . ." Ogden, who had a fine regard for the professorial trade and expected much of pedants, was shocked that this ignoramus had credited him with writing something written by Gelett Burgess in 1902, the year Ogden was born, and he so indicated in a sarcastic letter to the professor. All he managed with that gesture was to enrich the professor, because a few years later he learned that the letter had been offered for sale by a book dealer for $25.

That mistaken-identity incident was another indication of the poet's growing fame. The wide sale of seven books of poems, to say nothing of the more ephemeral publication of most of these poems, first in magazines, had brought Ogden a national reputation as well as a living. Book reviewers in every corner of the continent and even across the Atlantic were familiar with the name. He had also been heard on national radio network shows several times, which gave him another sort of exposure to the general public. Thus Ogden had become what in the world of publicity is known as "a property" and as such he could be marketed in a number of ways. One way was the lecture tour, an inviting trap because the four-figure gross fees seemed very handsome.

Ogden had been approached in the fall of 1940 by Harold Peat, a New York lecture agent, with assurances that he could make a pretty penny in talking to college groups, ladies' clubs, Knife and Forkers, symposia, and business clubs. All he had to do was travel around and deliver a few of his own jokes and read some of his verses. The agency would take care of all the details, make the bookings, make his travel arrangements, collect the fees, and publicize his efforts in the local press of whichever Podunk he was gracing with his presence.

The negative side was that lecturing meant constant travel, wear and tear on the digestive system by a succession of rubber-chicken lunches and gluey roast beef dinners, and long absences from the family.

To Ogden, as much possessed by his wife after nine years of marriage as he had been on his wedding day, this latter stricture was by far the worst. But there seemed to be little alternative.

His life that fall of 1940 had been completely in disarray. Wellesley College had written him in the summer to ask him to come up and read his verses. He had not even answered the letter, so confused were his affairs that it had gotten stuffed into a drawer when he was between trips to the West Coast. That omission was of a piece with his actions that summer. If by winter he had settled back into life in Baltimore, he had realized that it would take some time to restore his literary markets, and by spring he had steeled himself to accept the lecture tour he hated to contemplate.

In 1941 Ogden went on the lecture circuit. The first tour began in October, was broken early in November, resumed after a week, and lasted until December. The first stop was at Worcester, Massachusetts. He confided in the reporter from the *Worcester Telegram* that this was his first appearance on any stage anywhere, and thus assured himself a very good writeup, for how many times a year did Worcester, Mass., get a first in anything. It wasn't planned; Ogden had the innate innocence of children and poets. In this, his maiden interview, he told the story of the confusion between himself and Mrs. Parker, and he delivered a few other brief lines. When it came time to make his appearance, he was at his most amusing. He told these stories again, and he read some of his verses.

The next stop was Buffalo. The train took him up there. He then walked through a station that seemed to him larger than the Sante Fe Station in Los Angeles and came out on Paderewski Boulevard. A taxi took him through what impressed him as several miles of Poland. But when he got to the Hotel Statler he found himself assigned to a pleasant corner room on the sixteenth floor with large windows on two sides. He had time for a bath and a shave, and then a reporter from one of the newspapers came to interview him. This was always valuable, for it tended to sell books, as well as draw attention to the lecture.

His appearance that day was at a luncheon, which, fortunately, was held in the Statler Hotel dining room. At noon he went downstairs, found the lunching businessmen, wearing their huge badges that announced their names, nicknames, and business affiliations, and the fact that they belonged to the Greater Buffalo Advertising Club. He sat down at the speaker's table to one of those prefabricated chicken lunches. Then he had the pleasure of listening to the club officials carrying on their weekly business. Surreptitiously he read a copy of *Advents,* the club's weekly newspaper, and with considerable interest saw how he had been advertised.

There was something about Nash's poetry that seemed to bring out the poet in everyone assigned to write about him. He had already encountered reviews in rhyme, and newspaper interviews in rhyme, and letters in rhyme, ad nauseum. Here was some more:

The first name is Ogden, the last name is Nash
The man who writes stories and verse, just for cash.
He's serious, funny, witty and droll.
The verse pads his purse with a sizeable roll.
And the vitamin tonic that flows through his pen
Is a humorous ticket without scratching, amen.

An hour given to Ogden Nash, which he will crowd into thirty short minutes or so. You can leave before that if you gotta go. But it will pay you to stick like a pup . . . good stuff and common sense to it. Ogden Rhyme Nash, the middle name you see above is one we thought up in our labor of love to pass the test of the famous car.
Welcome, Og . . .

Finally the club's business was accomplished, and the chairman of the day turned to the entertainment. That was Ogden. The program chairman was ordered to stand up and introduce the guest. The introducer dwelt entirely on the vast amount of money that the poet must be earning by the practice of his versifying and speechifying, to say nothing of his Hollywood scriptifying. Ogden got up and did his little routine, and everybody laughed in the right places—mostly—and where they seemed befuddled he gathered that they somehow felt that it was their own fault, because by rule of Rotary, anyone who made as much money as he did doing what he did had to be a success, and who could quarrel with success? The luncheon ended, a few of the clubmen cast admiring glances at the speaker over their shoulders as they departed to return to making money, and the program chairman thanked him and said kind words about the performance. Then Ogden was on his own, to rush back upstairs, grab his gladstone, speed down in the elevator, cross the lobby, get a taxi, and hasten to the station to catch the two o'clock train for Rochester.

At Rochester he was pleasantly surprised to be met by the program chairman in charge of the lecture. The committee had not done much of a job, because they had to try three hotels before Ogden finally found a room; it was in the hotel where the Baltimore Orioles stayed when they came to Rochester to play baseball. (The Orioles then playing Triple A ball, not big league.)

The lecture, like everything else in Rochester, was to be held at the Eastman Company plant. There, the long arm of history caught up with him, and he met one of his old co-workers from the streetcar advertising days in New York. Nothing would do, of course, but that they celebrate old palship by having a drink, so Ogden brought him back to the hotel bar and they did. Finally, he wrenched himself away and collapsed in his room, until he regained enough strength to write Frances a letter.

The schedule those little gnomes in the New York office of the lecture agency had put Ogden on was merciless. He had to get up the next morning at four-thirty to catch a train bound for St. Louis. That meant delaying shaving and toothbrushing for the train ride. He got downstairs, paid his bill, and scurried out to find a taxi, which sped to the station, as he prepared to catch the St. Louis train as it came through Rochester and stopped for a few minutes. But the St. Louis–bound passenger train was behind a freight that had just gone off the track east of town, killing the engineer of the freight train and tying up the whole line. What to do? Ogden could not find any station officials at that time of day; in fact, he could find no one at all who spoke English. Finally, someone in authority showed up and told him to go back to Buffalo and see if he could get to St. Louis from there. So unwashed, untoothbrushed, unshaven, he piled himself and four bags into a day coach and set off for Buffalo. There he caught another day coach to Cleveland, where he found a train to St. Louis. Soon he was aboard. He cleaned up and then lurched down the corridor to the dining car to get a drink, soup, broiled chicken, and cheese and crackers. Then he returned to luxuriate on his compartment couch, where he revised the speech he was supposed to make in Tulsa. At St. Louis he caught the Will Rogers Limited on the Frisco Line, bound for Oklahoma, and that night he slept like a kitten in his Pullman berth.

In Tulsa, Ogden was to make two speeches, one to a men's club and the other to the Women's League.

He was met by both the chairman and the chairwoman. They took him to the Hotel Tulsa, left him alone for an hour, and then picked him up and took him to the luxurious Tulsa Club for an elaborate luncheon. Then they took him sight-seeing around town, to look at oil wells and other spots of cultural importance: the oil-built skyscrapers and the Frank Lloyd Wright house owned by the proprietor of one of the local newspapers.

The schedule gave Ogden a little time that afternoon to finish revising his lecture. Then he had to meet at the hotel with the girls of a high school creative writing class. As usual there were questions about how to write, one of the subjects that really did not delight Ogden. The way to write, he had discovered, was first to read, and then to write. And then to write and then to write and then to write. What upset him most of all, and always would, were the people who intimated that they knew it was all very easy and that he really ought to share his secret with them so they could become great writers. He later recalled a young man who had been assigned a paper on Nash and his works by a high school English teacher; the youth demanded that Ogden send him his works.

Finally, the invaders left, and Ogden had time to prepare for an evening session and a reception.

The evening session turned out to be a cocktail party for about three hundred men, at the Tulsa Club again, then the dinner, the speech, and a reception. His program chairman suggested that the two of them did not want to sit around with a gang of men and drink and led him out the back way. They got into the car, and Ogden thought they were going to his sponsor's house, but no, the chairman said they were going to call on two very nice girls named Dorothy and Cathy. So they drove and drove until they came to a lighted bungalow where the chairman stopped the car.

They went into the bungalow and met Dorothy and Cathy, who seemed to be nice girls, but not very bright. They talked about baseball, and Dorothy said that this year she had been given a ticket to the world series and had gone to Belmont Park for the game. Ogden sat upright in a straight chair, very uncomfortable, preferring not to wonder what was supposed to happen with Dorothy and Cathy. His sponsor hemmed and hawed, and Dorothy and Cathy sat on the couch and looked at each other, and smiled enigmatic smiles. Ogden sat and looked at his briefcase. The sponsor suggested that they ought to liven things up a bit by drinking a bottle of champagne he had left at the bungalow earlier in the day. Ogden arose and said he had to get up very early the next morning, and he would have to be excused from the champagne. So the party broke up without ever having happened, and Ogden got back to his hotel to ponder the mysteries of Tulsa, and his sponsor went he knew not where.

The next morning Ogden was up early, working nervously on his speech for the 2,300 ladies of the ladies' club. After his performance, which again seemed satisfactory, he was taken to a bookstore, where he autographed books for an hour. Then came the luncheon session with the ladies.

The big session was covered by a reporter from the *Tulsa World,* and once again, the journalists, this time the headline writer on the copy desk, could not withstand the temptation:

Nash Makes Premiere
As Orator at Dinniere

There was something about Ogden's verse that created such monstrosities; he brought out the incipient versifier in almost every man who handled letters, for it always looked so easy after Ogden had done it. And the imitators seemed totally unconscious that their little apes of the Nashian japes reached for the perigee of puerility.

The reporter could not stand the strain either. He opened by quoting one of Ogden's oldest rhymes, which dealt with the nousiance of making a living, which interfered with his insouciance. At least he was quoting Nash, not trying to one-up him.

That afternoon's speech, however, found Nash one-upping himself. He had written a poem called "The Mind of Professor Primrose," which dealt with a Harvard professor who had won virtually every prize known to man, from the Nobel to the Davis Cup, and who was a bastion of American culture. But the professor, said Ogden, could keep few things straight. He would leave church for a smoke, and say his prayers at the theater; he entrapped the baby and bounced the mice on his knee. He always thought he was teaching at Yale. After a number of years of this confusion, his wife one day announced that it must cease. There was a way to resolve the professor's problem, a way for him to straighten out his rotten memory. There was an organization dedicated to just such problems: the Pelman Institute. The professor's wife prayed, nay, demanded, that he enroll immediately in the Pelman Institute and put his brain to rights.

And so the professor said he would do it, and he sent off a letter. Then he disappeared. The professor's wife said that was just what she expected, and she rearranged the furniture and lived happily for seven years. Then one day she was on her way to visit Chicago, and she stopped in Schenectady and saw a Pullman porter who was brushing off a tip and trying to put a traveler into his pocket. She looked very carefully at the porter, thought she recognized him, and asked him if he was not Professor Peabody, the long missing Professor Peabody. He admitted that this was so.

What had happened to him, said Mrs. Peabody. What did he learn at the Pelman Institute?

"Lawzy me, ma'am," said the porter, in rich porter's tones: he thought she had said Pullman.

Well, the way Ogden wrote the tale in verse, it was very funny indeed and would be to two generations of readers. (Not the third generation, for in the 1950s the American sense of humor took a decided turn, and ethnic jokes about any but WASPs became too hot to handle.)

But what liberties Ogden always took with his own work! Originally it had been Professor Primrose, whose story was delineated in *The Primrose Path*, the last of the Simon & Schuster books. Now it was Professor Peabody.

Ogden had also re-run a poem he wrote while at Doubleday. Originally the verse had been "in praise" (not much) of Dan Longwell, the advertising manager of Doubleday. Then, when Ogden had included the verse in *Hard Lines*, Dan Longwell became Mr. Linthicum and the poem had appeared as "Songs for a Boss Named Mr. Linthicum." Having revealed little so far, Ogden then told his admiring audience how he worked, which was: Read telephone directories. Read dictionaries. Write notes on yellow pads. Make doodles. Write more notes.

The notes could be anything. They might consist of names: Pauncefoot, Prickett, Daingerfield.

They might be advice to Ogden Nash to use his time better, a thought that engaged him all his life.

They might be philosophical comments: the hope of finding a really good razor (this before the advent of the Atra); the saxophone, he noted, was shaped like the human gut and made about the same sound. Do birds know where they are going? And the emergence of women created emergency for men, a thought he expressed in a number of ways in those days before male chauvinist pigs were perceived by their female opposites.

Or the notes might be rhyming words (Nash-style): pranksters and ganksters, Samaritan and Sheraton, careless and heirless. Chambers of Commerces and Norman Thomases.

There might be just a germ of an idea. Once he jotted down Horatius, and then hop down, chop down, pop down, prop up, chop up, mop up. A few lines farther down this particular page was another idea: dignity in the barber's chair. That's all, no elaboration. The elaboration, if ever, would come later, and the result would be a funny verse.

Having told the ladies so much, and having read a poem, Ogden had given them what they wanted, insight into the life of a real honest-to-God writer who got paid for what he did.

He was a big success in Tulsa. Now on to Omaha.

13

What Does an Aging Poet Do for the War Effort?

Ogden arrived home in Baltimore just in time for World War II. He was as indignant and furious as any American at the Japanese attack on Pearl Harbor. For although he stayed away from controversy in his writings, for the most part, he was a moderate liberal, moderate supporter of the Roosevelt administration, at least in the early years. He kept that to himself, but occasionally some of his opinions crept through. In *Hard Lines* he had taken after publicity-seeking politicians in his jape at Senator Smoot of Ut. and noted that Tammany cooks spoil the broth. In *Happy Days* he had put a spike into the Roosevelt administration's National Recovery Act price-fixing program with a pointed verse. In 1932 when the stock market gave some sign of arising from its two years of somnolence, he celebrated the rise in stocks with a poem. He had also pricked in that book at people who did not vote. When Lindbergh had crossed the Atlantic, Ogden had cheered. When Lindbergh and his wife, the former Anne Morrow, had journeyed adventurously around the world by air, he cheered. But when Lindbergh in the late 1930s and early 1940s became a spokesman for America First, the faintly pro-Nazi, and more anti-British patriotic organization that worked against American entry into World War II, Ogden Nash's feelings erupted, and he penned a short verse linking Lindbergh, Gerald Nye, and Senator Burton K. Wheeler in a most unseemly cabal. The poem never got finished, for Ogden sensed that he was not cut out to be an indignant man, but an amused one, and he had said a number of times that the writer

109

of light material who let his bitterness show destroyed himself. Any time he became outraged, he advised himself to lie down until the fit passed, and usually he was smart enough to take that advice. In serious matters he likened himself to the twelfth man on the football field, who does nothing but get the team into trouble.

With the coming of war, Ogden wanted to volunteer for service. He was nearly forty years old, married, with two growing daughters, and he was so nearsighted that he could not pass an eye test without glasses. He was, in other words, the sort of physical specimen whom the military forces could quite nicely do without.

Still, Ogden hoped, and in January 1942, he sent a biography and tentative application to the Navy, hoping to be enlisted in the U.S. Naval Reserve. It was a forlorn hope, the days went by and nothing happened. So in February he went on a lecture tour once more. He started this time in St. Louis, and then went to Waco, Texas, and to San Antonio. There he met a distant cousin, a lady, who arranged a party at *the* Mexican restaurant in San Antonio, advertised by her as so good that the rich Mexicans drove up from Mexico to eat there. The Texans arranged a very hot lunch, obviously hoping to get a rise out of their guest. But not Ogden. He had been in training, for at home in Baltimore, Carrie, the family cook, had a passion for Tabasco sauce. So Ogden devoured every morsel, without a hiccup or a groan. After lunch they took him to see the Alamo, the old Spanish governor's house, and the Mexican quarter. He had a fine time.

Then it was off to Kansas, to Detroit, Saginaw, and Indianapolis.

The Navy did not come through with an offer so Ogden settled down. He decided to devote himself, at least partly, to good works and accepted the presidency of the Children's Aid Society for Baltimore.

There was more lecturing that spring of 1942. The United States Treasury Department asked Ogden to become a war bond salesman, and he tried. His role was to appear on a platform with other celebrities and to read a poem. Most of these appearances were at war factories and large public gatherings, and the audiences were much more interested in pretty actresses and singers than in poets. Besides, Ogden was not very adept at arousing patriotic fervor. So try as he might, when Ogden became involved emotionally, his humor turned to bathos, and he was the first to recognize this distortion.

In the summer of 1942 he was recording some of his poems, which meant trips to New York. The whole family had moved out to the Leonard's summer place in Salisbury, on the Maryland Eastern Shore. From there Ogden went up and down, sometimes with Frances but usually not. She seemed never to have developed much taste for New York.

Once again, then, the Harvard Club became Ogden's home away from home.

Ogden's eighth book, *Good Intentions,* was published that year. One could safely say that by this time, after twelve years of national and international success, Ogden Nash had become pretty close to what George Whicher in *The Atlantic Monthly* called him: "God's gift to the United States" in the field of humor. Whicher said Ogden was the finest literary comedian since Will Rogers. In the 1920s the Nashian rhymes, with their outrageous misuse of the English language, had caused a flurry. His brittle humor of that period had been perfectly suited to *The New Yorker* and to the mood of the country. But with the sobering of the panic of 1929 and the following hard times, Ogden's targets had changed from the elite and the fleeting. He was moving along that road from Park Avenue to Main Street.

"He has," said Whicher, "a keen eye and a keener nose for what is broadly ridiculous or slightly affected in current ideas and manners, particularly those of metropolitan society . . ."

But Critic Louis Untermeyer was not quite so pleased with what he read in this latest book. "Far from his best," he said of Ogden's verse in his first paragraph. Something, he said, was missing, and he suspected it was the old spontaneity. All the old Nash mannerisms were included—the rhyming of vestibule and indigestibule, for example—but Untermeyer's impression was that the collection was sketchy, and, flinching a little at the thought, "dog tired and dull."

And then, before his review was finished, Mr. Untermeyer had second thoughts. He ended up saying that the more he thought of *Good Intentions,* the more he thought of it, and the better intentions he thought it had. Ultimately, he asked the reader to ignore the first paragraph of his review.

The *New York Herald Tribune*'s Thomas Sugrue had no such qualms at any point in his review of the poems. He saw this book as a departure from the past. He had been able to consult that collection of poems from Ogden's first five books, brought out as *Verses from 1929 On* by Little, Brown in 1940 to fill the gap left by the lean years of screenwriting. What had happened was this: Little, Brown and Company, having taken over the publication of Ogden Nash's works, had been somewhat embarrassed not to have the whole. Furthermore, the old books were now out of print. So Little, Brown took over the rights to the whole oeuvre from Simon & Schuster, and in 1940 brought out his collection. From this point on there would be many reprints. In fact, Ogden would use material over and over, sorting out the topical poems that did not repeat well and leaving them by the wayside.

A major change in Ogden's approach to his poetry coincided with his return from the Hollywood scene. The silence of those years 1937–39 had not been altogether unsalutary, for when he began to come out of it in 1940 it was a new, more philosophical Nash, not so much concerned with the personal complaints of papa, husband, reader, writer, drinker, diner, sleeper, sufferer, and taxpayer, as with the reactions of society in general. Before, he had viewed situations with a feeling of personal identification. Now, he was able to look upon them benignly, the commentator standing on the next-door planet and seeing all. Critic Sugrue suggested that Ogden "had moved from the lyric to the descriptive stage of his talent. Later he will enter the didactic period and finally, it is hoped, he will reach the ripeness of the epic."

Nash had, said the critic, stopped quarreling with nature and females. In this, critic and poet seemed to agree that both were powerful natural forces. The observation suggests, though probably quite wrongly, that Thomas Sugrue knew the man Ogden Nash very well. For indeed, many of Nash's attitudes had changed. During the frustrating courtship of Miss Leonard in the late 1920s, Ogden had indeed seemed to be at war with women, particularly this one woman. Early married life had pitted him against neighbors—he once wrote a poem, "I Do Not Like the People Upstairs"—and against airplanes, remittance men, and self-seeking politicians. He had envied the rich. He had found Arthur Brisbane, William Randolph Hearst's editorialist, a purveyor of platitude. He had been bemused, amused, annoyed, upset, and off balance. He had insisted on being the breadwinner of his family, although his wife had an independent income. He had lived in New York, although his wife much preferred her own Baltimore.

Now, Nash's private life was seemingly peaceful, and the poems much less frequently spoke of quarrels or states of siege. He got on very well with his in-laws, and would dedicate *Many Long Years Ago* to his mother-in-law. His life was so fragmented by six-week Hollywood rentals and the hotel-cum-Pullman life of the traveling lecturer that he had accepted the offer of the Leonards to live all together as an extended family in the Leonard's big house on Rugby Road. He was, in other words, feeling a sense of security in his marriage and certainly in his profession by this time.

In *Good Intentions* Ogden makes peace with the Collector of Internal Revenue (there was a war on, remember) and declares war on Japan. He had already declared war on that country in a poem about the Japanese, who first enters your garden, then brings in his relatives, and then tells you that it is now his garden. That poem was to the war what "Candy is . . ." was to the Flapper generation, a classic. It lasted and was used in 1969 by David Bergamini, author of a book on World War II Japan, as his theme-setting front piece.

In 1942 the Nash children still flash through the pages, but the poet is not overwhelmed by them as before.

Daughter Isabel had a sniffle that was immortalized in one small poem. But that was all. No pandering to children marked these pages. The poet had made peace with the cantaloupe and the parsnip, but never with parsley, which he still found gharsley. He was no longer so angry with trains and slipshod hotels as he had been a few years earlier. He erupted with affection for Frances, his wife of eleven years, but he confined the volcanic action more or less to the proper times and places, anniversaries, St. Valentine's Day, and birthdays. He still recognized the war between men and women but tended to look upon it from above. It was not the personal quarrel of yesteryear when in "I'm Sure She Said Six-Thirty" he wrote of the protective coloration given those who loiter. The advice was for the masher, safeblower, shoplifter, and mugger. If a cop came by all the loiterer had to do was announce that he was waiting for his wife.

Experience had taught Ogden well. With all that railroad travel in the Hollywood and lecture years, he knew a great deal about trains, and some of his experience was passed along in "We Don't Need to Leave Yet, Do We? Or, Yes We Do." This poem is the story of two sorts of people: the sort who allows an hour to get half a mile to the railroad station, and the sort who allows five minutes. This difference extends to virtually every aspect of their lives: the theatergoer who eats dyspeptically at six o'clock, and the theatergoer who sits down at eight, planning to make an eight thirty curtain and who announces that there is all the time in the world. The problem, said the poet, is that these opposites always marry one another.

Nash was still friendly to dogs, and particularly to his own Spangle. But the Noachic procession of animals that passed through his work, particularly his fifth book, *The Primrose Path,* had more or less disappeared, or at least the caravan made only cameo appearances. That meant the giraffe, the camel, the caribou, and the wombat. The dragon, however, would remain—not the "Dragons Are Too Seldom" dragon of *The Primrose Path,* but another, more domesticated creature, first met with Ogden's children, who would later reenter Nash's life. The poet, having accepted the fact that he is a failure at doing the children's school homework, as was proved in "Ask Daddy, He Won't Know," had metamorphosed. Now the philosophical sage was at hand.

ASK DADDY, HE WON'T KNOW

Now that they've abolished chrome work
I'd like to call their attention to home work.
Here it is only three decades since my scholarship was famous,
And I'm an ignoramus.
I cannot think which goes sideways and which goes up and down, a parallel
*   or a meridian,*

Nor do I know the name of him who first translated the Bible into Indian, I
*   see him only as an enterprising colonial Gideon.*
I have difficulty with dates,
To say nothing of the annual rainfall of the Southern Central States,
And the only way I can distinguish proper from improper fractions
Is by their actions.
Naturally the correct answers are just back of the tip of my tongue,
But try to explain that to your young.
I am overwhelmed by their erudite banter,
I am in no condition to differentiate between Timoshenko and Tam o'Shanter.
I reel, I sway, I am utterly exhausted;
Should you ask me when Chicago was founded I could only reply I didn't
*   even know it was losted.*

14

One Touch of Venus
Is One Pouch of Gelt

By 1942 Ogden Nash was sitting pretty. *I'm a Stranger Here Myself* had sold 70,000 copies. His new book, *Good Intentions*, went into multiple printings, and by year's end would sell 35,000 copies. He had recovered the important magazine markets sacrificed during the Hollywood years, and his agents had found new markets. He was now also published in *Mademoiselle*, a slick fashion journal, *Look*, the picture magazine, and *This Week*, a Sunday newspaper supplement that took him into newspapers from New York to San Francisco. He had completed the trip from Park Avenue to Main Street, and he had become America's comic poet laureate.

There were more lecture tours that winter and spring. In May he did a sketch for radio called "Who Sat in My Chair?" which paid him $180. He followed that with others: "Victory Garden," "Planning a Vacation," "Sense of Humor," and "The Man Beside You on the Train." He adapted "The People Upstairs Next Door," from his poem about noisy neighbors. There were several more radio scripts, produced at the rate of almost one a week, from May until mid-September.

Ogden did not then know it, but he was again moving into a period of poetic silence. Radio occupied him fully all spring and summer. At the same time he was in touch with composer Kurt Weill and his old Hollywood cellmate S. J. Perelman and producers Cheryl Crawford and John Wildberg about a musical. On August 16 he went to New York for some serious discussions and stayed to do some preliminary work on the project, which would be called *One Touch of Venus*. He remained in New York until September 14. Then it was back to Baltimore and more radio sketches. The sketches would continue until near the end of 1943.

In November 1942 Ogden went up to New York again, and then to a house Kurt Weill had taken in Rockland County on the west bank of the Hudson River. There he began to work on the lyrics for Weill's score. Just before Christmas he returned to Baltimore. At that point it seemed that Marlene Dietrich would take the female lead in the musical and that rehearsals could begin early in 1943.

Ogden really preferred staying home with his family but the Treasury Department got him again for another bit of war bond propaganda, and that unleashed one of the poetic reporters of Baltimore, the *Sun*'s Paul Scalera, who came to interview Ogden and then wrote his report in what he imagined to be Nashiana:

> . . . He now intends to divide his yearly schedule into six months of book work and six months of play work
> Provided life on Broadway doesn't call for too great an expansion in gay* work.
> As for Hollywood he says it's too much like a "community project" for an individualistic writer and vows he'll never return to the land of Goldwyn, Metro, and Paramount.
> "A dime in the East is worth a dollar in the West," he avers and won't go back even for a millionaireamount.
> He'll keep up radio work because it pays him well, "but it really makes me sweat" he asserted, for he's as bashful
> As he is Nashful.
> "The chief reason I'm in town," said Mr. Nash "is to appear at this book and author war bond rally Tuesday night at the Maryland Casualty Auditorium."
> "You'd better put that at the top of your story. That's more important than anything else," he added, and it really seemed to worium.
> So turn this upside down, dear reader, or stand on your head, if your dignity isn't offended.
> And then you'll know what Mr. Nash intended.

Such reportorial nonsense seemed to titillate newspapermen, and Ogden bore up with enormously good grace. Although he often held private readings of the dreadful rhymes of his imitators he never attacked

---

*"Gay" then meant only high-spirited.

them. At least Mr. Scalera got in the who, when, what, why, where, and how, in this rhyming way condensing the whole Nash career into less than two columns of newspaper type. And no matter what Ogden thought of the quality, a couple of newspaper columns sold some books. He did hope to get back to verses again, but the work on the musical was endless.

It dragged on and on, and so did negotiations over royalties, money raising, and casting. Ogden returned to New York and renewed his acquaintance with Sid Perelman. They hid out in a room in the Harvard Club for several days and worked out the libretto, using those lined yellow pads of Ogden's, and taking it word by word. Perelman came away from the encounter somewhat awed by Ogden's scrupulous, deliberate writing. ". . . as all his verse attests; he abhorred the slapdash, the hackneyed turn of thought, the threadbare phrase. Insofar as work can be pleasurable, I can't imagine anybody with whom one could feel a closer rapport. His understanding was so quick, his mind so fanciful and allusive, that it enriched whatever it touched."

In 1943 the tempo of work on *One Touch of Venus* grew faster. Endless meetings, endless correspondence, endless consideration of every line, every word, every bit of music.

Producers Crawford and Wildberg were having difficulty in finding the necessary backing for the show and Alan Collins and Leah Salisbury of the Curtis Brown agency were trying to work out the problem. The three authors, Weill, Nash, and Perelman, had agreed to take a total royalty of 10.5 percent of the gross weekly box office receipts as their compensation. That meant 3.5 percent each. The producers said they were having trouble finding money and that they would not be able to make it unless the writers would take less. So Weill, Ogden, and Perelman reluctantly agreed that any time weekly gross box office receipts exceeded $19,000, the three authors together would accept a reduction of ½ of 1 percent of the gross income over that figure. Thus, if the play were a hit, the backers would be more highly rewarded.

By autumn, the vehicle—as they say—had been assembled. Mary Martin was playing the female lead, and John Boles, the male lead. Kenny Baker was the juvenile. Osano Sato, was making her debut as a dancer. Agnes DeMille was the choreographer. Elia Kazan was the director.

Despite many weeks of rehearsal, the show was very ragged and the opening dragged like the Queen of England's train. Producer Crawford was very unhappy. She said they had to take the show somewhere to work on it and see if they could make it go. Director Elia Kazan concurred. The writers had to go along to make the changes in lyrics and lines demanded by the director and producer. A lot, of course, would depend on the audience reactions during the out-of-town tryout. New Orleans was considered for the workup, but, in the end, they decided on the more familiar territory of Boston, the theatrical bush league where a thousand plays and shows had been honed for Broadway.

So Ogden went to Boston, along with Weill and Perelman, and the producers and the director and the cast, to Boston's Shubert Theater. They were supposed to be two weeks or so, but the show dragged. The report filtering down to New York was that producer Crawford and director Kazan were stalking around the Shubert Theater with ropes in hand, whether to hang themselves or each other was not quite made clear. But the idea was very clear that *One Touch of Venus* was going to be a dog.

It was too slow throughout. The songs fell flat. The audience did not laugh when it was supposed to laugh.

And that was the advance notice *One Touch of Venus* got back on the Great White Way, revealed in the hints the reviewers loved to drop in the gossip columns. So it was no wonder that the producer and director were distraught. Weill and Perelman and Ogden were under the gun. They had to rewrite and cut, and add, and change the pace, each of these a major surgical act. Somehow it was done, and the show staggered through the Boston experience.

Frances was expecting Ogden home long before Thanksgiving, but when the Boston massacre was over, Ogden had to stop in New York to hear recordings of the changes in music and lyrics and make sure that the producers, director, choreographer, singers, dancers, and other authors agreed that all was as it should be. That was in mid-November, with Frances's birthday and Thanksgiving coming up, and his failure to get home when he said he would annoyed Frances no end, a fact she did not hesitate to let him know. He wrote her a long, apologetic letter, explaining, but also stating firmly that he was not going to rush his job and make the result mediocre. He knew only one way to work: that was at his most careful, and that was the way it was going to have to be.

Finally, he got home, just at about the time the new changes emerging from the New York recording sessions were referred to the writers. Nash and Perelman split the script in half to make the corrections. Perelman had his half finished in no time and sent it down to Ogden, who was to do his share and then send the whole back to the agency for delivery to the producers. But Ogden delayed, and delayed, as he sweated over the changes. Back in New York, Producer Crawford grew testier as the time grew shorter and was in danger of losing her temper altogether. Finally Leah Salisbury was appointed by Alan Collins, with the concurrence of Weill and Perelman, to be a committee of one to sit on Ogden's doorstep until he delivered the final script to her. On December 9 she gave him a deadline of December 14. He did not make it, but he did send it off five days before Christmas 1943.

One Touch of Venus opened in New York at the Imperial Theater. It was reviewed for *The New York Times* by Lewis Nichols, who found himself pleasantly surprised. The New York season had been such a dud that even the war and the absence of any number of theatrical figures could not excuse it. Nichols said the feeling along Broadway had been that there was no season for 1944. But all that changed when *One Touch of Venus* opened. Mary Martin wowed the audience, and Osano Sato gave them reason to sit up in their plush seats. Kenny Baker, heretofore known to New York as Jack Benny's tenor and straight man, turned out to be a real singer and an actor to boot. What a surprise it all was.

Having poured out that much sugar, Nichols had to add a little salt. The book, he said, was not what it should be, but, even so, it was so much better than anything else that had come along all year that it had to be regarded as good. As for Ogden's lyrics to Kurt Weill's songs, "soft and sweet" was the verdict, "if sometimes, perhaps, just a shade confused." To paraphrase Ogden: What the hell did they expect from a fantasy that brings Venus, not Venus de Milo, but the real honest-to-God goddess, down to earth where she falls in love with an earthling, thus beckoning all the complications that the Roman pantheon could imagine? The audience was lucky the lyrics and book made any sense at all.

At least the critics didn't pan the show. Lukewarm praise for the mechanics was better than cold water, and Mary Martin (Peter Pan) absolutely took New York in thrall once again, having been greeted suspiciously by the Broadway crowd after a Hollywood stint.

Hadn't hurt her a bit, was the unanimous verdict. And on that, *One Touch of Venus* survived and prospered.

Ogden's involvement with the show lasted for years, and like the Hollywood involvement before it, the musical took so much emotional effort and provided so much money that Ogden's flow of poetry once again dried up. Most of the problems now concerned rights and money; the British dramatic rights, the Hollywood film rights, the book publishing rights. All these involved endless negotiation, because of the complexities of the three-author cabal that had produced the show. Kurt Weill went to Hollywood, which made it even harder. Fortunately, the three authors got on well and created virtually no problems for one another. The British and film rights were the big issues of 1944, as the show rolled along. In 1945 other foreign markets began to emerge, including the Spanish language, for South America, and the Swedish. But as agent Collins said, because of the Berne Copyright Convention and the "take" of all the various agents who would be concerned, it was just as well to forget the licensing of the show in translation; it was a fine commentary on the complexities introduced into twentieth-century life and literature by agents and lawyers.

Ogden was as busy as he wanted to be, which was sometimes not very.

Maybe he was not becoming very, very rich, as he had dreamed in the 1920s, but he was becoming very, very comfortable, and it showed. As for Ogden's chosen role as Poetus Americus, the result was dismal in the extreme. He produced only fourteen poems in 1944. In 1945 and 1946 together he produced only eleven poems.

The Nash failure to produce a large body of poetry was concealed from the Nash reading public by Little, Brown. Having nothing new to publish and knowing of the existence of the ready market for Nash's work, Little, Brown persuaded Ogden to put together what in art would be called a retrospective show, verses culled from all his published work. *Many Long Years Ago* was brought out in October 1945, cannily planned for the Christmas trade. It got good reviews, probably better reviews than a rehash deserved, at least by American standards of the day. There was a logical reason for this special treatment: the original five volumes of Simon & Schuster books were so long out of print that they threatened to become rarities. Here America was in 1945, which meant a whole generation of Nash fans who had never been exposed to the early poems of the 1920s and early 1930s. Furthermore, by this time Ogden had achieved a special place with reviewers, which virtually immunized him from negative criticism. That was natural enough, for Ogden Nash was *sui generis.* He had produced a style that remained inimitable, although the host of would-be imitators continued to send a flow of fake Nashiana through the editorial rooms of the magazines.

The *New York Times Book Review* critic Russell Maloney called Ogden "poet laureate of a generation which had to develop its own wry, none-too-joyful humor as the alternative to simply lying down on the floor and screaming."

What America had produced, said he, was Ogden Nash, "an urbane articulate Donald Duck, an Alexander Pope with a hangover, a Rabelais who you could introduce to your sister."

The success of *One Touch of Venus* seemed to offer a whole new future to Ogden and S. J. Perelman in writing musical comedies for the Broadway stage, later to be made into motion pictures. Along the Rialto Ogden became acquainted with Vernon Duke, another songwriter, and thereafter was involved in a number of attempts to duplicate the great success of *Venus.* Producer Cheryl Crawford brought Nash, Duke, and Perelman together to write a new show: it was called *Forty-Five Plus.*

The summer of 1945 found the Nash family living at West Chop on Martha's Vineyard, where the absolute proof of Ogden's standing in the community was shown: he managed to get a telephone when no telephones were available. The Nashes had a big house with a cook, and the only drawbacks Ogden could see were a stony beach and fish seven days a week.

Vernon Duke was summering that year on Nantucket, so the collaborators traveled back and forth on the Nantucket–Martha's Vineyard ferry.

Samuel Goldwyn wanted Perelman and Nash to come back to Hollywood to produce a vehicle for Danny Kaye. They talked about it, but nothing emerged. And then, in the autumn of 1945, Ogden went on a lecture tour again, pressed by the lecture agent and by his publisher. A Nash lecture, combined with an autographing session at a local bookstore, was always good for the immediate sale of one or two hundred copies, and the impact usually lasted several weeks in each community that Ogden visited.

The first tour of that year took him up the East Coast from South Carolina to New Hampshire. The second was arduous, Ogden wrote to his friend Dan Longwell. Because of the length of the tour, he persuaded Frances to come along with him this time. They went to Wisconsin, Michigan, Ohio, Illinois, New Mexico, California, Idaho, and then to Washington. He did not then know it, but except for the long running *One Touch of Venus,* with all its spinoffs, summer stock, community theater, and all the rest, his musical comedy career was ended. Collaborator Vernon Duke had been a big Broadway name in the days of the Ziegfeld Follies. He was a superb musician, his real name was Vladimir Dukelsky. All his life he had alternated between the serious musical world and that of Tin Pan Alley and had done so successfully. He continued to be successful in the 1940s and 1950s, but in the serious musical world, not on Broadway. He and Ogden made several tries, but nothing came of them. Perelman slipped on a banana peel or two, recovered, got into television for a while, did some more motion picture work, including *Around the World in 80 Days* that won him a raft of prizes, and then moved back into the saner world of magazines and books, where he remained until his death, ever a staunch friend of Frederic Ogden Nash.

15

❦

Stumbling into the Sweet Bye and Bye

Out of the effort to work out a new musical with S. J. Perelman came a show called *Sweet Bye and Bye*. The year was 1946.

The producer was Nat Carson and the director was Curt Conway. Perelman and Al Hirschfeld, the cartoonist, wrote the book. Vernon Duke wrote the score, and Ogden wrote the lyrics.

Ogden's lyrics had rhymes like walrus and ten million dalrus, headache tablets and soft-shelled crablets. At first the show was called *Futurerosy*. It was a disaster.

The show began with troubles. After *Futurerosy* had been in rehearsal for ten days, it lost its leading lady, Pat Kirkwood. She was replaced by Dolores Gray. The show went to New Haven, where it bombed. The authors went back to work and the name was changed to *Sweet Bye and Bye*. Leading man Gene Sheldon was replaced by Erik Rhodes. Ten minutes were cut out of the show, and it went to Philadelphia, for a three-week run.

Philadelphia's playgoers responded nobly. The house was packed on the night of October 21, 1946, as the overture ended and the curtain came up at the Forrest Theater.

Baltimore Sun critic Donald Kirkley had gone up to Philadelphia for the opening night, but obviously wished later that he hadn't. Ogden's lyrics, he said, were "typically bright, witty, and amusing for the most part, with an occasional touch of tenderness and sound sentiment in the more romantic numbers."

There was a good deal of dismay, however, after that Philadelphia opening. The play was set in New York on the Fourth of July 2076, with the digging up of a time capsule buried at the world's fair in Flushing in 1939. The idea was to give a bright look at life in the future.

"What lies ahead," said Kirkley, "in one respect is pretty grim, especially for drama critics, because in the year 2076 musical comedies appear to follow the same boy-meets-girl formula which has plagued generations of theater goers."

The audience must have agreed, for the laughs were few and far between, and the final applause was exceedingly sparse.

Ogden said he was not discouraged. They ought to have seen the condition of *One Touch of Venus* after the Boston opening, he told Kirkley.

It was back once more to rewriting, and then the play went to Hartford. It bombed again, and this time after opening night of a two-week stand, the producers saw that ticket sales thereafter were sparser than the laughs on opening night. So at Hartford they said good-bye to *Sweet Bye and Bye*.

"The thing just crumbled away, night after night. It was like watching a corpse disintegrate under your hands," said Ogden.

Despite the enormous disappointment, Ogden did not give up. He and Vernon Duke vowed to try again. They also put together a recording of Ogden Nash's "Musical Zoo," which Duke set to music in 1947 under his real name.

They worked on another play idea. Ogden was interviewed at about that time by Joseph Cloud, a reporter for the *Baltimore American*, who came to the house for the talk. Cloud found his playwright-poet in the living room, between the two dogs, the Bedlington terrier Spangle and a new addition, an enormous German shepherd named Krag.

True to the form of interviewing poets, reporter Cloud wrote:

Ogden Nash
Writes for Cash,
Precisely as you
Would expect him to.

And, said the reporter, he and Nash had one thing in common, Franklin P. Adams had once printed a piece of Cloud's poetry in "The Conning Tower."

But as for Cloud's readers, he warned:

That, which although not golden, glitters
Will get rejection slips and give you the jitters.

As one poet to another, reporter Cloud delved into Ogden's secrets and learned that for years Ogden had believed that he had invented the "long, straggling line" as a poetic form, only to learn this year that "other and better writers have used the same device."

This becoming modesty was not put on. Ogden was feeling very glum that day, and his outlook was not much improved by the reporter's probing about the death of *Sweet Bye and Bye.*

"I was pretty lucky with *Venus,* I guess," he said finally, and then turned to a brighter subject: his 1938 book of poems, *I'm a Stranger Here Myself,* had topped the 100,000-copy mark in hardcover, his publishers had written.

Faced with such indications, Ogden was moving back into writing for the printed page. He found a new market in *Collier's* weekly, and for his prose at that. The editors of *Collier's,* along with other magazines, were developing the short, short story. Ogden sold them "The Other Mind Reader" for $600 that year. He sold another short story, "Victoria," to *Harper's Bazaar,* another fashionable women's magazine.

As for poetry, he was writing more for *The New Yorker* than he had for years. *The New Yorker* had become the symbol of New York's cognoscenti, rich enough, and debonair enough, to match Harold Ross's most glittering dreams. The magazine was wealthy, and its contributors profited. Ogden was now getting $350 for a *New Yorker* verse.

Most of his poems now tended to be longer than in previous years, but he still offered the brief poem, and he still dredged back into the past, sometimes to rewrite old poems. For example, back in the Doubleday era his friend and mentor Dan Longwell had once been invited down to the Carolinas by Nelson Doubleday to go duck hunting. Dan had begged, borrowed, and bought the necessary equipment: shotgun and camouflaged clothing, waterproof boots, decoy ducks, and an instrument which, when blown, produced a quacking noise, supposedly reminiscent to a drake of the call of a lady duck. He had gone south to Nelson Doubleday's duck club. There he and other hunters had been punted out in a duck boat to a duck blind in the midst of a body of water, and there had sat, half freezing, in the dawn's early light, awaiting the arrival of ducks.

Longwell had returned to Long Island prideful with the duck tales. Ogden had been mightily amused, and had written a little poem about it. Now, faced with a shortage of Nash poesy for his audience, he had dusted it off and used it, and it would be in the collection for his next book. There was nothing dated in the late 1940s about his verse written around 1928.

A duck is a duck is a duck, and a hunter is a hunger is a hunter, even until the twenty-first century. So also a reader is a reader is a reader, and to nonhunters the concept of grown men spending enormous sums of money and effort to shoot something they can buy at the supermarket at a dollar a pound, prepared for roasting, without blood and guts, feathers, head, feet, and tail, and without birdshot to be either removed by hand or on which a diner is likely to dislodge an inlay—for grown men to do all that is something for grown women to laugh about.

Getting together enough verses for a book now became a perennial problem. When Ogden looked back at his own production in the mid-1930s he was astounded that he had managed to do so much. Some of that thirties work still was being fed into the publishing machinery late in the following decade. Who could tell? The moment a pundit claimed he could distinguish a new Nash verse from an old, he would find out that the "new" verse was simply one written in 1929, one which had been dusted off. For all his life Ogden thought nothing of refurbishing a verse to bring it up to date. If in the 1980s some of Nash's poesy began to seem dated, it is only because we no longer had the master but his heiresses to smooth up the verses for reconsumption. Thus, in the twenties he had written the verse "A Bas Ben Adhem" ("Down with Ben Adhem," to non-French speakers), a spoof on the then immensely popular poem: "Abu Ben Adhem, may his tribe increase . . ."

Ogden's theme was that unlike Abu Ben Adhem, he did not like his fellow man, a thought he pursued for five verses. But when "Abu Ben Adhem" went out of style in America, "A Bas Ben Adhem" ceased to make much sense.

Over the years Ogden did a good deal of tidying up of his verse for new uses, and many of the pieces fell by the wayside. In the 1930s his poems were larded with references to Sloane's furniture store on New York's Fifth Avenue; smocks, which ladies donned at home by the millions in the 1930s; snoods, which they wore on their heads in preference to hats; one-way streets, the city planner's 1920s answer to auto traffic; the "new" breakfast cereals of the 1920s, which meant Professor Kellogg's Corn Flakes and National Biscuit Company's Shredded Wheat; double features, invented as moviedom's answer to the Great Depression; and mustard plasters, which were still a common treatment for colds.

But by the 1940s all these things had either become so commonplace as to be uninteresting, or had gone and been forgotten.

The point is that nearly all of Ogden's verse was topical, but some of it was also philosophical, as well. The public's frequent attempt to place Ogden Nash as merely a writer of light verse seems always to have been the bemusement of the more serious literary critics. But, just how was one to look upon him? *New York Herald Tribune* reviewer David McCord, a poet himself, denied that the Nash poems he read (and liked) were really poetry. He could find an argument there with Archibald MacLeish, poet, Pulitzer prize winner, librarian of congress, and perhaps the most celebrated American poet since Robert Frost. Poet MacLeish never considered Ogden as anything but a consummate artist. Despite the remarks of some lesser critics and their struggle to come to grips with an unknown quantity, the American people of the late 1940s continued to embrace Nashism. He was still the master of the quatrain, still the ringmaster with the snapping whip to end a thought. And he was still capable of offering something written years before, perhaps with a change or two, perhaps not, and seeing it go over with an enchanted public, and, perhaps more pleasurable to the author, with the critics, who feigned to watch the "development" of his style. The style really had not changed that much, although Ogden had certainly changed in his approach to life, and that is what the critics must have meant. The reviewers themselves had changed, too. For example, in the 1930s when confronted by Nash's first book, *Hard Lines*, *The Times* of London suggested that this poor oaf had best go back to school to learn how to use the King's English. But by the 1940s, as the British editions of his books kept coming along, London greeted them with as much enthusiasm as did New York and Atlanta.

"Mr. Nash is a most ingenious and amusing critic of frailty and absurdity," said *The Times Literary Supplement*, in discussing *Good Intentions* when it was published in Britain. "It would be a mistake, however, to think of him merely as a funny man; like James Thurber, he has a Democritean streak which entitles him to the respect due to a philosopher."

The Times also quarreled with American reviewer Sugrue, who had professed to see Nash moving from the specific to the general, from the lyric poet toward the epic, ringing all the changes as he went. What the English loved most about Nash was his treatment of "the vicissitudes and eccentricities of domestic life, as they affect a gentle, somewhat bewildered man," and they found him "most endearing when he is most deeply involved." For all of this read "American drollery."

The year 1948 was not very productive for Poet Nash. Once bitten by the theater, it is difficult for a writer to break away. Early that year Ogden began work on a new musical, but it came to nothing. He could afford the speculation because royalties were still coming in from *One Touch of Venus*. He did pause to write some poetry. *The Saturday Evening Post* was encouraging him to write longer poems, for which they paid $350. Every Christmas one of the big magazines would want a seasonal poem, and each year the price kept going up. It hit four figures and continued to rise. This meant, of course, that Ogden had to be Christmassy in July, a task he found difficult but not impossible.

In 1948 he was Christmassy just before taking ship with his wife and daughters, bound for Paris to spend what his friend Sid Perelman called "fairy money," part of the reward from *One Touch of Venus*. They put up at the Hotel Georges V, Paris's second-most exclusive and best known to Americans of the period. The motion picture producers and other celebrities of Ogden's world would hardly be caught anywhere else. On the first day Ogden made the mistake of taking his harem to lunch there. Stunned by the check ($15), he vowed not to repeat the error. Thereafter they would lunch—cheaper and better, he discovered quickly enough—at virtually any Paris restaurant.

They went to the Café Cirque Medrano, where Ogden was introduced to the delights of a Chicken Kiev whose buttery center spurted across the plate. They went to the Comédie Française to see *Cyrano de Bergerac*. They bought a Michelin guide and followed it around Paris, window-shopping in the Faubourg St. Honore. The girls, seventeen and sixteen, fell madly in love with a young man who smiled at them, and the passion lasted until their mother took them to fashion designer Jacques Fath's opening in the Faubourg. The girls quickly spent their every franc on clothes.

On September 1 Ogden spent an hour with Andre Kostelanetz, discussing a new musical venture. Kostelanetz was planning to produce a radio show and record of Saint-Saëns's *Carnival of Animals*, and he wanted Ogden to work with him on verse, to write and voice it. They discussed to their hearts' content, undisturbed, for the Nash women were back at the couturier's, undergoing fittings.

On Sunday the family went to the American Church in Paris, an Episcopal establishment. Ogden and daughter Isabel took communion. It wasn't often that Ogden mentioned, even in his notes, his religious feelings. But they were there. He was a more or less faithful churchman; it just took some transcendental event, like a trip to Europe, to bring it out.

On September 5 they boarded the *De Grasse* and were spirited back toward New York and reality. Then, after a few brief weeks at home in Baltimore, Ogden went up to New York to meet with Ken Englund and Vernon Duke. The object was to produce a sort of revue, which they called *He and She*. It was to consist of playlets and songs, with the lyrics by Ogden and the music by Duke. They included "It's Ho for the Open Road," "Call Me a Family Man," "A Little Love, a Little Money," and "The Lama." For a time the three were violently enthusiastic about the prospects, and J. S. Robbins and Sons said they would undertake publication of the score, the book, and lyrics.

But the *He and She* project died aborting, as did other Nash-Duke plans. There would be several more Nash casts at the theater, the Off Broadway production of *The Littlest Review*, with Tammy Grimes and Joel Grey, which never made it past Off Broadway, and *Two's Company*, which broke down, too. Finally, at the end of Ogden's life he would be working on a new sort of musical, called a "wordsical," with the composer Milton Rosenstock. But he did not live to see the finished show, called *Nash at Nine*, which was produced only after his death.

The end of 1948 was occupied by piecing together another book of verse, this one called *Versus,* which Little, Brown would publish in 1949.

It had, after all, been seven years since Ogden's last real volume of verse. The bibliography would not indicate that; it showed *The Ogden Nash Pocket Book* for 1944, and of course *Many Long Years Ago,* the rehash of the first five books, for 1945. *The Selected Verse of Ogden Nash*—brought out by Bennett Cerf in 1946 in one of his Modern Library inexpensive editions—was another rehash.

Nash fans had always been exposed to "new books" during the period, but the truth was that most of the work was warmed over.

In 1949 Ogden and Andre Kostelanetz did get together to produce for Columbia Broadcasting Company the show they had discussed in Paris—Saint Saëns's *Carnival of Animals,* for which Ogden received $1,000.

A few more poems, more lectures, and more work on the abortive musical ideas, and some final tidying up of the new book had to be done.

The new book reflected, as always, what Ogden had been doing for the past few years. The first verse was a remnant of the *He and She* musical attempt, called "The Lama." The title was changed to "I Will Arise and Go Now." It was a celebration of the lamas of Tibet, who had no need for material possessions, even unto penicillin, and it told of the Nash intention to arise and go off to join the lama in his ignorant bliss.

Ogden had been suffering his usual bouts with the wicked Maryland winters, which promise so much in December that the hydrangea and the forsythia happily send forth their buds, only to see them rudely assassinated by $-30°$ F weather (wind chill factor included) that sweeps in during January and may remain through February. The thaw comes early in March and the benighted Marylanders each year celebrate spring, until Cherry Blossom week (when Washington's gift from the Japanese government blossoms along the Tidal Basin) only to be overwhelmed by a snowstorm. The snow becomes slush, and sleet and fog, the crocuses croak, the tulips sprout in the snowdrifts, and the daffodils shudder in the chill. Finally spring comes on the afternoon of April 29, and lasts three hours, when a heat wave breaks the spell and it is summer.

Ogden had always paid obeisance to the gods of colds and storms, and *Versus* was no exception. But many new elements had entered his life in recent years.

The latest trip to Europe produced a poem: "How do You Say Ha Ha in French?" It was a Nashian discussion of the pretensions of the American traveler in Paris.

He reached a bit further back to include a memory of that summer on Martha's Vineyard, in the house at West Chop with the pebbly beach and all that fish. He wrote of the trials of a lyricist, who finally gave up the musical theater to write radio commercials.

After many years of experience the truths about Maryland weather had suddenly come to him, and he revealed what the chamber of commerce had so long concealed, that in Maryland spring is not; it is merely a hiatus between winter and summer. And he went on quite properly to examine the Chesapeake summer, caloric as Chungking, or hotter than the hinges of Hades in a peculiarly sweaty sort of fashion, and to remark on the peculiarities of his fellow Marylanders, who seemed surprised each summer to realize that it was H*O*T.

The rest was of that fine potpourri that Ogden always served, ridiculous glances at mundane situations, and mundane glances at ridiculous situations, eminently satisfactory to those who contemplate the vagaries of the Species Americanus. In all this, there was one new note. It was 1949. Ogden Nash was forty-seven years old, he loved his wife, and he loved his daughters too, and he wrote about them lovingly. All that was as of yore. What was new were poems in which the philosopher, with a certain consternation, regarded the changes in his life. First was the poem "Let's Not Climb the Washington Monument Tonight," in which he ruminated on new frailties he had observed in the human race: the golfers' stomachs sticking out over their belts (or under), the singers off-key, the umpires at ball games getting younger, the homebody refusing to visit friends overnight. He noted that nobody knew who he was talking about when he mentioned Babe Ruth and Al Capone, and even his old dining companion, F. Scott Fitzgerald.

The second poem of this ilk made note of the fact that his poor little dog, so spry ten years ago, was now old and half-blind. There were similar references in a poem about television watching and in one called "The Middle."

THE MIDDLE

When I remember bygone days
I think how evening follows morn;
So many I loved were not yet dead,
So many I love were not yet born.

What they added up to was Ogden's realization in 1949 that at forty-seven he had become the archetype of the middle-aged man.

16

How're You Gonna Win That Pulitzer Prize When Everybody Says You're Unique?

In the beginning of 1949 Ogden Nash was not a happy man. His failure to connect with an idea that would make a successful Broadway show still rankled. He was having difficulty readjusting to a life less exciting than that of the past five years. He was haunted by his failure to win awards. Others walked off with National Book Awards and Pulitzer Prizes, but not Ogden. That was the trouble with being *sui generis*, with whom could you compete?

One reason for the failure of the Pulitzer committee to bring forth an award for America's funniest poet was that those busy fellows had not time to consider whether or not Ogden's was proper poetry, and the staff did not enlighten them.

Ogden began to refer to himself only half humorously as "a minor literary figure."

Like many apparently phlegmatic people he bottled up these emotions, and they emerged in the form of rashes and intestinal problems. From this point on he was to have more than his share of the latter.

In the spring of 1949, recognizing his rotten state of mind, he and Frances decided to take an extended trip to Europe, bringing the girls along. The trip would serve as the Nash daughters' "Grand Tour," which all proper young ladies of the Anglo-Saxon world took in Frances's day.

They booked with The French Line for the maiden voyage of the *Ile de France*, which would sail on July 30 from New York.

The family went to New York a few days early, where they saw *South Pacific*, a bitter reminder to Ogden of the tenuous hold that he had attained on Broadway. But, at least, they had dined that evening at the Drake Room and Cy Walter, the pianist, had recognized Ogden and played two songs from *One Touch of Venus*, which cheered him up a little.

The *Ile de France* sailed at 11:15 on the morning of July 30. It was a hot day, New York was suffering through a heat wave, and the Statue of Liberty shimmered in the heavy air. When Liberty had disappeared in the haze, the Nashes went down to the first luncheon sitting and then to their cabins. The *Ile de France* had been tied up at the Hudson River pier for three days, air conditioner off, and the cabin was like a steam bath. Frances, who was efficient about such things, did the unpacking, while Ogden hovered about hotly and ended up taking three showers to try to cool off. He recovered somewhat, however, when the girls took him down to the salt water pool for a dip.

It remained very hot, and the prospects for a happy voyage looked dim to the Nashes: they did not see anyone they knew, and the crowd appeared to Ogden to be mostly of the racetrack variety, especially the young men.

That evening Ogden ran into Bruce and Beatrice Gould, the editors of the *Ladies' Home Journal*, and he found Harry Scherman, president of the Book-of-the-Month Club, and his wife. Also, Joseph Wechsberg of *The New Yorker* had come along to write up the maiden voyage for the magazine. Ogden grew more content to find that he was among his peers.

Like fireflies the girls quickly attracted swains and out of the woodwork appeared the better sort. The girls paired off for entertainments, and after a little examination the old folks heaved sighs of relief at the caliber of the escorts.

On August 1 everything improved. The Nashes woke up to find the ship off the Grand Banks, speeding along through a magnificent cool mist. Out came sweaters and woolens, and the senior Nashes retired to deck chairs for much of the day. Ogden began to feel better, even the rash on his hands subsided.

The ship landed them at Southampton on August 5. Then they went to Nice. From there they hired a 1945 Cadillac and driver to take them down the beautiful coast road toward Genoa. The driver spoke no English, but this time Ogden had recovered enough of his schoolmaster French to be understood, and they carried on something of a conversation. The main subject was *les douanes,* and the driver was voluble in his warnings that the Italians made things dreadfully difficult. The party could expect to be delayed for two hours at customs, while the Italian officers went through their luggage with small combs.

It seemed a discouraging prospect, but there was nothing to be done, unless they wanted to turn around, and that retrogressive idea was vetoed. So they came up to the border in the Cadillac, and the drive braked to a stop at the barrier, prepared for the worst.

Ogden smiled pleasantly and gave a cigarette to the carabiniere who came up in his splendid uniform. Ogden asked if the carabiniere could please, swiftly, begin the search of the luggage.

"Signor," said the officer with a sweeping gesture, "I have already examined the luggage." And he lifted the barrier and waved them through. Ogden gave the carabiniere a package of American cigarettes, and got a salute in return. The driver watched all, goggle-eyed, and still seemed unable to believe, as he drove them to their hotel in Genoa.

After seeing the sights in Genoa, they went to Florence, and then to Siena and Assisi and finally to Rome. There the girls came down with what hotel porters called a touch of summer stomach, but it didn't last. They went to the Vatican and to Hadrian's Villa, they rode up the Appian Way to the catacombs, and they trudged through the Forum. They visited half a dozen magnificent churches, and they went to the opera, to hear *La Traviata*, in a performance outdoors, set in the ruins of the baths of Caracalla.

They went to Bologna, and then to Venice where they stayed for a week, "doing" everything from the pigeons at St. Mark's to the gondola rides and art museums. Ogden was virtually on a light wines regimen, drinking Chianti for the most part. To have a martini, as he did in Rome, was a rare event.

On August 29 they went to Paris once more, and again stayed at the Hotel Georges V. Again, Ogden drank a martini, otherwise he was on his very good behavior.

When the Nashes returned to Baltimore from the exciting voyage, Ogden began to do a little writing, but not a great deal, for a new lecture tour loomed. Again Frances went along. The tour took them to Fond du Lac, Wisconsin, where he spoke in the Jewish temple, and then autographed a hundred copies of books the members of the audience had. It was on, on, to Evanston, Grand Rapids, Chicago, and then to New Mexico where they tarried a little. After that came San Francisco and one of the most ghastly luncheons that Ogden could remember, all dingy chicken salad and rancid crab meat, after which he had to perform once more.

From San Francisco they went to Los Angeles to stay at the Biltmore Hotel. Ogden had several engagements, but Los Angeles had the charm at least of housing some old friends, so they were able to break the monotony of the tour.

After several years of addressing large groups, particularly large groups of women, Ogden had grown inured to the process. Sometimes he even liked it, if the audience reacted with sufficient enthusiasm. What he had come to like least of all was the female provocateur he encountered occasionally, who asked him how he "really" felt about talking to women's clubs. The implication was clear that if he said he liked it, he must be lying. How did he *really* feel?

Ogden had thought long and hard to work up an answer to that question. He had, in St. Paul, addressed a crowd of 7,500, that is seven thousand five hundred women all in a crowd. That was seven and a half percent of a hundred thousand women. He had been worried at the outset about boring seven thousand five hundred women for one hour. But, as he walked from his hotel to the auditorium, he considered the problem. Not to bore seven thousand five hundred women for one hour was comparable to not boring one woman for seven thousand five hundred hours. He had been married for twenty years, more or less. He felt he could assume that at least one hour a day for twenty years he had not bored his wife. That came to seven thousand three hundred hours of not boring one woman. Mathematically, then, he should be able to not bore seven thousand three hundred women for one hour, leaving only two hundred bored women in the audience, and as everyone knew, there were a few harridans in every crowd, just the sort of people who would ask that question.

Sometimes the lecture tour took Ogden to enlighten so many; sometimes it took him to talk to so few. On December 10, 1949, he was in Portland, Oregon, a city of four hundred thousand people. From there he and Frances went to Mount Vernon, Washington, which was the real hustings; Nash's appearance was before an assembly of the Skagit Valley Junior College, an institution whose total student body and faculty numbered in the hundreds. On this occasion Ogden also labored under unusual difficulties. His appearance was in competition with a basketball game to be fought against Skagit Valley's deadliest rival. And besides that, a triple murder and suicide had just occurred in that community, and apparently not many people were eager to go out at night. So the audience consisted of a handful of the faithful, who came bearing Ogden Nash books to be signed, and tried to make up in friendliness for the paucity of numbers.

That night in Skagit Valley was in every way the low point of the trip. Then it was on to Seattle, where Ogden's spirits were raised a little because he sold fifty-five books at an autographing party and signed another fifty copies, which the bookseller said he would sell the next day.

The book was *Versus*, which was just out that fall and was getting the usual good reviews.

His old friend Christopher Morley reviewed *Versus* in the *Saturday Review of Literature*. Ogden, said Chris, was a "great temographic historian."

If Morley's word was "demographic," then it referred to that branch of anthropology that deals with the life conditions of communities of people. No one could disagree.

"Ogden," said he, "plunges the needle with such generous and hyper-gelastic opiate that even as we perish we bless his name."

What Christopher Morley was saying, in all his literary erudition, was that Ogden, the great historian of the people, "can remind us better than any other writer, what has gripped us in our hideous and hellbound civilization."

Whew! How many of even the erudite *SRL* readers—you know, the kind who knocked off the Double-Crostic in half an hour—could fathom the author's prose? Maybe it was no wonder that in his later years Christopher Morley had ceased to be a boy wonder of the fictional scene, and enfant terrible to the New York literary coterie (Columnist O. O. McIntyre particularly disliked Morley and his works and did all he could to destroy The Foundry in the 1930s) and became a magazine editor and judge of the Book-of-the-Month Club.

But there was no denying the fact that even if a reader could not parse all of Morley here, he got the idea, for at the end, the reviewer suggested that the only thing to do was buy the book and invite a few friends for fireside reading.

Fortunately the average reader in St. Paul or Mt. Vernon, Washington, did not have to trample through Chris Morley's prose, dictionary in hand, to understand what Ogden Nash was up to this time. David McCord's review in the *New York Herald Tribune* was typical and a lot easier going. McCord was still having trouble identifying Nash, but he knew something spectacular when he saw it, and that is what he said:

"Opening a book by Ogden Nash is something like opening a bottle of champagne: (1) it makes a pleasant noise, and (2) it is highly charged with volatile stuff. All his verse is set in italic, a more volatile type than roman. A stanza practically takes off the page as you look at it."

And more:

"Once you have granted that the author of *Versus* is like unto no other writer dead, living, or likely to be born, you're not interested in criticism, you care not for reappraisal, you don't want even the good things pointed out. Did I say the good things? I mean the better things. You want to find them for yourself."

The reviews were always good for Ogden's ego, which needed inflation from time to time as he worried more about his place in American letters. He already had a few props. The Harvard association served him well. He had been elected to the American Society of Composers, Authors, and Publishers in 1943. He had been elected to The Century Association of

New York, that meeting ground of publishing's elite. In January 1950 he was elected to the National Institute of Arts and Letters.

But still no prizes came his way.

His disappointment was generally well concealed, except perhaps at home. His manners were ever impeccable, and he was as kindly as a man without full-time secretarial service could be in responding to a relatively large volume of mail. Author Dale Kramer, who was writing a book about *The New Yorker*, asked Ogden to give him a hand, and Ogden agreed readily. The trouble, however, was that Kramer wrote on August 15, and Ogden replied on October 31. That was the way his correspondence went; off to Keokuk one week, and on the road for six, it was hard to keep the letters moving, even if they did not get stuck in a drawer for many weeks. He did help Kramer as much as he could when finally they met. But in 1950 Harold Ross and *The New Yorker* and the Jesus crowd seemed a long, long way behind.

It was in one town and on to the next. The lecture invitations came by the dozens, by the scores. Some came from the agent. Some came directly to Ogden and were referred to the agent. He was regarded as one of the hottest of platform properties. He changed agents, joining W. Colston Leigh and Associates, the leading lecture bureau of the United States.

From May 1950, he was on the road again, Iowa, Texas, and stops in between. He didn't much like the tours although he was genial and usually pleasantly impressed by the people. But on this spring tour of 1950, for example, he ran into the sort of personal problem that bothered the lecturer. A number of Ogden's old friends had decided to honor Christopher Morley with a dinner at the Coffee House Club in New York on Morley's sixtieth birthday. Ogden would dearly have liked to have gone, to have wassailed over old times, and to dredge up memories of the Deviled Ham and Lake Ronkonkoma Association, but on the date in question he was deep in the heart of Texas, and all he could do was send a telegram to the lucky devils carousing in New York.

The poems were coming a little faster, the longing for Broadway now submerged and the false glitter of Tinseltown pushed firmly behind him.

It was the 1950s, inflation was driving up the cost of everything, and Ogden's income was also pleasantly inflated. New markets came to him again: *Flair* magazine paid him $500 for a poem. *Life* paid him $2,000 for a piece. His *New Yorker* rate went up.

Logically, the poems should be middle-aged poems now, composed by a middle-aged poet, but were they?

They were not. "The Private Dining Room" was a tale told in verse of a young Ogden Nash and one of his youthful pals in a private dining room with two young women. They had drunk large quantities of champagne and dined sumptuously on pickerel and mackerel and grew pickereled. When the young man sobered up the two young women were gone. This was hardly a tale Ogden would have told Frances in the days of courtship, but now in the well-to-do comfort of middle years, he could put it on paper, bring a good laugh and enjoy it himself, and no harm done. This particular poem would be the title piece of his next new collection.

When Ogden did write about a proper middle-aged subject, as in "Peekaboo, I Almost See You," he did so in a manner calculated to get a laugh out of anyone who could read. For this middle-aged man was troubled by the fact that his arms were no longer long enough to hold the telephone books that he liked to read, so he could read them. So he went to the eye doctor, and the eye doctor told him he needed two pairs of glasses, one for reading and one for walking around, and bought two pairs and then when he wanted to read, the reading glasses were upstairs when he was downstairs and vice versa. When he wanted his seeing glasses he could not find them because they were somewhere where he was not, and he could not see well enough to find them without having them on.

Of such trials were many poems, of middle age and a New Year's hangover. But among these plaints were signs of all the old stuff: a poem about the hamster, and one about the toucan and one about mules. He dealt with the caterpillar and the duckbilled platypus and the cuckoo. Dogs kept creeping into his poetry as they always had, accompanied by chipmunks and Republicans and Democrats. Had he subtracted those poems that declared him to be in middle age, and substituted others less personal, no reader would have guessed how old Nash was.

Indeed, Ogden was writing, and the writing of 1949 and 1950 showed a definite improvement in cheeriness. Meanwhile, Little, Brown, who knew a good thing when they saw it, particularly because of the constant sales stimulation of the lecture tours, was busily turning the presses with collections and subcollections and special collections. *Family Reunion* came out in 1950, as Ogden toured and toured. He was, as the nineteenth-century critics used to say, at the height of his powers. But when had he not been? Certainly he was not producing at the furious rate of the 1930s, but what he did produce was solid and eminently satisfactory, and sometimes, as in "My Trip daorbA," a tour de force. That particular poem was based on the fact that on his recent trip abroad he had courteously ridden backwards nearly everywhere, on the jump seat of the Cadillac going down to Italy, and backwards in the trains so his daughters could ride frontwards and see the sights.

What greater love . . . but of course when he got home he also produced a hilarious verse out of that experience, a poem that describes Europe (eporuE) as it was seen by a man riding drawkcaB, from eciN to emoR and back again, rhyming quite certain with emaD ertoN and hard to judge with taes-pmuJ.

MY TRIP DAORBA

I have just returned from a foreign tour,
But ask me not what I saw, because I am not sure.
Not being a disciplinarian like Father Day,
I saw everything the wrong way,
Because of one thing about Father Day I am sure,
Which is that he would not have ridden backwards so that the little Days
*   could ride forwards on their foreign tour.*
Indeed I am perhaps the only parent to be found
Who saw Europe, or eporuE, as I think of it, the wrong way round.
I added little to my knowledge of the countryside but much to my reputation
*   for docility*
Riding backwards through ecnarF and ylatI.
I am not quite certain,
But I think in siraP I saw the ervuoL, the rewoT leffiE, and the Cathedral of
*   emaD ertoN.*
I shall remember ecnerolF forever,
For that is where I backed past the house where etnaD wrote the "onrefnI," or
*   ydemoC eniviD, and twisted my neck admiring the bridges across the*
*   onrA reviR.*
In emoR I glimpsed the muroF and the nacitaV as in a mirror in the fog,
While in ecineV I admired the ecalaP s'egoD as beheld from the steerage of an
*   alodnoG.*
So I find conditions overseas a little hard to judge,
Because all I know is what I saw retreating from me as I rode backwards in
*   compartments in the niart and in carriages sitting on the taes-pmuj.*

17

No More Creamed Chicken, If You Please—or If You Don't

Lectures! Lectures! Lectures! In the early 1950s the lecture tour was Ogden's way of life. Not that he liked it more, but he certainly was in greater demand, particularly now that he had the W. Colston Leigh agency to represent him. They sent him up one side of the country and down the other, then crisscrossing back. A month or so on the trail, and then he would squeeze some time off to come back to Baltimore and regain strength for the next ordeal.

He went to Kansas City, where he was interviewed by a *Kansas City Star* reporter who was more than a little awed by this tall, slightly stooped, and legendary figure, particularly when he asked why Ogden lectured (expecting to get a high fallutin' answer), and Ogden told him "for money."

The interviewer was further nonplussed because the man everyone said was the prime funny poet of the land did not profess to be a poet or funny. He professed only to be a writer. He didn't like lecturing because he did not like to get up and talk to people, and that was because he did not have anything to say. So he ended up lecturing on himself, which made him uncomfortable.

As for his writing, times had indeed changed. When he began in the 1920s, life was easy and laughter came quickly. The 1920s era, of course, was before the sense of chaos (Ogden's word) overtook the world in the 1940s. It was not so easy to laugh any more.

That whole concept was new to the youthful reporter. He was impressed by Ogden's words and by Ogden's pithy way of speech, calling his oeuvre not poems but "stuff." The stuff, the reporter reminded his readers, was now included in many a poetry anthology and in college textbooks.

When that interview appeared, out of the woodwork sprang an old termite from the Barron Collier car card advertising, or salad, days in New York. A few years earlier, Ogden would have gotten rid of this relict of a long-forgotten past swiftly, but the years had mellowed Ogden, and he spent a couple of hours of pleasant reminiscence with his old acquaintance before he caught his train that day.

From Kansas City, on this lecture tour, Ogden went to Oklahoma City. If Ogden needed proof that his appeal had crossed the generation barrier, he once more had it in Oklahoma City. He was interviewed. The reporter went back to his desk and wrote. The next day in the newspaper Ogden read another sample of The Brassy Trashery of Imitation Ogden Nashery:

I met the so-called master of the tortured word
   Who hails from Baltimore
In Room ten twenty nine in the Hotel Biltmore.
He was not expecting me just then, but quick as a flash though,
He extended his hand to me, which I took and said
   "Hello, Mr. Nash-o."

And this went on for nine more paragraph . . .

Ogden sent this little gem home with the suggestion that Frances assemble a crowd and read it aloud. A badly wanted hitchhike murderer had just been arrested in Oklahoma City that day, and as far as he could figure out, every reporter in town with a lick of sense was down at the jail.

After Oklahoma City the lecture tour took a turn downhill. The itinerary given Ogden by the agency said he was to speak the next day in Tulsa, so he went to Tulsa. He showed up at the university office, where he was supposed to check in, and was informed that the lecture was not until the next day. He looked at his itinerary. That's not what it said. Furthermore, his train and hotel reservations for McAllen, Texas, the next stop, were for that night.

Ogden had to get a hotel room and change all the reservations and wait twenty-four hours, twiddling his thumbs and worrying about what he was going to say and how they were going to like it. As usual, the reception was positive, and he went as happily as he could on to McAllen.

It was an unsettling life, but there were also consolations. After McAllen, he went to Dallas, where the bookstore owners did him proud, and he autographed hundreds of copies of his books. He made his usual speech and then was taken to lunch by Margo Jones, the Dallas theatrical entrepreneuse. Then he saw a performance of *The Willow Tree*, in her theater-in-the-round. Then he had dinner with Stanley Marcus, the doyen of Dallas's famous department store.

Later, on this same tour he visited the King Ranch and saw the Santa Gertrudis cattle they were breeding there. The King Ranch people entertained him royally at the ranch and at the country club.

A few days later, though, Ogden found himself in New Orleans, which had just iced over. He was sliding around the Vieux Carre on something he would rather have in his drink, ice. The five-hour train ride from Corpus Christi had taken him ten and a half hours. After New Orleans he had to go to Houston, which was also unusually frigid. That train was also late because of the cold weather. Next came Montgomery, Alabama. The frozen train got him in two hours after the scheduled time of his lecture. The university rescheduled the lecture, but the lecture hall was also frozen, and for the first time in his life Ogden lectured in his overcoat.

Finally, Ogden broke the ice barrier and made it to Florida, where the weather improved distinctly. But the ordeal was far from over. He still had to go to Indianapolis, and Terre Haute, to DePauw University where they lodged him in a girls dormitory.

Reviewing this painful procession, Ogden later could recall a few highlights, such as the scenery of New Mexico, and the success of most of his talks, and the pleasure of autographing books and knowing they were sold. But against that, sometimes it was seven lectures in ten days and very little leisure in between. When the leisure came, too often it was in the wrong place, at the wrong time, with the wrong people. The lecture tour was not the life he would have chosen.

When not on tour, ever hopeful of regaining the head of steam generated in the 1940s, Ogden was working on lyrics for a new musical, *Wedding Day*, a spoof on high-fashion magazines. His partners this time were Vernon Duke, who was doing the music, and English writer Leonard Gershe, who was doing the book. Ogden spoke hopefully of a Broadway production in 1953.

In 1952 the poems were fewer, longer, and better paid. *Life* paid $2,000 for "The Father in Law of the Groom," which had to do with daughter Linell's wedding to John Marshall Smith in Baltimore that October. *Life's* Washington office had noted in the Baltimore papers the announcement of Linell's engagement and suggested that when the daughter of the nation's No. 1 humorous poet got engaged, it ought to make a good story for the magazine. The young couple-to-be had been appalled at the thought and *Life* had been persuaded (by Ogden) to back away. Ogden had promised *Life* that they could do something about the wedding: the magazine could reprint "Song to Be Sung by the Father of Six Months Old Female Children," which Ogden had written way back when he lived in New York and worked for Farrar & Rinehart. Ogden had improved on the idea and now wrote a sequel—how it was for the father of the bride twenty years later. Twenty years later! If there was ever a labor of love, here it was: the only reason for the work was that Ogden wanted to give the bridal couple a wedding trip to Bermuda.

Sales of $750 and $1,000 for a poem were not uncommon. Still, the output was limited by the lecture tours. It was a hard path to walk, producing enough poems to keep the collections coming, so the collections could be milked by autograph parties and mention of the book at all the lectures. Unlike the author tours that began after television had grabbed America in a hammerlock, Ogden's interplay of the spoken word to sell the written one was immediately and constantly effective. Each lecture tour alone had to account for several thousand direct and indirect sales of Ogden Nash collections.

Little, Brown brought out *The Private Dining Room* in the fall of 1952, and—one might almost say as usual—the reception was excellent. *Time* magazine echoed previous reviewers' finding that Ogden Nash was unique among writers. "The difference between Nash and his imitators is that somewhere in the cunningly dislocated gears of his lines he imprisons a patented point of view."

And there was more of this in *The New York Times*, the *Herald Tribune*, the *Saturday Review of Literature*, *Harper's* and *The Atlantic*; wherever books were reviewed. Ogden's work got a notice, and it was almost invariably a good notice. The greatest triumph came from across the water in England, where the *New Statesman and Nation* admitted reluctantly that "he supplies us with the best light verse now being published." That meant in the English language. Coming from a stern Socialist point of view, and a magazine that was not notable for its affection for Americans, this was nearly the ultimate in high praise. It had to be tempered, of course, by the observation that Ogden had taken the traditional path of the American humorists, presenting himself as "incompetent, well-read, out of touch with the loud commercialism of modern life, a chick-pecked rooster on an asphalt run." At times, said reviewer Frank Houser, it would be possible to wish he were more adventurous and less "fuddy-duddy."

That is almost a direct quote of the poet. In one verse he referred to himself as a "middle-aged fuddy-duddle duck." In another poem Ogden confessed that he preferred to be with people over fifty. But the rollicking tone of the young was still with him. His treatment of America's foibles was like a fun house mirror, but underneath was the moralist, notebook in hand, studying Homo sapiens and wondering how close really was he to Neanderthal man.

In 1952 Ogden made a few big sales to *Life* and *Cosmopolitan*. *Life* paid him $2,000 that spring for "With My Own Eyes," he made two $1,000 sales to *Cosmopolitan*, and *Life* paid him another $1,500 that September.

In 1953 and 1954 Ogden's literary output seemed to hit stride at about thirty pieces and poems a year, most of them selling in the $300 range, but with the occasional big sale.

Many changes came to the family. Linell was married and settled in Baltimore. Isabel, having "finished" at Miss Porter's school for rich young women in Connecticut, had begun again at Bryn Mawr College. All very proper for the daughter of a proper Baltimore society family, as the Leonards most certainly were. The Nashes moved back to New York, to 333 East 57th Street. And they now summered at Rye Beach on the New Hampshire coast. But these were almost ports of call for the busy lecturer. Often Frances accompanied him on tour these days, and often they were feted by businessmen and faculty of various institutions, as at Purdue University, where Ogden spoke in March 1953. He left his notes behind that night, perhaps because Professor Richard A. Cordell of the Department of English startled him with a word he did not know: oscitant (drowsy, lazy, somnolent, careless because of the above). But all was forgiven when the professor gave a party for the Nashes, and then Ogden hurried back to New York to consult his dictionary. He mentioned the matter in his thank-you note to the Cordells; such things as a new word to be twisted about were life's blood to the poet.

Another change came to the Nashes in the fall of 1954. Daughter Isabel got married to Frederick Eberstadt. It was a small wedding held in the chapel at St. Bartholomew's Episcopal Church on Park Avenue. After Ogden had given away the bride, he gave the pair a party at the 57th Street apartment and shooed them off on their honeymoon.

Ogden did not have to write many poems to remain comfortable. By 1954 his life had assumed an easy pattern, if one could subtract the dratted lecture tours from it. Several books produced handsome royalties each six months. He now had also become an anthologist. In 1952 J. B. Lippincott paid him the ultimate publisher's honor for a writer of any sort by asking him to put together an anthology of "good-humored verse." Honor it was, because publishers in the last half of the twentieth century are anything but eleemosynary institutions, and to use their words, a project had to be "sufficiently commercial" to attract their interest. With the rise of the university publishing houses, the old "gentleman's occupation" of publishing had lost its spats and took no further responsibility for the furtherance of "literature." In other words, if there wasn't a good chance of it making money, to hell with it. So, when someone at Lippincott wanted to put out an anthology of verse, eyes turned to Frederic Ogden Nash, the primest of prime versifiers, the most commercial property in the poetry business.

Ogden selected a hundred and seventy-five humorous verses, including eight of his own. His own selections concerned animals—the wapiti, dogs, cats, ducks, panthers—germs, Professor Twist, whose wife was eaten by a crocodile, and Isabel (Nash), who had thrilling adventures with a bear, a witch, a giant, and a doctor. What might have been interesting to Nash readers with long memories was that he did not include a single poem from Dorothy Parker or Samuel Hoffenstein, although many long years ago he had dedicated his first book to them and several times afterward had told interviewers that these two writers had been primary factors in the development of his poetic style.

Gone commercial? Hell, yes. Why should Ogden not join the rest of America in pursuit of a buck? All restraint gone, he wrote a poem in praise of vermouth for the Joseph Katz advertising agency ($750) and a promotion piece for the *Reader's Digest* ($1,000).

This year, 1954, was also the year in which Ogden decided that he was going to give up the lecture tours. The girls were educated and properly married off, and Frances had her independent income. The need was not nearly so great as it had been ten years earlier, so he announced in his foreword to the Lippincott anthology, *The Moon Is Shining Bright As Day*, that he would forego the creamed chicken circuit in the future.

18

The High Hopes of a Low Poet

Alas for the high hopes of a low poet. Ogden did not manage to free himself from the chains of W. Colston Leigh and the lecture tour, for the 1950s saw a major change in American life and letters that had serious effect on Ogden's literary markets.

The name of the change was television.

Late in the 1940s television had spread across the Eastern Seaboard, and many thousands of sets were sold. In the 1950s television stations sprang up across the country like field mushrooms; by 1953 a town of 60,000 people might have two stations. The coaxial cable was perfected, which made it possible to telecast from coast to coast; the stations began to tie in with the networks, and the damage to the delicate media competitive balance began.

The first to be hurt were the newspapers. Gleeful television types were predicting the day when newsprint would disappear altogether; the citizen would get his news from a newspaper facsimile cast up on the silver screen. But the newspapers pulled up their socks and concentrated on local advertising in two areas that television could not match: food and classified. The weakest newspapers began to collapse, and the cities saw merger after merger. The *New York Sun* went down. The *Brooklyn Eagle* flew away. Eventually the newspaper situation would be completely changed; in Ogden's youthful publishing days he had eleven New York newspapers to deal with. But as cigarettes and beer, soapsuds and automobiles moved from the printed page to the tube, the decay of newspaperdom began. The *New York World* had already become part of the *World Telegram* and then the inroads of TV caused it to become the *World Telegram and Sun,* and finally the *Herald Tribune-World Telegram-Sun,* a title too heavy for any vessel to bear through the journalistic storms, and it sank. Finally, a few years later, New York newspaper competition, which had been the spice of the life of the city, disappeared almost completely. All that would remain would be *The New York Times,* the *New York Post,* and the *New York Daily News.* The process was well along in the mid-1950s.

So, too, came what seemed to be the collapse of radio and the dissolution of the old established national "general interest" magazines. As the national TV networks gained viewers, the magazines could not compete with the unit cost of exposing advertisers to population, the numbers game.

Liberty was the first to go, along with such second-raters as *Click* and *Pic.* Then in 1956, the Crowell-Collier magazine empire disintegrated and that meant the end of *Collier's,* the *Woman's Home Companion,* and *American* magazine. Two of these had been regular markets for Ogden Nash, and they were no more. They would be followed by *Look,* and finally by *Life* and *The Saturday Evening Post.*

The process was gradual, but in the middle 1950s Ogden was feeling the erosion of his markets. He had made a considerable amount of money from radio sketches, and from radio appearances on national broadcasts. The latter were becoming virtually troglodytic. Radio was saving itself by turning to music and news. The shows on which he had appeared: "Information Please," the Bing Crosby hour, the Rudy Vallee hour, the Charlie McCarthy hour, were gone or going.

Fortunately, *The New Yorker* was stronger than ever, and Ogden's line rate went up some more. Eventually, he was getting nearly a thousand dollars per poem from *The New Yorker.* But tastes differed and Ogden's poetry had a certain eclecticism of subject so that not all poems appealed to all editors. This factor grew stronger as time went on, too; the markets shrank, the competition among magazine writers grew so fierce that most magazines stopped completely the practice of reading over-the-transom manuscripts or ideas. Ogden had an agent, one of the best in the business, but even he felt the pinch in the 1950s, so the lecture tours remained an unpleasant part of Ogden's life. He did cut down, trying to limit the tour to one month a year.

Another sort of market was beginning to emerge for Ogden, however. His first book, long forgotten by virtually everyone but the author, was *The Cricket of Carador,* a children's book. In 1950, at Little, Brown's urging, he had collected a number of his poems about family life, and they were many by that time, and the result was *Family Reunion.* That was so successful that the next year he collected more poems about and for children, and the result of that was *Parents Keep Out: Elderly Poems for Youngerly Readers.*

In the 1950s the grandchildren began to emerge, which gave Ogden a new field of observation. As he was quick to note, a child of your own and a grandchild are not the same. So, he had more ammunition and a new audience, too. The first indication was "Fee Fi Ho Hum, No Wonder Baby Sucks Her Thumb," Ogden's poetic tale of a small female grandchild and her two favorite books. One told the tale of a little boy who lost his cap and looked everywhere for it and finally found it on his head. The other told the story of a little girl who lost her shoe on a train and bedeviled everyone until finally she found it in her suitcase.

This was funny? The poet was not amused, particularly since the grandchild visited the grandparents at their rented summer place on the New Hampshire beach, and Grandpa was often corralled in his little hands-off corner of the living room and dragged away for a reading session.

At this time Ogden was beginning to feel a certain paranoia, a common writer's ailment from which he had largely escaped over the years because he hit it big with his first book, and from then on it was never a backward glance. Now, however, there were some sidelong glances. He had kept this stand open for more than twenty years, and all he had to show for it was a certain amount of pelf, which never seemed to stick, and a membership in the National Institute of Arts and Letters. That would have been enough for the average writer, but Ogden was not average in any way. He had a large ego, if one concealed. What rankled was to read year after year of the prizes won by other poets, and never to see the name of Ogden Nash on the Pulitzer Prize list, or propping up the National Book Awards.

He was not the only one so puzzled. Clifton Fadiman of the Book-of-the-Month Club felt the same way and had been known to say so. But the Pulitzer committee plodded along its own mysterious path, and spring after spring went by, and the name of Ogden Nash never came to the top.

He had settled into a routine, now, this "minor literary figure." Ideally it would be winter in New York, one lecture tour, then summer and early fall in New Hampshire. In 1956 he found a summer place in New Hampshire that suited him to a T. He rented a house at Little Boar's Head in the town of North Hampton, a summer colony that contained a number of people Ogden liked. Summers were easy and happy times. The gathering spot was Bunny's Sandwich Shop, where the sunburned crowd assembled in sneakers and cotton knit shirts for lunch and sometimes for dinner, if there was not a dinner party, or nobody took a sudden craving for lobster, which meant going to a restaurant. He decided that New Hampshire was his spiritual home and spoke about being buried there. Ideally, he could go up in May and not come back till October.

But the ideal could not be achieved. W. Colston Leigh was a hard taskmaster, constantly thinking up new ways to milk Ogden's talents, and the resulting money was too much for the author to pass up. It was more like three months on the lecture trail than one. As he wrote Katerine White at *The New Yorker,* he simply found it impossible to write while on the road. The best he could do was read the telephone books and his other odd bits of source material and make notes of his meanderings to use at a future time, and that he did. The meanderings began again that spring; he was off on another lecture tour of the Midwest. At least this time he had the good fortune of stopping by Neosho, Missouri, where his old friend Dan Long-well had moved after retiring from the Time, Inc. organization. Ogden per-suaded the Longwells to rent a house at Little Boar's Head, too, and so the summer of 1956 was spent with children, grandchildren, and old and new friends.

In the fall it was back to 333 East 57th Street, but then the road again in November. Christmas was a sad and worrisome time, for Ogden's mother-in-law was operated on for breast cancer. It was a hard period for every-one. In their eighties, the Leonards had given up the big house at 4300 Rugby Road several years earlier as much too large for them and had moved to 3908 North Charles Street in central Baltimore. Mrs. Leonard came out of the operation very well. That worry was over just before the end of the year. Ogden scarcely had time to turn around, for he was off on January 5 for a week of speaking engagements in Minnesota. Home again, then off again in February to Oklahoma and Kansas.

Ogden's busy life was complicated by another new adventure: this was the beginning period of the celebrity television panel shows. They leaned heavily on New York's resident celebrities. Franklin P. Adams was one. Polly Bergen was another, Bill Cullen, a third. Ogden almost always had a place on the panel of one of the shows, which changed its name from time to time. He also appeared for "guest" spots on others. This took at least one evening a week when he was in New York.

The fact was that it was easy to make money with a lot less effort than the real work of writing, and so the writing was largely left undone. And, in order to keep up with the demands of his publishers, he had used up virtually everything he had written anytime. His poetic cupboard was almost bare.

In the winter of 1957 Rolfe Humphries of Amherst College was trying to put together an anthology of unpublished poetry by prominent poets as a money-raising device in behalf of a creative writing foundation. In Febru-ary he wrote to Ogden asking for something. When Ogden got back from Oklahoma and Kansas he replied that he was enormously busy complet-ing a manuscript for Little, Brown and had no time to take on an extra assignment. That statement was true, but it was not the half of it. That year he and daughter Linell were doing a special Christmas children's book for Little, Brown's publication. Ogden wrote the poem: "The Christmas That Almost Wasn't." Linell did the illustrations. They were nice illustrations, amateur, but nice, and Little, Brown did them the favor of reproduction in full color.

Ogden was also reading proof on *You Can't Get There from Here*, his new volume of collected verse. *The Moon Is Shining Bright As Day*, the poetry anthology for children, had been so successful that Lippincott had asked Ogden for another anthology, this time of stories. So he also was putting together *I Couldn't Help Laughing: Stories Selected and Introduced by Ogden Nash*.

Rolfe Humphries did not accept that refusal as final and asked Ogden if he had not time to write something, could he please contribute some unpublished gem out of his ragbag. Ogden was properly shamed and looked all around the house, in his famous drawer and even deeper, but there was nothing, he had to report, and it left him feeling empty.

In truth, Ogden Nash was a kindly man, and he tried to help out where he could, if the seeker was a person of merit. He could not bear the procession of high school students who wrote "send me your works," but when a promising writer wrote, he responded nobly. But he steered others to markets, and if he liked something that someone sent him, he was quick to give a quote for publication. It was the sort of editorial backscratching that had helped so much to hurl Ogden into instant celebrity in 1931, and he continued it, although the practice was generally dying out in the literary trades as markets shrank and writers became more self-centered and jealous of one another.

After a very busy early spring, Ogden and Frances set sail for Europe at the end of April aboard the Holland America Line's RNS *Ryndam*. Little, Brown had sent ahead to the ship a little present for Ogden, a $25 gift certificate good at the ship's bar. With martinis at 35 cents, Scotch whisky at 30 cents, and Dutch gin at 10 cents a glass, Ogden faced some difficulty in using up his credit before they arrived. As American celebrities, the Nashes were seated at the table of the Dutch captain, a jolly old gent who looked like Winston Churchill. They were surrounded by a Dutch couple and the sister of one of the proprietors of 21, Ogden's favorite New York restaurant, which he had frequented since the days when it was a speakeasy and the bosses were bootleggers.

The ship stopped at the Azores, which turned out to be a drag, because the weather was too cold for enjoyment ashore. They did tour St. Michael's Island. Ogden and Frances spent a day in Madeira, and then they arrived in Spain and spent two days at Malaga. That visit, too, was unpleasant because of the weather. Then it was on to Lisbon, where they properly toured the city's museums and historic spots.

On May 15 they arrived in London. Ogden bought clothes on Bond Street, and Frances bought presents for the children and grandchildren.

They ate at Prunier's London branch, and at the Ritz, and they went to see Agatha Christie's *The Mousetrap*. Malcolm Muggeridge, the editor of *Punch*, gave them tea at the magazine's offices. They had cocktails at Claridge's with Bruce and Beatrice Gould of the *Ladies' Home Journal*. They played tourist again and went to the National Gallery and visited Eton College and Windsor Castle. Ogden was interviewed by the British Broadcasting Company. They were two weeks in London, having a wonderful time, except that toward the end, Ogden became sick and ran a fever. The doctor diagnosed the ailment as internal upset. Ogden was dosed, and he recovered to go to Amsterdam and Rotterdam to sail home.

Then it was time to set stakes at Little Boar's Head for the summer. All those books began coming out in the fall, and there were the usual reviews and interviews. Ogden had always been extremely sensitive to publicity, and he continued to be that way, no matter how much his work was celebrated by the critics. The slightest negative would throw him into a funk. There were few negatives, but Richard L. Schoenwald, writing in the highly intellectual *Commonweal*, ventured one or two remarks that at best could be called faint praise.

Nash, the critic said, was the perfect composer for poesy for America because "he does not laugh too hard, he does not cry too hard."

"No one," said the critic, "could profitably turn out amusing verse in the American setting in any other way . . . When everyone owns the same fin-tail 1957 model, the cheapness of its chrome can't be poked at too hard. The age demands a nice, balanced, thoughtful, undisturbing writer."

Ogden had said much the same himself at various times on the lecture trail, but it hurt to have another repeat the truth, particularly if it was at his expense.

"Nash accepts America; America reciprocates. He is what a poet ought to be, his fans exclaim. They never see more than the surface because there is nothing more to see. Nash never cuts into the depths. His readers behold the surface selves of their neighbors . . . They have not been reading poetry. True poetry does not come when the poet says, Let there be a little light, but not on the dark corners."

Much as it hurt, Ogden could not but agree. As he said himself, he had sometimes been moved to violent indignation at some outrage, but if so, and he wrote, it came off unsuccessfully. He envied the poets who could feel deeply and express themselves on social and political evils.

"But I'm not one of them, and it's wrong for a pussycat to get mixed up with tigers."

Even when such criticism cut deeply, Ogden recognized its validity. But the unkindest cut came that year from Mother Nature. After that bout with intestinal-whatever, Ogden knew he had been very sick and he so wrote his old friend Charles Duell on his return from London. The summer passed pleasantly at Little Boar's Head, but in the fall he had a recurrence of the intestinal trouble and finally underwent some tests. The doctors discovered that he had acute polyps, as he wrote Dan Longwell, and that he would have to have them removed. On February 2 he entered Baltimore's Union Memorial Hospital, full of fears and trepidations.

19

A Plugged Nickel Says My
Polyps Are Cuter Than Yours

Before Ogden went into the hospital in February, that Simon Legree of lecturing, W. Colston Leigh, sent him off on another tour. Probably it was the best possible therapy for it kept him from worrying overmuch about what was going to happen. But he worried enough, and on the eve of his incarceration he sent a plaintive note to Dan Longwell about his polyps, saying bravely that the doctors said they were not malignant, and ending with the words that the operation would immobilize him for just a few weeks. Well, almost ending thus; he pinned on another thought: he *hoped* he would be in touch with Longwell and his wife again. The letter gave the impression that Ogden feared very much that he was about to meet his maker, whom he now began to refer to as "Dodger Thomas."

Despite Ogden's worst fears, the operation was a success. Recuperation took several weeks and caused Ogden a good deal of emotional pain. He was, he said, suffering from myopia, astigmatism, dyspepsia, gout, arthritis, and abdominal problems that were the delight of physicians and surgeons. He had always been a hypochondriac.

Now, making light of his troubles, Ogden did not banish them, but at least he put them at arm's length, examined them, and got some verse out of them.

By summer Ogden was well enough to get up to Little Boar's Head for a time, and he relaxed, but in the fall he was back for a busy season. He was putting verses to Prokofiev's suite "Peter and the Wolf." He was writing that one Christmas poem every year. He now had a new market, *Sports Illustrated*, which paid well for his verse. He and Frances took a cruise to the British West Indies, and he sold an article about it to *Holiday* for $1,500. The lectures took him out to Los Angeles again.

The year 1959 was more of the same, although the lecture tour took him no further west than Denver, but it was again up and down. Little, Brown, short of poetic ammunition (he produced only about twenty poems and articles that year), brought forth *Collected Verse from 1929 On*, for which he had culled his entire poesic past and had revised and rerevised some poems to bring them up to date or to make them dateless.

One reason that W. Colston Leigh retained a stranglehold on the lecturing business was that he kept coming up with new ideas. His 1959 suggestion to Ogden was that he vary his routine by doing some Christmas reading of his own poetry and that of others. So Ogden also became a verbal anthologist that year.

That was also the year that Ogden really stepped out in the field of juvenile literature. The occasion was the publication by Little, Brown of a heavily illustrated revision of the long Nash poem "Custard the Dragon," which had first appeared in *The Bad Parents' Garden of Verse* in 1936. The idea actually went back much further and probably ought to be attributed to Dan Longwell. For in the Doubleday days, Longwell had really been Ogden's greatest source of encouragement, and, while Ogden was still living in New York, Longwell had suggested that he write a book of children's verse that would banish Winnie-the-Pooh, the A. A. Milne classic set that had dominated the children's verse market since the 1920s. But Ogden had put the idea aside, and Milne had kept the hammerlock in the 1930s, 1940s, and 1950s. Times having changed, and tradition in America having relatively the same staying power as a low-rise building on Park Avenue, many publishers racked their brains for a new approach to this market.

One thing was certain, most children's book editors in the 1920s and 1930s and 1940s didn't know very much about children or what they wanted. Children's books were bought by other people to give to children, most children not having ready access to $3.95.

One of the great revolutions in books came when fathers and mothers began to be selected as children's book editors. One of the first books to crack through under this new approach was *Little Bear* by Elsie Minarek. When Ogden came up with *Custard the Dragon* he, too, began to widen that market.

The successors to Mr. Little and Mr. Brown could not have been more pleased.

One reason that Ogden was so successful in writing for children is that he *knew* children, having been an acute observer of his nieces and nephews and then his own progeny and now his grandchildren.

He had written poems about children for nearly thirty years. He had written children's poems for his own children, and some of these had been published in magazines that were not for children. After the publication of the books *The Bad Parents' Garden of Verse* and *Elderly Poems for Youngerly Readers,* he had begun to get letters from schoolchildren. He had not paid a great deal of attention to all this, but slowly he had come to the conclusion that there was something important here, and, particularly after the success of Ogden's Lippincott anthologies, Little, Brown agreed.

Ogden knew one secret about children that had escaped most librarians: children are real people, and even before they can read they can think and they do not like to be treated improperly by infantile adults. Ogden never wrote down to children, or to anybody else for that matter.

Custard the Dragon represented a new approach to dragons; Custard, a very sensible dragon, felt the need (doesn't everybody?) for a little security. In a pinch he became a very brave dragon indeed, while his pals Belinda and Ink and Mustard and Blink all finked out and then came back when the battle was won to tell one another how brave and smart they were. Children got the message: this was the way it really was in the world inhabited by big sisters, big brothers, fathers, mothers, and other people. The pinafore set loved the book.

Ogden began to expand his market for children's verse, which could not have brought much joy to the counting house on Beacon Street. In 1960 he published *Beastly Poetry*, with Hallmark Editions. Another publisher, Franklin Watts, a long-established children's book house, paid him an advance of $2,500 for *A Boy Is a Boy.* That was a coup. He also got $3,500 from *McCall's* for the same work.

Ogden was reaching an entirely new audience, and an appreciative one. From Mr. Trombly's fifth grade (address not preserved) he received a poem written by the class, addressed to him and about him. The class also sent a letter, suggesting that it would be better if more people wrote his sort of poems and "not so much about crooks and things." Ogden expressed his agreement to Mr. Trombly's fifth grade. Maybe, he said, those people would get tired of such writing after a while.

Ogden finished with his spring lecture tour in the first week of May 1960, and the Nashes went to Baltimore for a week, then back to New York for a month, then to Little Boar's Head from June 15 to September 15.

The next year, 1961, along came another Lippincott book, *Everybody Ought to Know: Verses Selected and Introduced by Ogden Nash.*

This book was really another departure. The earlier Lippincott anthologies had been confined to lighter stuff, but Ogden held that children are capable of reading Swinburne, so Swinburne was there. The Swinburne poem was "The Chorus from Atlanta to Calydon." Browning was there with "My Star." Alfred Tennyson contributed "To Christopher North." Whitman and Coleridge, Byron and Kipling, all were there. After *Everybody Ought to Know*, no reader would ever again be afraid of the classical poets. Also there were poets of modern day: Sandburg and Frost, Hilaire Belloc, Don Marquis, and e. e. cummings. And, wonder of wonders, so, at last, was Samuel Hoffenstein, with a verse from *Poems in Praise of Practically Nothing*, which read so much like Ogden Nash's funny verse. Ogden Nash was there with two, one the little poem about the hunter trying to outwit the duck, which he had written for Dan Longwell, and one of his favorites, the very serious end piece of *Hard Lines* that had brought Ogden compliments from Stephen Vincent Benét: "Old Men."

Seeing Ogden's new round of success, Little, Brown got the idea. The success of *Custard* brought about their request for a new book about the dragon by their favorite poet. He obliged, for an advance of $1,250, and in 1961 they had *Custard the Dragon and the Wicked Knight*. It was another Nash book eminently satisfactory to Custard's fans. Indeed, Winnie-the-Pooh had something to worry about.

In the summer of 1961 the Nashes did not go to Little Boar's Head. They had business afoot and stayed in New York. They had sold their apartment on 57th Street and bought a new one on East 81st Street, in a much quieter neighborhood. Temporarily they were staying with Isabel and her husband on Park Avenue but would spend part of the summer with Linell and her family in suburban Baltimore. In the fall they expected to move into the new place. Ogden took time off from a busy writing schedule to accept an honorary degree from Adelphi College. It was like a spring rainfall to his ego.

Ogden was very busy with his new children's books, and he had amassed about enough poems for a new adult collection. This would be called *Everyone but Thee and Me*.

He was finishing up the two children's books, *The New Nutcracker Suite and Other Innocent Verses*, for Little, Brown, and *Girls Are Silly*, for Franklin Watts.

There was just time to move from 57th Street to East 81st Street, which was no easier than moving from Baltimore to New York, when Ogden had to be on the road again and would stay there most of the time, holidays excepted, until the following spring. It was, he said, the most exhaustive schedule yet, devised by his ravenous agent. From Vermont to Washington he went, from Montana to Florida, with countless stops in the middle, including a most instructive week among the Mormons in Salt Lake City.

On his return to New York, he rested and caught up on his correspondence, which was months behind.

He had come home with his spirits renewed. He felt for the first time that his sickness was ended, and that, in spite of all, he was not about to meet Dodger Thomas just yet.

By summer, Ogden and Frances had returned once more to Little Boar's Head. This year, there was a difference. After years of renting, they bought a house there on Atlantic Avenue, with an eye to winterizing it so they could spend most of the year in the rural atmosphere.

New York City was in the throes of a cultural revolution that did not appeal to the Nashes. The city had been multiracial for as long as Ogden could remember. But in the 1950s the old neighborhoods began to break up. Particularly after the 1956 school desegregation decision and the emergence of Martin Luther King as leader of the black civil rights movement, the changes came fast. Blacks began to flock to the cities. In 1957 the number of U.S. cities with a population over a million rose to seventy-one as compared to sixteen in Ogden's boyhood days. New York was a major destination of those seeking opportunity. The upper west side, along West End Avenue and Riverside Drive, had been the lair of the very, very wealthy in Ogden's youth. In the 1940s it became the dwelling place of the middle class. In the 1950s Harlem began to move south, and moved, and moved until it lapped at the edges of Central Park. Low-cost government housing filled in most of the interstices between the avenues.

The march of changes continued:

1957. The Little Rock school desegregation crisis.
1958. U.S. population is 179 million, but 5 million are unemployed. The "beatnik" movement spreads from California across the world.
1959. Stanley Kunitz's *Selected Poems* wins the Pulitzer Prize.
1960. John Betjemann, *Summoned by Bells*, autobiography in verse. John Updike's *Rabbit, Run* is a bestseller. The United States has 85 million TV sets, which is more than one per household.
1961. J. D. Salinger's *Frannie and Zooie* is a bestseller. Racial consternation and conflict in Birmingham.
1962. e. e. cummings dies. James Meredith and federal marshals integrate the University of Mississippi. Boris Pasternak's *In the Interlude* is the poetry talk of the year.

In the meantime came the second part of the cultural revolution: the wave of Puerto Ricans who swept into the city, filling up all the holes in Harlem, and then scattering wherever warrens could be unearthed or pried from landlords eager to cram six into a room, on the lower east side, and then the middle east side up to 34th Street, and through the west down to Greenwich Village. Most of the old "village" had become enormously expensive; no longer did one find there the charming, if cold-water,

hutches of artists and writers, but the fortified castlets of television producers and expensive celebrities. If you were a writer you had to be James
Beard to afford a Greenwich Village house.

Ogden observed this movement without pleasure, but it was not the only
movement that disturbed him. He was an unfortunate man in one sense;
the America in which he had been a child had been a simple straightfor-
ward country, dominated by people of his own kind. He had watched all
this change in New York City and, to a lesser extent, in the rest of metropolitan America. No, he was not mistaken through ignorance; few Americans had traveled more across the land than Ogden Nash in the 1940s and
1950s. The cultural revolution was in full swing, America was dividing up
like a giant amoeba into a nation of hyphenates, Anglo-, Afro-, Hispanic-;
there the conflict was most apparent, and the primary battlegrounds were
the streets of New York City. It was the sort of change that had caused
James Thurber to write *My World, and Welcome to It.*

Along with that conflict Ogden early sensed another, the disintegration
of family life. In Ogden's quiet way, he was appalled, and his poems began
to show, more than ever before, a concern with the meaning of this social
change.

When *Everyone but Thee and Me* was published, it was greeted by the critics almost precisely as usual. In *The New York Times* Morris Bishop repeated
the accustomed litany: "Ogden Nash is the only American except Walt
Whitman who has created a new poetic form and has imposed it on the
world." He gave credit for this to the influence of Swift and Gilbert. He
said nothing of Parker and Hoffenstein. Nor did he say creation of a form
would indicate that a poet would be followed by others who would write
in the same vein, but with their individual styles. There *was* a rub. For anyone who tried to follow Ogden's style was immediately labelled a poor
imitator by the magazine and book publishers. With his odd rhymes and
rhythms Ogden remained *sui generis;* his poesy could not be called a form
because it could not develop a creative following.

Critic Bishop did suggest that Ogden deserved more serious analysis
from the academic community than he got, probably because "serious"
poets by this time seemed to have deserted rhyme as senseless, while
Ogden retained it as essential. Bishop repeated the portrait of Ogden as
court jester, the wise man pretending to be simpleminded. He also made
the now usual complaint that Ogden spent too much time on easy jokes.
Yet, he, too, was a happy reader. He wound up the review: "Yet at his best,
Beau Nash is at everybody's best."

John Mason Brown, in the *Saturday Review,* was a little more prescient
than Morris Bishop. He paid the usual homage to the versifier, the "Mississippi of metrics" who had "remained his buoyant, unpredictable and
unique self." But he did see a little something new: Ogden's "Come, Come,

Kerouac. My Generation Is Beater Than Yours." Among other ripostes, he thrust at the "progress" in aviation. Two Wrights, said Ogden, had made a wrong.

But critic Brown and the rest failed to sense the major change that had occurred in Ogden's approach to American life. In the early days he had been concerned with love, marriage, and children, and the foibles of women. All these concerns remained. In the middle days he had been concerned with the materialistic development of America. These concerns remained. They were augmented now by a basic concern that Ogden was feeling about the deterioration of the quality of life in America. "Come, Come, Kerouac . . ." was far more than a jab at the Wright brothers. Ogden had first taken such a jab in 1931 in *Hard Lines* in "No, *You* Be a Lone Eagle," when he suggested that the cause of humanity would have been better served had the Wright brothers gone into silver fox farming or tree surgery than airplane inventing.

Critic Brown had noted but one of Ogden's main complaints about the decline in the quality of life in the name of "progress." The others named in that one poem: the Europeanization of American taste (headwaiter had become maitre d'); the retrogressive nature of U.S. television (radio jokes about Bing Crosby's horses became TV jokes about Crosby's children); the homogenization of sport, baseball czar, football czar, and coming czars; and the complication of such machines as the phonograph to become the hi-fi.

That was just one poem. "The Spoon Ran Away with the Dish" was devoted to the puerility of television commercials; the vehicle was a dishwasher soap ad. "Is There an Oculist in the House" considered the American policy that led us to fight the Italians, the Germans, and the Japanese, and in 1962 to befriend them. But more, the snapper to Ogden's poem was at the end, where he considered the growing war between the generations with his usual helpless consternation.

There were the usual briefs, such as a four-liner that warned husbands to admit when wrong and shut up when right, and the consideration of the problems of shrimp love in a translucent shrimp world. And poems of the day, sometimes tied to the news of the world, such as one triggered by a newspaper note about Soviet purchase of Cypriot citrus fruit, and one triggered by Henry Kissinger. There was a plaint about picnics, which indicated that Ogden had gotten a bit long in the tooth. But it was so easy to mistake irritation of the spirit for irritation of old age. One whole section of the book was devoted to "The Mother Tongue," and his concern for the bowdlerization and downright corruption of the English language by professors, bureaucrats, and hyphenated Americans. There was no mistaking Ogden's meaning there. He was beginning to speak more openly on social issues that had troubled him for years. The pussycat was showing some signs of growing into a tiger.

20

It Takes a Heap of Doggerel to Keep the Home Fires Burning

Near the end of the year 1962 Ogden was pleased to learn that *Everyone but Thee and Me* was selling very well. The advance sale, based on Ogden's reputation, was 13,000 copies, and that had been followed by reorders of 5,000 copies in the first four weeks after publication. The book had also been chosen as an alternate selection by the Book-of-the-Month Club for March 1963. All this bolstered his ego as did the fact that Franklin and Marshall College had awarded him an honorary degree.

By finding new outlets for his work, Ogden was surviving the great media change very nicely.

He was not getting multiple sales on his long poems, as he had almost always achieved with short ones. For example, "A Boy and His Room," which Franklin Watts had published as a book, had first been published by *McCall's* magazine earlier in the year; he had received $4,000 for it. *Family Circle* magazine paid him $5,000 for a 540-line poem. *The Atlantic Monthly* was buying poems from him, *Sports Illustrated* was a regular market, *Life* was only an occasional purchaser but a very high-paying one.

In 1963 Ogden's poetic output for magazines was very slight indeed—eight poems in all, and there was only one book, another retread of Ogden's old verse put out by Little, Brown. *The Adventures of Isabel*, it was called, and it was based on poems he had written for and about his children a number of years earlier. But those poems were of the timeless variety; the vagaries of human nature was their key.

The reason for Ogden's lack of productivity lay deep inside the physical man. By June he had completed his spring lecture tour, taken care of a few New York chores, and then headed for Little Boar's Head. The Nashes would have the grandchildren up in waves that summer, and other guests when possible. Linell's daughters came first. But this summer Grandfather Nash was not much of a sport. He had not been at the beach long when his belly began acting up again. He was sick much of the summer. He got some work done; he produced a Christmas poem for *Holiday* in June and he got off a prose piece to *The Saturday Evening Post*. But his gut troubled him enormously, and finally in August he gave up and went to Boston where he entered Massachusetts General Hospital for tests and treatment of his intestinal complaint. The doctors kept him for two weeks and then said he was suffering from colitis. This meant no more martinis, not even any more Chianti. A thirty-five-lecture tour was already scheduled for the fall; it had to be canceled since the patient was directed to have complete rest and a very bland diet. So Nash went back to Little Boar's Head to spend the off-season until October 15.

In the fall the Nashes returned to New York. The six weeks of lying about brought enough recovery so that work could begin once more. Most of Ogden's work was now being done on assignment, not speculation. *Sports Illustrated* ordered a "golf poem" for a special issue planned for the summer of 1964, previewing the National Open Tournament.

Little, Brown wanted a book for 1964. Once again, what they got was mostly retreaded, but Little, Brown was not dismayed. The publishers now knew that in Nashiana they had a multigenerational market. He had been writing for more than thirty years, and many of the old poems would run once again, to be greeted as "new" by a new generation of readers. Ogden revised here and there still, again cutting out the names and events that would date the work. So, *An Ogden Nash Bonanza* was published that year. It consisted of poems from the five volumes: *Good Intentions, I'm a Stranger Here Myself, Many Long Years Ago, The Private Dining Room,* and *Versus.*

The year also brought another "new" book, but it was again a compendium of work done, old poems with a theme: *Marriage Lines, or Notes of a Student Husband.*

It opened with "Love Under the Republicans"—a poem that had first been published in book form in *Hard Lines* in 1931. There were fifty poems in all, some culled from Ogden's valentine greetings to his wife on their thirty-fifth Valentine's Day, some from place card poetry, and some from personal poetry, to piece out the collection of old poems republished.

As with everything that Ogden touched, *Marriage Lines* was financially successful, but this time it was not quite as successful as usual with the reviewers. Perhaps they had seen some of these poems too many times.

Some reviewers merely noted that many poems had appeared before. Some implied that this collection did not represent the best of Nash.

Besides those two books, 1964 brought an increase in Ogden's output of work for magazines, from eight items the previous year to eighteen.

At Little Boar's Head, grandchildren filled the house for the summer. After several revisions, the house could accommodate a dozen guests comfortably: five guest bedrooms upstairs, with host and hostess living in grandparently splendor on the first floor with their private bath. Swimming and sunning and all the delights of the shore were theirs until fall, when Ogden and Frances went to London once more.

J. M. Dent, Ltd., Ogden's London publishers, had gone to great trouble to arrange a promotion and publicity tour of England that was expected to create an enormous stir for the book.

The Nashes were in London, then, when *The Sunday Times* reviewed Ogden's *Marriage Lines*.

The Sunday Times was not impressed.

"Ogden Nash in his heyday was as witty as [Hilaire] Belloc. *Marriage Lines*, old admirers must admit with a regretful sigh, suggests not so much heyday as heigh-ho. Technically Mr. Nash is less brilliant: the polysyllabic lines, the remote and execrable puns, are more laboured; but what strikes chill in these 'notes of a student husband' is the wholesale trading in sentimentality. But not all the genius is gone, and this is still a book for collectors."

When Ogden saw that review he was furious.

He wrote a letter to *The Sunday Times*, pointing out that he had made it quite clear these poems were mostly old ones. (He had not; in the introduction to the book he had been less than forthright with his readers. Ogden had referred to his notes penned through the years. He had not said the notes were not poems, but he had not said they were poems either.) *The Sunday Times* reviewer, not being familiar with the American publishing practice of wringing every dollar from viable materials, had accepted the work as new work and criticized it accordingly. The result was partly transatlantic cultural clash and partly time clash between 1964 and the 1930s and 1940s when most of these lines were written.

Even when these particular poems had first come out in various books, Ogden was occasionally accused of supersentimentality (a feeling this biographer shares) and an uxurious infatuation with Frances Leonard Nash, which he never got over. Most twentieth-century men—most American men, at least—found it hard to express deep love in words. Ogden was the great exception, and frequently he was taxed more than praised for it, both home and abroad. On this occasion he suggested that the lines the reviewer did like were those most recently written. Even that was not quite true; the lines quoted were from "The Perfect Husband," which had first appeared in book form in *Versus* in 1949.

And thus was the matter left, with no great harm done, save to Ogden's ego.

This damage was soon forgotten in a greater crisis. The excitement of the promotion efforts was too much for Ogden's weakened digestive system. He collapsed just after the first of November and had to be admitted to the London Clinic.

After two weeks the doctors let him out to go home to America. He thought he was all right, but he was not. New Year 1965 came, and he was still suffering from intestinal distress.

The lecture agency was told there would be no more tours at all. The television appearances also came to an end for a different reason; the "What's My Line," and "Masquerade Party" sort of panel shows had mostly run their course. Ogden was not disappointed. He was nearly sixty-three years old, and he had to be careful of his health. So if his big earning days seemed to be behind him, the change was acceptable.

Furthermore, Ogden was fed up with a New York that bore only a skeletal resemblance to the city he had once known and loved so well that in *Hard Lines* he had declared that he wanted the whole city all for himself. It was no wrench for him, then, to go back to Maryland where Frances could be near daughter Linell and her family, who were now living on a farm outside Baltimore and raising ponies, dogs, and Arabian horses.

In March they began the move to 30 Olmstead Avenue, a large garden duplex apartment in a new development on Olmstead Green, the grounds of the former golf course of the Baltimore Country Club. It was delightful, they found, after the dirt and violence of New York.

Baltimore welcomed the prodigal back with enthusiasm. Mayor McKeldin wrote him a welcoming letter. Governor Spiro Agnew asked him to become poet laureate of Maryland, an honor of Ogden refused. The *Baltimore Sun* sent a reporter to find out why he had come back.

"New York just got too depressing," said Ogden. "Everything was getting so expensive . . . $9.90 for theater tickets a year from now . . . $12 for a bunch of lilies of the valley . . . traffic worse and worse."

The plan was to spend five and a half months there and six and a half months at Little Boar's Head. The Nashes would become "citizens" of New Hampshire, and thus "synthetic New Englanders."

Surprisingly, the first months of 1965 proved extremely lucrative for Ogden. He received a $3,500 advance against royalties from Little, Brown for *The Animal Garden* and another $3,500 for *The Mysterious Ouphe* from the short-lived Hale Publishing Company. Merrill Lynch, Pierce, Fenner, and Smith paid him several thousand dollars for a poem they used in a promotional advertisement.

But what Ogden still hoped for in his mature years was again denied him:

in the spring Ogden was again overlooked when the Pulitzer Prize for poetry was announced. Added to that disappointment was a turn of the screw. Poet Phyllis McGinley had won a Pulitzer Prize earlier. This spring she was to be celebrated on a cover of *Time* magazine and *Time* asked Ogden to supply some material for the cover story. He did not. But by May the disappointment had washed away in the anticipation of the months at Little Boar's Head. Once more Ogden looked forward to a house bursting with grandchildren and friends. In the winter the Nashes had brought in carpenters and painters and plumbers to add to the amenities of the house so the Nashes could spend more time there and less in Baltimore.

They arrived at North Hampton at the end of May, expecting summer weather but got winter instead. On went the furnace, and they shivered away the end of spring and the beginning of summer. It had been the habit of Ogden and some of the other hardy Rye Beach residents to swim in the sea every day, starting with the arrival of spring. But the polar bear syndrome had to be abandoned this year. The furnace was roaring away on the Fourth of July. A few days later the weather warmed up and the remainder of the summer was pleasant. In the fall Ogden and Frances drove inland to the White Mountains to see the foliage turning, and then at the end of October went down to the new apartment outside Baltimore.

The year had been most successful in every way except for the coveted Pulitzer Prize. Ogden had been elected a fellow of the American Academy of Arts and Sciences in Boston, along with Vice President Hubert Humphrey and Cardinal Cushing. He learned of it by reading the story in the *New York Herald Tribune*. At first he did not know what it was all about, and it took ten days to discover that this Boston organization had a distinguished history: John Adams had been president, so had John Quincy Adams and Charles Francis Adams.

As 1965 drew to a close, Ogden had reason to be pleased with his literary output. No longer burdened by the lecture tour, he had produced twenty-eight poems and prose pieces and had sold them for $20,000. Combined with the advances and royalties from books, which had to more than equal the fees, that gave him a very substantial income.

Ogden was just then considering the sale of his personal papers to the Harry Ransom Humanities Center at the University of Texas at Austin. Any great library, and that included the Library of Congress, would have been delighted to have them (and later the Library of Congress asked and was disappointed to learn they had been sold). Ogden had decided to sell his papers while he was alive to enjoy the fruits of them, and the University of Texas, which was well endowed and "buying up everything in sight" (as one competing archivist put it a little bitterly), was negotiating for them. Dan Longwell held a number of papers from the past, including the minutes of the Nassau and Suffolk County Deviled Ham and Lake

Ronkonkoma Club, Ogden Nash, permanent temporary corresponding secretary. Ogden asked for these, and Longwell cheerfully gave them up, although his own papers would go to Columbia University.

Ogden now kept up a lively correspondence with Dan Longwell, reminiscing about old times, sending him limericks that Ogden composed on nights he lay awake, and gossiping about family matters. Longwell was really almost family to Ogden. They had grown up together in Rye, New York. Longwell was older, but he remembered the kid who used to play with his sister; that bond had helped Ogden get that first Doubleday job, and the closeness had persisted since. Now, in the later years of the two, both men ill and feeling very mortal, the closeness increased.

Christmas 1965 was a time of joy and sadness. Daughter Isabel and her husband came down from New York, and Christmas Eve for the whole family was spent at Ogden's place. Next day they all trouped over to daughter Linell's house for Christmas dinner. It seemed to Ogden to be like an old-fashioned Currier and Ives event with overtones of Dickens. That was the joy. The sadness came five days after Christmas, when Mrs. Leonard died. She was ninety-one years old, and her death came as no surprise, but the finality of it was a wrench for Ogden and particularly for his wife, for mother and daughter had been extremely close all Frances's life.

The festive atmosphere and excitement of the holidays had raised hob with Ogden's internal plumbing. In January he underwent extensive X-rays. The result showed that he had a kink in his lower intestine and that it could be corrected only by surgery. The prognosis was excellent, the doctors assured him; it was a simple operation and they thought that the excision of this sharp turn would relieve his symptoms. Ogden agreed in principle to an operation to be performed sometime in late winter or early spring.

The symptoms, however, did not let up, so he could not stall. On March 2 Ogden entered Johns Hopkins Hospital. He had very little confidence in the outcome. He was, he said, taking a big gamble. But the operation was successful, the kink was removed, and he was sewed up, loaded with cortisone, and the doctors told him he would recover nicely. His surgeon even delivered the verdict in Nashian verse.

As the doctor said, Ogden would heal nicely, but he would not heal quickly. By May he was still wobbly. That month he and Frances headed for Little Boar's Head. This summer they expected to be relatively free of grandchildren, for on Mrs. Leonard's death Ogden's daughters had come into some money, and both families were planning trips abroad that summer.

But in fact, the Nashes kept house for three to five grandchildren, among others, all summer long. This, as Ogden wrote Dan Longwell, meant that a lot of verse was needed to get them through the summer. He produced enough: $5,000 worth of Christmas poem for *Family Circle*, $1,500 worth of Christmas poem for *TV Guide*, $1,250 from *Venture* for a poem, $3,500 from *The Saturday Evening Post*, and $2,000 for stories. The *Reader's Digest* paid him $4,000 for a promotion piece to be used in their advertising—more, he noted, than they paid for similar editorial material.

He also made a deal with RCA Victor Records to put out two records of Nash poems.

Only in one place was Ogden having difficulty: *The New Yorker*. In the past few years he had sold them fewer and fewer poems.

In the late 1940s Ogden's stock with *The New Yorker* had risen to its zenith. In July 1947 the Curtis Brown agency had asked the magazine to pay Ogden more than it had been doing in the past. This request created something of an internal crisis, because while Harold Ross brooked no interference by the business office in the editorial functions of the magazine, the business department was the final arbiter of money matters. So when the offer came up from the business side and was less than the agency had asked, Ross was all atwitter until he learned that Ogden had accepted.

Ross wrote Ogden that he was both pleased and relieved that Ogden had not balked. Ross had gone to bat for Ogden with the business office, with limited success. But he was delighted as he could be that Ogden would remain a contributor. Ross said that he didn't want to run the magazine with Ogden out of it.

That was 1947.

Ross continued to be a Nash booster. In October 1949 the magazine had purchased that tour de force, "My Trip daorbA," the backwards account of Ogden's backwards journey overseas. It had occasioned one of Ross's rare fan letters. Thereafter all had gone well, the limitation on the Nash poetry in *The New Yorker* being largely Ogden's because he was busy then with his hopeful ventures into the musical theater, and his lecturing.

But in 1951 Ross died suddenly on an operating table, and *The New Yorker* went into a state of shock. William Shawn succeeded Ross as editor.

Ross's was a very hard act to follow. In 1946 he had been the one who had turned the entire issue of the magazine over to John Hersey's report on Hiroshima, something no other magazine had even thought of doing. He had established a unique sort of magazine. The new generation had to try to carry it on. Shawn had been given credit for the Hiroshima coup, but Ross was still final authority.

In the years that followed 1951 many readers began to believe that *The New Yorker* had become a stodgy imitation of itself. The most devastating criticism was that of a flamboyant young *New York Herald Tribune* reporter,

Tom Wolfe. When that attack was made, Ogden rose loyally to the defense of his old employers, claiming that the attack was sheer nonsense.

Over the years Ogden had sold less and less to *The New Yorker*. Because of the musicals of the 1940s and 1950s and the lecture tours of the 1960s, Ogden was not producing very much poetry anyhow, and *The New Yorker* bought a reasonable amount of it. He had never expected to sell them everything he submitted, although the rejections had always puzzled him.

But after Ogden's first illness, the tone of some of his poetry changed, and from that point on, the relationship of the poet and his oldest market changed, too.

21

From Piddletrenthide
to the Preakness

Ogden Nash's difficulty with *The New Yorker*, the magazine more responsible for his success than any other, began in 1960. Before that year he had not always clicked; a number of his poems had been returned to him, always a painful matter for Ogden; but every writer grows familiar with rejection if not inured to it. Usually *The New Yorker* rejects had been circulated by the Curtis Brown agency to other magazines and were published. If not, Ogden preferred not to believe much of what editors said, and he simply saved the poems that no editor liked and used them to fill out the chinks in his books. To Nash aficionados this practice was a source of delight, for it meant every book brought them something no one had seen before. To Ogden it was satisfactory. Unlike some writers who accept the ephemeral judgments of editors as gospel and despair, Ogden believed in himself. He was not only confident but frugal, and except for prose, for which he had never developed a book outlet, there was almost no waste at all.

During that 1960 trip to England, Ogden had picked up a copy of *Country Life* magazine, to find an advertisement that caught his fancy:

DORSET—8 miles Dorchester in the valley of the River Piddle. Kiddle's Farm, Piddletrenthide. A small mixed farm with small period farmhouse. dining/living room, kitchen, 3 bedrooms, bathroom.

Back home, Ogden composed a poem about Piddle's Farm, saying that if he had the money he would buy it and leave the noisy, smelly city of New York, forsaking the smog and the Internal Revenue Service, and live happily ever after in Piddletrenthide in the Valley of the Piddle.

He sent this poem to the agency, and they sent it to *The New Yorker*. It was rejected. So were a number of others. These days that magazine's decisions about Ogden Nash's work were very often negative.

Ogden had taken on a temporary secretary that year, and instead of a hardworking stenographer he had gotten a young woman from Bennington College who had literary ambitions. She loved to be in the presence of the Great Author, and she loved to talk. But she never, Ogden concluded, listened. Also all the agility she had learned in modern dance and whatever else at Bennington had not been transmitted to her fingers. Somewhere, in that modern education, they had left out the English language, and she had never learned to spell. Thus, when he dictated, she made mistakes in spelling. When he told her to send something parcel post, she sent it to Marcel Proust, who had gone to his eternal rest in 1922, the year that Ogden was writing car card advertising. She couldn't type and she couldn't think like a secretary and she couldn't . . .

Finally Ogden unlimbered this elfin creature and set about finding a new secretary. What he wanted was a young woman who had grown up in Feeble Bluff, Nebraska, and who had never heard of James Joyce. He wrote a very funny verse about this encounter called "The Quick Frown Sox", but *The New Yorker* editors did not like it.

There were more rejections. On April 19, 1965, another rejection: "Never Was I Born to Set Them Right."

Ogden had written a long poem, mentioning some of the elements of the post-1945 society that particularly irked him. The nonbook. The antihero. The hot air machine that replaced the paper towel in public restrooms. Fluorescent lights over mirrors. Odd-shaped bottle openers that did everything but open bottles. Toll booth baskets that the driver could not quite reach. Self-mailing aerogrammes. And, last, the abandonment by the Internal Revenue Service of the courtesy to the taxpayer of a franked envelope in which to send his tax money.

No, said *The New Yorker*.

If *The New Yorker* had mixed feelings about Ogden Nash in the 1960s, the compliment was certainly returned by Ogden. In 1966 he spent several hours with Roy Newquist, who was writing his book *Conversations*, a revealing series of sketches of literary figures. Newquist asked Ogden several questions about the contemporary literary scene. As to humor, Ogden said the level had fallen sharply. *The New Yorker*, once famous for the prose pieces of Robert Benchley and Frank Sullivan, no longer had anything like them. Their place had been taken by what Ogden called the self-pity school. "Most of these young men have the distinct feeling that nothing awful has ever happened except to them."

What he wanted to see was some joy of spirit, but he did not find it in the pages of his favorite magazine.

Indeed, Ogden was musing in these 1960s about the deterioration of the society all around him. It was easy to be wry, but hard enough even for him to laugh loud enough these days to be heard over the ridiculous, the unconscious humor he saw distributed all around him.

He did not, he once told a reporter, write poetry. "I write comment in verse," he said.

As he grew older the comment became a little sharper than it had been, but at his worst he was hardly a cantankerous old man. Late in the 1960s when his contemporaries were damning college students for their open opposition to the Vietnam War, Ogden took a longer view.

"In the old days," he said, "people criticized students for being too uncommitted and doing nothing but panty raids and goldfish swallowing. Now that students are deeply involved in politics and so forth, the older generation criticizes them for being too committed. I believe in a little more tolerance. They're all going to grow up and become poops like we are anyway."

And about television, he was a little bit ambivalent, just a little bit. "I growl at it . . . but it's always possible to turn it off. The industry ought to be ashamed of 80 percent of its stuff, but the other 20 percent is excellent."

Long a Thurberian warrior in the ranks of men in the war between men and women, he decried the endless victories of womankind and the emasculation of men. His cry, these days, was more of whimper for a battle lost; he knew where he stood, and he lamented it, but he warned his constituency to lie low and take it, at least for now . . .

That feeling led him to escape from time to time in male company to the race track. Oh, how he did love the Preakness! Every year in the later days Ogden was a guest of the track on Preakness Day. He once wrote a poem "All Roads Lead to Pimlico." And in 1958 he had cemented his relationship with Maryland's racing world with this poem:

> *At Santa Anita and Hialeah*
> *The horses begin to get the idea.*
> *They loosen their muscles at Tropical Park*
> *And take the baths at Hot Springs, Ark.*
> *They skip the rope at Jamaica and Bowie*
> *In April going, half good, half gooey,*
> *And finish their roadwork jogging through towns*

All the way from Keeneland to Churchill Downs.
They've sworn off smoking, they've sworn off drinks,
Their condition today is the pinkest of pinks.
And for what are they working up to this zenith?
For the Preakness, children, on May seventeenith.

There were, of course, areas in which Ogden's field of vision was blurred: after that early experience in the 1930's of flying across country and actually going most of the way by bus and train because of bad weather, he had taken a real dislike to air travel. Finally, he decided he would not fly any more. And he didn't. Often he went to the racetrack with his friend David Woods and with Tom White, a young reporter for the *Baltimore News American*. One day they went to Laurel. On the drive there Ogden was witty and loquacious, talking all the way. Once they hit the track, his nose went into the racing form and stayed there. He would hum as he studied the statistics, and he would talk only to share some observation about a horse. If he lost the first race, the humming would grow louder. If he lost more races, the volume would increase. Tom White never learned how high it might go, because generally Ogden was a lucky horse-player; losing streaks did not last long. On the day at Laurel, he abandoned his handicapping "system" to bet on a horse named Clytemnestra, because the mythological name appealed to him. She paid $18.40 to win, and did.

On the way home, pockets jingling, Ogden was a happy man, talking steadily again about this and that. They got caught in a traffic jam on the Baltimore-Washington Expressway, and when they came to a dead stop, Tom White suggested that they should have chartered a plane. Ogden sniffed:

"Planes are nothing but flying coffins," he said.

It was one of the opinions he never changed.

In the summer of 1965 he had been invited down to Washington by Larry O' Brien, special assistant to President Johnson, to attend a ceremonial bill signing, and he begged off because he was in New Hampshire and could not get there in time via the Boston and Maine Railroad and the New Haven line.

He loved trains, and he lamented the shrinking of America's railroad system, as he lamented the loss of so many of the civilized niceties.

The crime and the dirt and the cultural clashes of New York had finally driven him out of that city. He now found Baltimore nearly as intolerable, except for the track, and he yearned to spend the year around in New Hampshire, but now that he could do so, the Little Boar's Head house being winterized, his health precluded it. Yes, what he called the indications of senility had made their appearance, but he recognized these signs, and joked about them. The problem was to differentiate between his own feelings as an aging man, and the real outrages of a society gone mad.

What the editors of *The New Yorker* recognized as a crotchety poet was not that much changed. He did a poem on the cricket. He did a poem on April Fool's Day. He did a very funny poem on paperback books (the only thing the Russians had not claimed to have invented, he said). He did a poem on the vicissitudes of a TV golf watcher. A moose appeared on Rye Beach one day, and he did a poem on that. He did a whole flock of limericks.

The New Yorker did not like the moose and *The New Yorker* did not like the limericks. (He sold them to *Punch*, the English humor magazine whose taste had not changed quite so remarkably over the years.)

Ogden was not the only one who now found *The New Yorker* much changed. Another was S. J. Perelman, who had been on that scene as long as Ogden had. Perelman was so disgusted by what he saw that he could hardly make fun of it any more. He was invited to a commencement at Brown University and was not happy to find there John Updike and John Cheever, two of his least favorite writers, but favorites of *The New Yorker* crowd. He escaped the scene, he reported to Ogden, just as quickly as possible.

Perelman and Ogden shared much besides what could be called middle-aged prejudices, or observations on a sick America, depending on your point of view. Ogden wrote a foreword to Perelman's new book, which would come out in 1966, *Chicken Inspector #23*. Nash recalled the old days at MGM, where one of the pair's bits of recreation was watching Joan Crawford bicycling on the lot beneath their window. Ah, those were the days. All the pain was now submerged; the idiocy of a Hollywood trying to make an epic movie out of *How to Win Friends and Influence People* was small potatoes compared to an America where a best-selling book was a nonbook of lists.

In this desert of cultural aberration there were a few beacons of sanity. Perelman, said his friend Ogden, was one of them.

The kind judgment could also be applied to Ogden, and was by Perelman, who wrote Ogden that his poetry was the joy and despair of Perelman's existence.

But not *The New Yorker*'s.

By 1966, Ogden wrote Dan Longwell, he was engaged in a constant battle of wits with the editors of that magazine, in which, he averred, the wit was all on his side. He was averaging one acceptance to nine submissions, and most annoying to him were the reasons given for rejection, which he found stuffy.

And so it went, with monotonous regularity the rejections came along. "Who Put That Spokesman in My Wheel" was rejected as not funny. "The Entrapment of John Alden" failed at *The New Yorker*.

Even when the editors of *The New Yorker* liked something, there was revision to be done, as with "Ill Met by Fluorescence." Ogden complied, possibly because this was for the fortieth-anniversary edition of *The New Yorker*, and he wanted to be represented there.

The next success was "Notes for the Chart in 306," a Nash poem that was as unfunny and stark as anything he had ever written. It certainly was a compelling work, another reminder that had Ogden chosen a different path he would had been a powerful serious poet, instead of a philosopher who hid behind the laugh.

The editors of *The New Yorker* said they wanted Ogden Nash's light verse. But these days, when he submitted it, too often it was the old story. And even when they succumbed to his rollicks, there continued to be reservations. Reservations became part of the game. Conditional acceptance was the new phrase. By the middle of the summer of 1966, Ogden was thoroughly disgusted. He sat down in the corner of the living room of the North Hampton house and wrote a sarcastic letter to his editor at *The New Yorker*. He had just received a July issue of that magazine containing a long poem by Robert Penn Warren, and the reference to stars falling through the heavens like dandruff caught his eye.

The poem, said Ogden, reminded him of the defunct *New York Daily Mirror*'s resident poet, Nick Kenny, an expert at creating the non sequitur. Surely, said Ogden, thinking like Nick Kenny, it had to be God's dandruff. After reading this, Ogden said, he realized why *The New Yorker* kept rejecting his comic submissions. They were certainly justified, he said, because his little rhymes were as nothing compared to such ridiculous lines.

When Ogden read over the letter, he decided there was a better way, and he put the missive aside and composed a poem: "A Visitor from Porlock, But, Alas, No Xanadu."

With rapier he assaulted the poet who had penned those idiotic lines. He then went on to discuss other idiocies; a country overstocked with electric squeezers where there was no fresh orange juice, the aspirin manufacturers for cramming up the surplus cotton crop into aspiring bottles so hard it had to be gotten out with scientific instruments, the states' legislators and their antiquated youth drinking laws. And more . . .

It was hardly the sort of poem, poking at another *New Yorker* poet, that the editors would be expected to like. But they bought it.

At this time in Ogden's life, *The New Yorker* really was not very important. From this point on it became less so. The new art form for him, recitals to music, was developing. He was asked to give many readings at colleges and civic functions. His poems were appearing in *The Atlantic Monthly, Boy's Life, Clipper, Ford Times, Gourmet, Holiday, Horizon, Look,*

Life, McCall's, Odyssey, the *Saturday Review, Signature, Travel and Camera,* and *Venture.*

He was poking fun at the Me Generation for their constant preoccupation with self, but he didn't forget everybody else, as in "Bet You a Nickel My Unhappiness Can Lick Your Unhappiness," which took on the mania for things marked "His" and "Hers"; crowded theater rows; faulty three-way light bulbs; and window envelopes. He had taken up birdwatching in middle age and found a new aversion to predatory cats ("The Bird Lover"). He found Ann Landers so brutal in her advice to the lovelorn that he wrote a poem about her. Traveling with the grandchildren by auto brought back the old days of traveling with the children by auto, or what Robert Benchley had once referred to as comparable to a third-class passage through Bulgaria, a thought Ogden seconded heartily in "Children Under 12 No Charge, And That's Too Much." He wrote about baseball, which occupied many of his television hours. He wrote more of his natural history poems, about elks and snakes, Tyrannosaurus Rex, hylas, hogs, and foolish dogs. He suggested in "Road Block" that lawyers had become so preoccupied with the law that they had forgotten why they were there, to serve people. Sometimes he remembered his boyhood, as in "From an Antique Land," which concerned the old days in Savannah and shiny motorcars. He had long found banks a good mark, and that habit had not changed. Now, in "Give-Away, Give-Away Banker Man," he spoofed the premiums banks gave to attract customers. Often he wrote about himself as in "He Didn't Dare Look, or The Puzzling Uniqueness of Mr. Saltbody's Meekness." He wrote about a common plight of middle-aged Americans in "Which the Chicken, Which the Egg," which had all the saltiness of that old poem about candy and liquor.

He speared the search for the stick-figure look in "If Ethyl Vanillan Be the Food of Love, Drink On." He poked fun at airline advertising—up, up and away, and fly the friendly skies—in "Is This Any Way to Advertise an Airline? You Bet It Is!"

Television advertising got its comeuppance in "Most Doctors Recommend, or Yours for Fast Fast Fast Relief." He attacked maraschino cherries. In "Sexual Politics Farewell: A Memo to Kate Millett, Shulaminth Firestone, Betty Friedan et al. (Al. Stands for Alice, not Albert)" he sounded the retreat of men from the battle of the sexes, men worn down by female belligerence and outnumbered. He still reminded his readers that there is a language called English, that gourmet is not an adjective, and that thrust, uptight, relevant, and clout leave something to be desired. He continued to be the conscience of America, the philosopher who had made his way from Park Avenue to Main Street and found he liked it a lot better down there. And he was still very funny.

22

The Poet Tilts at Windmills

In 1967 Ogden Nash was preparing his first collection of new poems in five years for Little, Brown to publish. The title: *There's Always Another Windmill*. No, there was not a poem in the collection by that title; it was a perfect representation of Ogden's relations with *The New Yorker*. Most of these poems had been seen by the editors, some of them purchased, but more turned down.

Life went along for the Nashes in their New Hampshire–Maryland ambivalence, a little more turbulent than in recent years. Ogden found, to his discomfort, that the intestinal operation had not cured his dyspepsia and gut discontent. Daughter Isabel came down with some strange malady, apparently poisoned by the toxic interaction of several medicines, and there were many anxious weeks until she recovered. But daughter Linell published a book on Arabian horses, which she raised for fun and profit. Rather, the book was a biography of a famous Arabian stallion. Little, Brown brought it out with high hopes, and Ogden did his best to push it with people like Harry Scherman of the Book-of-the-Month Club, but the world apparently was not panting for the biography of an Arabian stallion just then.

In 1967 only four poems were sold. Ogden worked mostly on children's books that year.

A long Christmas poem for book publication, *Santa Go Home: A Case History for Parents*, punctuated the juvenile parade. His major effort was *The Cruise of the Aardvark*, which had been commissioned by M. Evans & Co., a small New York house that marketed books through Lippincott. This experience with a new publisher was not entirely satisfactory. It was Ogden's first encounter, as author, with the "made" book. The idea had come from Herbert M. Katz, the editor of M. Evans. Sometimes an editor can supply an author with an idea, and the resulting book sails through production. Sometimes, the editor feels that his ideas have not been properly exploited, and then there is trouble. There were signs of trouble with *The Cruise of the Aardvark* from the outset. Mr. Katz wanted a book for children between six and ten, one that would conform to the demands of librarians. From the beginning Editor Katz said he wanted a work like Ogden's books of the past, but with a controlled vocabulary.

Ogden's instinct told him never to write down to children. His editor was saying the opposite, and Ogden should have been warned.

In the spring of 1967 Ogden delivered his manuscript. In a bibliographical note published by the Harry Ransom Humanities Research Center of the University of Texas at Austin, George W. Crandell called the manuscript a "draft." Editor Katz wanted some revisions largely to meet his original specifications for the book. As authors will, Ogden read the letter with annoyance; Nash's words of disagreement and other notes sideline the page.

Mr. Katz was a line-by-line revisionist of *The New Yorker* sort that Ogden knew so well. He was afraid of the big words tubuludentate (describing aardvarks), aesthetically, and extensile, all used by Ogden in his happy tale.

Ogden replied, all was finally settled, and the book was published with tubuludentate, aesthetically, and extensile.

In 1968 Ogden once more widened his horizons. His standing in the literary community was indicated by some of the commissions that came his way that year. There was little for *The New Yorker*, the same old sixes and sevens with the editors over what was funny and what was not. But *Life* paid him $5,000 to write captions in verse for a photo story about the Baltimore Colts football team. Poet Laureate of the Colts, they called him. He wrote verses for Ravel's "Mother Goose Suite," and contracted to narrate them in June at Lincoln Center in New York, with Andre Kostelanetz and the New York Symphony Orchestra. He also would narrate his "The Carnival of Animals" and "Peter and the Wolf" verses with the San Francisco Symphony Orchestra at the end of the year. For this the San Francisco Symphony would pay him $6,000. The British Broadcasting Company was then approaching him to do a film.

He was asked by Harper and Row to complete the late Edward Lear's unfinished work, *The Scroobious Pip,* and did. Hallmark brought out a new collection of old poems: *Funniest Verses of Ogden Nash.*

Ogden could always find time for a good cause. When St. Andrews-by-the-Sea, the Episcopal church in Rye Beach, was trying to raise money Ogden obliged with a fund-raising poem that brought in some checks. When Richard Armour, the West Coast humorist, wrote *A Time of Laughter*, a book of light verse, his agent, Paul Reynolds, thought a word from the old master might help sales, so he asked Ogden how much he wanted to write an introduction. Ogden set a fee of $200, but when he learned that Armour, and not the publisher, was going to pay, he said the fee would be nothing. (That was the old authors' code: anything to help another writer, nothing free to publishers.) Armour was overwhelmed and insisted on sending Ogden a case of Scotch whisky. The shuffling and shifting regarding delivery of this handsome reward became a minor comedy; Reynolds could not have the liquor store in New Hampshire deliver the goods because the liquor store was a state store that did not deliver. Reynolds wanted to deliver the whisky in Maryland, but Ogden did not know when he would be there. Reynolds was going to send a check, but the problem of gifts and the Internal Revenue code intervened. Finally, a check was sent to Ogden's cut-rate liquor store in Baltimore, and Reynolds got his tax deduction, and Ogden got his whisky. The correspondence on the delicate problem was ten times as long as the simple foreword Ogden wrote for Armour's book.

Ogden had never been much for politics. In fact, as he wrote a *Baltimore Sun* reporter who asked, he had always regarded himself as a mugwump, a term coined in the nineteenth century to denominate fence-sitters, and further defined in the twentieth century as a person who sits on the fence with his mug on one side and wump on the other. But not so in 1968. Ogden had a candidate for president. He was Eugene McCarthy, the erudite, friendly senator from Wisconsin. The alternatives, Republican and Democrat, aroused such strong feelings in Ogden that he and Frances traveled from Maryland to New Hampshire in the winter to vote for McCarthy in the now famous New Hampshire primary. He also wrote a birthday verse for the senator.

But the senator did not win. Nor did the Democratic party candidate in the fall of 1968. Richard Nixon won the election and came to the White House to inaugurate among all his other changes, a new policy that would dry up the river of children's books.

After John F. Kennedy had been elected in 1960 the administration had begun to build up America's school libraries by special grants that permitted those institutions to buy large numbers of books. This policy had resulted in a flood of publishing in the children's field, which Ogden's publishing history reflects. But as of 1968 the outlook was grim, for Nixon was pledged to cut out such fripperies. The next year he did, and the children's book market in America went into a tailspin. The "young adult" market, always a librarian's dream, suddenly became a publisher's nightmare. There was no such thing as a young adult book, the librarians suddenly decided, coming to their senses and recognizing a truth that Ogden had known for years, that children read according to their interests, and that big words were not the problem the educators had always made of them.

So, after 1968 the children's book market declined and declined, but Ogden's place in the history of it had been assured with *Custard the Dragon* if he never did another.

There's Always Another Windmill was published by Little, Brown and Company in the fall of 1968. Little, Brown, it is sad to say, seemed to have become somewhat careless about their most valuable poet. This new, relatively slender volume of Ogden Nash's poetry was bypassed as not very important in the Little, Brown scheme of things. But it should have been expected that taking Ogden Nash for granted was going to create trouble. The publishers seemed to have quite forgotten that before Ogden had been a practicing poet of the freelance school, he had spent eight years as a publisher, and he knew where and how the bodies were buried.

The way to sell books in the old Doubleday days was to jump on any bandwagon. If, for example, a book got a superb review in Chicago or Washington or Kansas City, Doubleday had been there, plastering the daily and Sunday newspapers with advertising. Time and again Dan Longwell and his assistant had proved they could take a book that might sell 10,000 if left to struggle by itself, and triple that sale with advertising.

October came, and *There's Always Another Windmill* slipped out into the stream of publishing. Ogden received a letter of congratulation from Katherine White, who was wintering in Florida. The review copies were sent out, and they elicited the usual excellent reviews. But a review hit but once, just one day, and that was the end of the free advertising. After that, it was up to the publisher to keep the sales ball rolling.

The days went by, and there was no advertising. It was just as if this was Ogden's first book, and it was going to sink or swim by itself as almost all first books had to do.

Ogden had seen the performance from close up too many times not to know the dangers. And in 1968 it meant more to him than it might have in the past, because he was slowing down and living on the income from his books. Off the lecture trail, he had no ready method of self-promotion. Little, Brown could, by inattention, not realize more than perhaps a quarter of the book's sales potential.

At the end of the first week after the New York reviews, Ogden sensed that the impact was being lost. There was no ad that next Sunday in *The New York Times Book Review*. Another week went by, and still no advertising. Every day more books by other authors were being published, and *There's Always Another Windmill* was slipping out of the public consciousness. Bookstores that had put it in the window would take it out to make way for books supported by publisher promotion.

Two weeks went by. No improvement. Three weeks, four. No advertising to support the reviews.

Finally, Ogden could bear the strain no longer. He shot off an angry telegram to Little, Brown. He had been loyal to Little, Brown for thirty years, he said, and he had consistently brought them large profits. Such treatment, he said, could only be a considered policy of betrayal.

Apologies were sent, but it was late. Ogden drafted a furious letter to Little, Brown noting the place he considered that he occupied in literature, a successor at least to Robert Benchley and James Thurber, and perhaps to Mark Twain. He had held his place in literature since 1931, and was still going strong with young people, which was what counted.

On sober reflection, Ogden did not send this letter, but gave the same information to the Curtis Brown agency to deliver personally, so he would not be in the position of blowing his own horn.

Little, Brown listened now.

All stops were pulled out. Advertising and promotion material was dreamed up and executed with remarkable speed. Copies were sent to Ogden Nash.

By the end of November, Ogden was slightly less angry, but only slightly so, and a new distrust of his publishers had sprung up. Whether or not the thirty-year relationship with Little, Brown continued would depend on the publisher.

By dint of some exceptional effort that did sell books, Little, Brown managed to rescue the situation, and Ogden did not move to another publishing house.

That relationship survived, but the relationship with *The New Yorker* continued to deteriorate. In late December it was the magazine's practice to list on a back page all the books published by *New Yorker* contributers over the year. It made a nice promotion piece for the magazine, because the list was always substantial. But the rule was that no author would be listed unless one-third of his book had appeared in the pages of *The New Yorker*. In recent years not a third of Ogden's work had been accepted by *The New Yorker*, although perhaps three-quarters of it had been offered to them. So Ogden's book was not on the list. It was nothing very important. Lord knew how many copies of a book that low-keyed notice had ever sold. But Ogden Nash, by 1968, was one of a handful of people of the early *New Yorker* crowd left in the main stream of publishing, and he was about to come to the fortieth year of his contributions to the magazine.

It seemed a little shabby.

23

Dodger Thomas Comes at Last

For some reason, Ogden's British agents, A. P. Watt and Son, concluded that J. M. Dent and Sons, Ltd., was not the appropriate house for Nash's next book to be published in that country. Ogden's personal agent in the Watt office so informed Ogden's American representative.

Ogden was told of the proposal, but Dent apparently knew nothing at all, and in 1968 they wrote Ogden about their plans to bring out *There's Always Another Windmill* in London the next year. Ogden replied with one of his usual cheery and often funny letters, giving absolutely no sign of what was going on.

The British agent shopped around London, and when the American counterpart went to the Frankfurt International Book Fair in October, he also talked to English publishers. Finally it came down to two: Chatto & Windus, a mossy old British publisher of impressive dignity, and Andre Deutsch, who was regarded as very energetic. The agent opted for the latter, and Ogden, who let his agents handle such matters, accepted the change.

So, in January 1969 J. M. Dent was informed that they were losing an author.

The Dents were astounded, flabbergasted, and nonplussed. Martin Dent wrote Ogden, referring to their recent chummy correspondence and asked: Why?

That was a hard and embarrassing question, because Ogden did not really know why, but he could scarcely say "Ask my agent." He had to fumble through an apologetic letter in which he said he was nearing seventy, he was concerned about the sale of his books in Britain, and did not feel that J. M. Dent and Sons were doing a properly aggressive job.

There was a good deal of nonsense in that letter. No Americans writer depended very greatly on income from British rights for his living. In the first place, the agents took a healthy percentage off the top. In the second place, Britain being a small country, the publishers had to be content with sales that would scarcely prompt an American publisher to issue the book. So Dent was cast off with no real explanation, and the baton passed to Andre Deutsch.

In the spring of 1969 Ogden continued to suffer from his internal complaints. It seemed that he would never overcome them. A lot of time was spent with doctors. He had been in and out of hospitals so much he could have written a book about them, and, in fact, he was doing so: *Bed Riddance* was in the works, a collection of verses celebrating his stays in Union Memorial Hospital, Johns Hopkins, Massachusetts General, and the London Clinic. He thanked seventeen doctors by name and several hundred nurses, nurses aids, lab technicians, X-ray specialists, dieticians, electricians, plumbers, floorwaxers, and surgical crews by inference for providing the research materials on which his sixty poems were based.

"Notes for the Chart in 306" was very definitely not included, for the shadow of Dodger Thomas was not to fall on the pages of a book designed to give a lift to the sick. Ogden dealt with boredom, sniffles, and getting to sleep and being-waked-up-to-take-your-sleeping-pill, and other diversions in the hospital. It was charming, laughing poetry, aimed primarily at the sickbed market.

Having put those wheels in motion during the spring, Ogden and Frances set off on the SS *Nieuw Amsterdam* in June for six weeks of sheer tourism in England, Scotland, and Ireland. The only hint of business was a stint promised in London in July at an international poetry festival, at which he had agreed to give two readings.

In the spring of 1970, the Nashes traveled again, this time staying abroad for another six weeks. There were more readings that year, more poems, more acceptances and more rejections from *The New Yorker*. Life had settled down to half a year in Baltimore; a trip abroad; summer on the beach; short trips to speak and read, and not too many of those; visits to the children; and too much time spent with doctors.

The poems now were reflective for the most part, the lines of a man with an enormous sense of humor and love of life, writing about the present with the wisdom of a longtime inhabitant of the past. He had once observed to Dan Longwell how nice it would be if they could just feel young again and not have to go to all the trouble of being young. By 1971, troubled with his intestinal pain, he would have settled for either. But he went on. He was asked to do many poems celebrating events. When the musician Rudolf Friml was ninety years old, Ogden did a poem to celebrate, a poem commissioned by the committee for the event. At long last, he was fulfilling the prophecy of critic Thomas Sugrue, made nearly thirty years earlier: "For Rudolf Friml on His Ninetieth Birthday" was pure epic poetry, leavened by a few Nashisms, rhyming nibble with Ish Kabibble, bed with drop dead, and mastheads with bastheads (meaning illegitimate sons).

Life was sweet. The grandchildren were a trial (all those teenage girls to be protected against their biological urges), but he wouldn't have missed that trial for all the world. He could still write funny verses about taking an auto trip with children aboard. He could still write about wild creatures and tame ones, the coelecanth, the lamprey, the hyena, the scallop. He was, in a phrase, the same old Nash doing business at the same old store. Like old port laid down properly, he was improving with age.

Everything went along more or less as usual, which meant topsy-turvy, hither and yon. He was supposed to make an appearance in Pittsburgh on April 7 for a poetry reading. What a problem! The virtual abandonment of America's railroad system had made travel extremely difficult for a man who would not fly. The only way to get from Baltimore to Pittsburgh by rail was to go to New York. He might do that. He might drive. He wrote the committee that was sponsoring the event for advice.

That letter was mailed on March 3. Two days later he wrote another. He had been to the doctor and had undergone a new series of X-rays. They showed serious inflammation of his lower intestine, and the doctor insisted that he go into the hospital immediately for surgery. So he had to cancel the reading. If all went well, and he said he expected it to go well, he would be out of action for three weeks, and it would be another month or so before he could face an audience.

So Ogden went into Johns Hopkins Hospital once again. The operation was successful, but the operation did not resolve the problem, it flared up again, and in May he was back in the hospital once more. The doctors operated, and he seemed to be coming along. But then he suffered a massive stroke. On May 19, 1971, Dodger Thomas finally slipped through the unlocked door of the room at Johns Hopkins Hospital and came for Ogden.

And so passed America's great humorous poet of the tewntieth century, a man whose gentle humor transcended events, and whose humorous funning more often than not held a grain or two of philosophical truth. The poem "A Necessary Dirge" was not his last, but in its warm look at the prickly nature of man and the universe this poem comes close to epitomizing the man.

A NECESSARY DIRGE

Sometimes it's difficult, isn't it, not to grow grim and rancorous
Because man's fate is so counterclockwise and cantankerous.
Look at all the noble projects that die a-borning,
Looking how hard it is to get to sleep at night and then how hard it is to wake
*   up in the morning!*
How easy to be unselfish in the big things that never come up and how hard
*   in the little things that come up daily and hourly, oh yes,*
Such as what heroic pleasure to give up the last seat in a lifeboat to a mother
*   and babe, and what an irritation to give some housewife your seat on the*
*   Lexington Avenue Express!*
How easy for those who do not bulge
To not overindulge!
O universe perverse, why and whence your perverseness?
Why do you not teem with betterness instead of worseness?
Do you get your only enjoyment
Out of humanity's annoyment?
Because a point I would like to discuss
Is why wouldn't it be just as easy for you to make things easy for us?
But no, you will not listen, expostulation is useless,
Home is the fisherman empty-handed, home is the hunter caribouless and
*   mooseless.*
Humanity must continue to follow the sun around
And accept the eternal run-around.
Well, and if that be the case, why come on humanity!
So long as it is our fate to be irked all our life let us just keep our heads up
*   and take our irking with insouciant urbanity.*

Notes

Ogden Nash's papers, as the reader will see by the acknowledgements section of this book, are far-flung, indeed. The greatest collection exists at the University of Texas at Austin in the Harry Ransom Humanities Center. Ogden sold this collection to the university a few years before his death. Columbia University's Butler Library also contains a number of collections that deal with Ogden Nash's affairs. I was able to use most of them, but the Curtis Brown collection was closed to me in deference to the wishes of Mrs. Nash. The Curtis Brown agency represented Nash during almost all of his writing years. The most extensive collection in this regard was that of Dan Longwell, Ogden's friend from boyhood.

INTRODUCTION

The commemorative tribute to Ogden Nash by S. J. Perelman is reprinted courtesy of the American Academy of Arts and Letters, New York.

The material for this preliminary section of the book comes from the various reviews and obituaries of Ogden Nash that were printed after his death, the notes of S. J. Perelman's eulogy, and the publications of The Century Association, and *The New Yorker* magazine.

1

The material about Ogden Nash's boyhood comes from notes in his own hand that are now in the collection of the Harry Ransom Humanities Research Center at the University of Texas at Austin. Another source is a long interview he gave Roy Newquist, which was published as part of Newquist's book *Conversations*. Ogden told Newquist, for example, that his eyes were very bad as a boy. The story of the prince and the mockingbird is a paraphrase of Ogden's boyhood poem, the sole surviving one, kept in a diary he wrote for a short while. Again, this paper is in the Texas collection. The note about his life at St. George's School comes from a letter written by George W. Wheeler, alumni secretary of St. George's School in 1963, a copy of which was kindly sent to me by St. George's. The quotation about what he had learned from Arthur S. Roberts is from a letter Ogden wrote Roberts on his ninetieth birthday. The notes about Ogden's early New York jobs come from the Newquist interview, as does the quotation about his early poetry. The assessment of *The Cricket of Carador* is also from Ogden's interview with Newquist.

2

The poem "Admiral Byrd" brought Ogden to local fame in New York City when it appeared in Franklin P. Adams's "The Conning Tower" column in the *New York World*.

The story of how *The New Yorker* got its name is from *Ross and the New Yorker* by Dale Kramer. The material about New York's literary scene and the Round Table crowd is from Edwin P. Hoyt's biography of Alexander Woollcott. The facts for the notes about Dan Longwell and the early years at Doubleday come from Ogden's correspondence and from a memorial speech he made to the Friends of the Columbia Libraries in 1970. The material about the various advertisements Ogden wrote comes from the advertisements as they appeared in the New York newspapers. The material about the Garden City period comes from the Newquist interview and the Longwell speech.

The material about Christopher Morley and The Foundry is from Nash-Morley correspondence, in the Nash and Morley papers at the University of Texas. The story of Ogden's unfinished novel is from my reading of that novel in the Texas papers.

The material about Ogden's pursuit of Frances Leonard by correspondence is from the letters at the University of Texas. Apparently Mrs. Nash saved virtually every letter Ogden ever wrote her, and there they are in the collection he sold to the University of Texas in the late 1960s. I have been constrained to paraphrase rather than quote since I was denied such permission by the Nash estate.

Over the years in various places, Ogden told various stories about that party at which he first met Frances Leonard. Sometimes the man involved was a Princeton graduate. But I prefer the tale of the Naval Academy midshipman as a matter of logic. Even had Ogden managed to move place cards around, it seems doubtful that he could have monopolized Miss Leonard that evening unless her escort suddenly became *hors de fete.*

The stories about various books and enterprises in which Ogden was engaged come from his letters to Miss Leonard. The thread of his life in that period is also taken from a reading of those letters. The great weekend that was to change Ogden's life is mentioned in his letters to her and also in a letter to Christopher Morley.

3

The notes about Ogden's work come from his letters to Miss Leonard, from materials found in his papers, and from other correspondence in the Texas files. The Prosper Buranelli tale comes from letters to Miss Leonard.

The quotations from the Dorothy Parker poems are reproduced courtesy of Viking-Penguin. The story of Dr. Jack and Charles Hedlund is from one of Ogden's letters to Miss Leonard, as are the tales of his meetings with the Doubledays. The material about the Nassau and Suffolk Deviled Ham and Lake Ronkonkoma Society is from the notes of the club. The story of the Admiral Byrd poem is from Ogden's speech to the Friends of the Columbia Library about Dan Longwell.

4

The references to Ogden's poems, such as "Spring Comes to Murray Hill," are from an examination of Ogden's published works. The notes about publishing in the 1920s are the author's own. The story about Edna Ferber and Dan Longwell is from Ogden's Longwell speech. The note about the dinner at the Park Lane Hotel is from a letter to Miss Leonard, as is the tale of Bayard Schindel, and the stories he told about Radclyff Hall. The clipping about the jealous fiancé is from the *New York World*. The story of the Currier and Ives book is from a letter to Miss Leonard, as is the tale about Rufus King. The picnic tale is from the notes of the Nassau and Suffolk County Deviled Ham and Lake Ronkonkoma Society, sometimes called the club. The notes about Dubose Heyward and Prosper Buranelli's tales are from letters to Miss Leonard. The material about Harold Ross, *The New Yorker*, and Ogden Nash in 1929 and 1930 comes from his letters to Miss Leonard, and several other sources: *The Years with Ross* by James Thurber, *Ross and The New Yorker* by Dale Kramer, and *Ross, The New Yorker, and Me* by Jane Grant.

5

Most of the material about the Dutch Treat Club comes from my own experience. The stories of Ogden's publishing activities come from his letters to Miss Leonard and other papers in the Nash file at the University of Texas. The notes about the various poems come from a reading of the works. The notes about Robert Benchley and F.P.A. are from Ogden's letters to Miss Leonard. The note about Ogden's pay raise by *The New Yorker* is from his papers at the University of Texas. The observation about Miss Leonard is my own.

6

The notes about Ogden and Lowell Thomas come from my own conversations with Lowell Thomas and from Ogden's papers. Lowell was being given a chance to take the job relinquished by Floyd Gibbons, reporter, pilot, and sometime soldier of fortune. The story of Ogden's disenchantment with Doubleday comes from his letters to Miss Leonard and other papers in the file, plus the Newquist interview. In that case, Nelson Doubleday was probably right about the sales possibilities of a book on Diendonne Coste. Virtually no one has ever heard of him since. The story of Ogden's rapproachment with *The New Yorker* comes from various sources, and the material about Ross's "Jesuses" comes from the Woollcott biography. The notes about Ogden's yearnings to become an independent publisher come from his letters to Miss Leonard.

The information about Ogden's relations with other magazine and book publishers comes from their letters to him in the Texas collection. The story about the Yale-Georgia football game and the Legionnaires comes from Ogden's letters to Miss Leonard. So does the tale of his weekend on Long Island with the Gawtrys. The discussions of Ogden's new book with Simon & Schuster are to be found in various places in the papers.

The sources for the material about *The New Yorker* are the various books about Ross and Woollcott, and the Nash papers.

7

The tales of Ogden's wining and dining by *The New Yorker* crowd are from his papers, particularly the letters to Miss Leonard. The letter from Miss Edna Ferber to Ogden Nash is published through the courtesy of Harriet Pilpel, attorney for the estate. Janet Flanner's remarks about Ross come from her introduction to Jane Grant's book. The material about Ross and Mrs. Parker is from the various Ross books and the Woollcott biographies. Ogden's relations with Ross were delineated in Ogden's letters to Miss Leonard.

The poem from Mrs. Parker comes from a fan letter she wrote Nash in 1930, quoted by permission of Mrs. Parker's agent. The Ferber incident was described by Ogden in a letter to Miss Leonard.

The fuss about publication of *Hard Lines* comes from several sources, largely Ogden's letters to Miss Leonard, the reviews of the book in various publications, and advertisements of Simon & Schuster in the New York newspapers. Ogden knew a large number of the important publicists of the time, through his connections with Doubleday, and he pulled out the stops to get good comments for Simon & Schuster's use in advertising his book.

8

Ogden's letters to Miss Leonard traced his activities as reported in the first part of this chapter. The poem written by E. B. White is included courtesy of Mr. White. The tales of Dorothy Parker are from John Keats's biography of Mrs. Parker and from Ogden's letters to Miss Leonard. The story about James M. Cain was recalled to Ogden years later by Cain, who remembered very well and wrote Ogden a note about it.

Ogden's movements back and forth from Baltimore to New York after his marriage were something of a mystery to me, and I was unable to get any answers from Mrs. Nash, so I reconstructed his activity as best I could from the available evidence. Mrs. Nash seems to have spent a good deal of her time during this period with her family in Baltimore, but some of it must have been spent in New York, because there are hiatuses in the letters from Ogden.

Most of the material about magazine sales comes from the little journal Ogden kept between 1930 and 1968, in which he noted his sales. His progress with Farrar & Rinehart is detailed in his correspondence.

9

Apparently Ogden Nash never owned a house in Baltimore, at least not in this early period. A lot of letters originated at 4300 Rugby Road, the house of the Leonard family. The Nashes did move into a rented house on Underwood Road for a time, and he wrote a number of hilarious poems about the trials and tribulations of the householder.

The poem "The Four Woods Colts" was also sometimes titled "The Four S.O.B.s," "The Four Bastards," and "The Four So-and-Sos." It is so out of synchronization with all the rest of Ogden's work of the period that it seems odd that it should have been included in his second book published by Simon & Schuster. But it certainly did make an impression at the Dutch Treat Club and off in Hollywood.

10

In reviewing *The Primrose Path, The Saturday Review of Literature*'s Ted Robinson did what scores of interviewers had done and would do, he yielded to the overwhelming impulse to copy Ogden's poesy approach. Robinson also came to the conclusion, based on the poem "The Secret Town," that Ogden could be a lyric poet if he really wanted to devote his effort in that direction. "The Secret Town" was another of Ogden's paeans to his wife.

Robinson also brought up the matter of Ogden as philosopher. It would be mentioned again and again by reviewers, but not much by philosophers.

The poems of *The Primrose Path* indicate that Ogden's encounters in the battle between men and women were quite frequent in these first years of marriage. At least one quarrel was serious enough to force him out of his usual attitude and to fight back, the quarrel conducted by cable across the Atlantic. There is no indication that Ogden triumphed in this clash.

11

Ogden's Hollywood era is delineated in his papers, and in the Newquist interview. Outside sources include S. J. Perelman's remarks about their writing partnership on *How to Win Friends and Influence People* at the Nash memorial services. Also Perelman was interviewed at length by Mr. Newquist, and some of that interview is germane to Ogden's life. The general notes about Hollywood are from my own experience.

Several articles in the *Baltimore Sun* and the *Baltimore News American* provided the rest, for Ogden was a favorite of the newspapers and was frequently interviewed.

12

Ogden went on the lecture trail with great reluctance, not so much because he knew how grueling it was going to be as because he was a homebody and hated to be away from Frances and the children. He soon learned to detest the lecture circuit. Eventually he wrote a number of poems that dealt with the ancillary problems: rundown hotels, bad meals, slow trains, and gushing hostesses.

Once again he encountered the irrepressible poets, even down to newspaper headline writers, who described him and his work in unbelievably bad verse.

13

Ogden's attempt to volunteer for the Navy in World War II is documented in a letter he wrote to the naval authorities early in 1942. His attempts to sell U.S. Savings Bonds for the Treasury were a failure, according to his own note on the subject and one or two letters to friends.

14

The notes about Ogden's book sales come from a letter to Dan Longwell in 1942. The material about *One Touch of Venus* comes from the Perelman papers, and from a collection of letters and documents relative to the musical in the Leah Salisbury collection at Columbia University. The story of the tryout of the musical in Boston comes from several sources, including Lewis Nichols, *The New York Times* reviewer and a longtime friend of the author's.

The tales of Ogden's other musical efforts are from the files of the *Baltimore News American* and the *Baltimore Sun*.

Ogden's friendship with Vernon Duke and his wife lasted all their lives, but Nash and Duke were never able to create the magic that would bring a show to Broadway. They did engage in some other profitable enterprises, but Ogden was to be frustrated in his desire to continue in the theater.

15

Ogden was a great conservator. Virtually nothing he wrote was wasted (after those juvenile attempts at plays and novels and short stories). He knew better than the magazine editors the worth of his verse. He was willing to revise a poem for *The New Yorker* and other publications, if they had bought it. But if they rejected it, he kept trying to sell it through his agent, and if everyone rejected it, he held it and put it into his next book of verse. No reviewer or reader was known to complain, which is a commentary in itself about the tastes and judgments of magazine editors.

In 1948 Ogden prepared for a new aspect of his career. Meeting Andre Kostelanetz in Paris, he was persuaded to write verse for Saint Saëns's "Animal Carnival," which Kostelanetz was going to air over radio. Thus began Ogden's readings to music, which were to culminate in a great triumph with the San Francisco Symphony Orchestra a few years later.

16

During the last years or so of Ogden Nash's life he recognized his own importance on the literary scene and was chagrined that the tastemakers and awardgivers did not. He yearned for the Pulitzer Prize he never got. He yearned for a

National Book Award. He wanted recognition and he got it in a way; election to the National Academy and Institute of Arts and Letters was a recognition. But as for the prizes, the real problem seems to be that Ogden's work did not fit a category. This business of being unique created the trouble. And he was and is unique, as I discovered. Partially in research effort (but honestly also driven by that strange malady that causes otherwise sane adults to think they can write like Ogden Nash), I sent a poem or two to *The New Yorker*. Here is one of them:

I traveled recently from Dallas to Dulles to National,
Which seems to me irrational.

The New Yorker rejected it as too close to Ogden Nash's poems. In cutting short my career as poet, *The New Yorker* made my point. Even fourteen years after Ogden's death, *The New Yorker* was still receiving imitations of his work and still rejecting them because they ape Ogden's style. Certainly that is evidence that Ogden Nash's work was and remains unique in American letters.

It is not simply a matter of humorous poetry. Edward Lear was a very successful humorous poet, but after his death Ogden was asked by Harper and Row to finish Lear's last book; he did so with no apparent difficulty. No one would be able to finish a Nash poem to say nothing of a Nash book. So, the defense rests. (But all of this is moot because *The New Yorker* of today bears no relationship to Harold Ross's magazine.)

Ogden's trips abroad in the 1940s and 1950s provided him with a good deal of ammunition for his poetry. It was on one such trip that he got the idea for his backward poem abut travelling around Europe backwards, "My Trip daorbA," which turned out to be a tour de force, showing how completely Ogden had mastered the English language.

17

A middle-aged Ogden Nash made a fine impression on the people he met. He was relaxed, and he had finally made the transition from Park Avenue to Main Street with good grace. There was no "side" to him. He had no pretensions to be other than a writer, and he kept pretty much to himself his resentment against the literary community for failing to honor him. Certainly he was not alone. Theodore Dreiser had been cast about like a waif for years, even thrown off the Doubleday publishing list as a writer of dirty books before Ogden arrived on the scene. Dreiser, too, had been denied the acclaim he sought and was overshadowed by Sinclair Lewis, F. Scott Fitzgerald, and Ernest Hemingway.

Ogden mellowed in his middle age and his poems, sometimes more sardonic than in the past, were also more philosophical. He always said they would not amount to much, that if he was remembered at all in later years it would be for the brittle couplets and quatrains of his youth.

It was really almost twenty years after *Hard Lines* that Ogden caught on with the British. The main reason was a change in English English that came about as a result of World War II. The invasion of millions of Yanks not only changed British drinking habits (ice), but it brought to Britain a new understanding of the American language as well as the adoption of many Americanisms. In 1931 *The Times* of

London had looked askance at Ogden's poetry, suggesting quite seriously that he had best devote himself to a study of English language. Twenty years later the London papers were saying that Ogden was writing the best light verse in the language, and they meant both languages, English English and American English.

18

Television revolutionized American (and world) communications. Its emergence in the 1950s destroyed the most popular general circulation magazines, relegated newspapers to a back seat, and for a time threatened the motion picture business. It also provided a new market for Ogden's talents, not as a poet, but as a personality.

Ogden was still ignored by the Pulitzer Prize committees and always would be.

19

The years 1961–68 were great years for librarians and writers and publishers of childrens' books, courtesy of John F. Kennedy's program of school library rehabilitation and the furtherance of that program during the Lyndon Johnson years. But it all came to a sudden end with the appearance of Richard Nixon in the White House. Library subsidy was one of the first programs he cut. By that time, however, *Custard the Dragon* had established Ogden Nash as one of the "greats" of children's literature.

The late 1950s and the 1960s brought unpleasant changes to American society. Crime and social problems made New York City uninhabitable for Ogden. He moved down to Baltimore only to see the same sort of changes overwhelming that once gentle city. By the late 1960s Ogden was thoroughly disenchanted with all American cities and looked forward to living in New Hampshire much of the year and somewhere in the warm South during the cold months. His observations about the social changes sometimes verged on the preachy as *The New Yorker* editors pointed out to him. He tried harder then to avoid the issues that upset him, for the disturbance would show and would affect the humorous turn of his lines. It is hard to write funny poems about muggings and racial strife.

20

Ogden's productivity decreased sharply in the last third of his life, a matter that he recognized more than anyone else. The bad London *Times* review of *Marriage Lines* upset him because he was in England at the time, and must have had something to do with his almost inexplicable decision to change British publishers.

21

Toward the end of Ogden's life, he and the editors of *The New Yorker* agreed less and less. He told Dan Longwell he was selling about one poem in nine submissions to the magazine. That did not mean they were lost. Most of them appeared elsewhere or at least in the collections. He told Roy Newquist of his concern for the lack of humor in that magazine and elsewhere. The quote about writing comment in verse comes from a 1968 interview with a Baltimore reporter. From the same interview is the quotation about students in 1968. The poem about the Preakness I was able to reproduce because it is the only poem I know whose copyright is not owned by the Nash estate. On May 7, 1958, the *Baltimore Sun* published this poem and a news story noting that Ogden had given the rights to the track.

"As an avaricious old pro writer," he wrote the Pimlico officials, "I assign you all rights in it if you can give me three good box seats for the Preakness and arrange with Joe Stevens a luncheon table for three in the Old Clubhouse." Permission to reprint the poem here was kindly granted by Pimlico's Director of Media Relations, Chick Lang, Jr.

The story of Ogden's trip to Laurel was written up in the *Baltimore News American* in the spring of 1971 as part of the reminiscent publicity after Ogden's death. S. J. Perelman's feelings about *The New Yorker* crowd were detailed in a letter to Ogden in the Nash collection. Ogden's remarks about Perelman are from his forward to *Chicken Inspector #23*. Ogden's remarks about his battle of wits with *The New Yorker* editors is from a letter to Dan Longwell in the Longwell collection at Columbia University. The Curtis Brown agency recorded with regular monotomy the rejection of Ogden's work by *The New Yorker*. The letters are in the Nash collection at the University of Texas. Ogden retained the unsent letter to *The New Yorker* about Robert Penn Warren's poem, but the real source of his irritation was not poet Warren but the editors themselves.

22

Ogden had very little respect for the complaints of *The New Yorker* editors, and they seldom caused him to make any changes in poems the magazine had rejected, but he maintained a steady equilibrium in his relations with the magazine. His foray with M. Evans and Co. in the children's book field was a trial for him. Little, Brown and even Lippincott had been much easier for him to work with. But all ended well.

In his years in Baltimore Ogden was a fan of the Colts football team, which was riding high and wide in those days, and of the Oriole baseball team. He also had a certain affection for the Boston Red Sox, based on his part-year residence in New Hampshire, which is Red Sox territory. He turned his interest to profit in at least two major poetical forays with *Life*, one on the Orioles and one on the Colts.

The quarrel with Little, Brown about their treatment of a prominent author is indicated in the Nash papers in the Texas collection. The quarrel was resolved, and no serious harm was done to the relationship, which persisted with the heirs after Ogden's death. Daughters Linell and Isabel combined forces to choose various poems for various new books brought out by Little, Brown, the most ambitious of which was *I Wouldn't Have Missed It*. This collection was introduced by Archibald MacLeish.

23

The reason for the Nash decision to leave Dent publishers in London was never explained to Dent, and is not apparent in the Nash papers anywhere. Andre Deutsch did not profit very much from the new acquisition, however; Ogden produced only one more book before his death. The end came quite suddenly, for on the eve of his final hospitalization he was planning a poetry reading in Pittsburgh, and his letter of regret (made available to me through the courtesy of the International Poetry Forum of Pittsburgh) indicated that he fully expected to be up and around again in about three weeks. But one operation led to another, he suffered from kidney failure, and when under treatment for that at Johns Hopkins Hospital he suffered a stroke. That's when "Dodger Thomas" intervened.

Bibliography

Adams, Franklin Pierce. *Nods and Becks*. New York: Garden City Publishing Co., 1946.

Adams, Samuel Hopkins. *Alexander Woollcott*. New York: Reynal & Hitchcock, 1945.

Allen, Frederick Lewis. *Since Yesterday*. New York: Harper & Bros., 1939.

———. *The Big Change*. New York: Harper & Bros., 1952.

Benchley, Nathaniel. *Robert Benchley: A Biography*. New York: McGraw Hill, 1953.

Ford, Corey. *Time of Laughter*. Boston: Little, Brown, and Co., 1967.

Gibbs, Wolcott. *More in Sorrow*. New York: Henry Hold & Co., 1958.

Gill, Brendan. *Here at The New Yorker*. New York: Random House, 1975.

Grant, Jane. *Ross, The New Yorker, and Me*. New York: Reynal and Co., 1968.

Hoyt, Edwin P. *Alexander Woollcott: The Man Who Came to Dinner*. New York: Abelard Schuman, 1965.

Keats, John. *You Might As Well Live: The Life and Times of Dorothy Parker*. New York: Simon and Schuster, 1970.

Kramer, Dale. *Ross and The New Yorker*. Garden City, N.Y.: Doubleday and Co., 1951.

Masson, T. L. *Our American Humorists*. New York: Moffatt and Co., 1922.

Morley, Christopher. *Off the Deep End*. Garden City, N.Y.: Doubleday and Co., 1928.

———. *Seacoast of Bohemia*. Garden City, N.Y.: Doubleday and Co., 1929.

Parker, Dorothy. *The Portable Dorothy Parker*. New York: Viking Press, 1944.

Perelman, S. J. *The Man of Perelman*. New York: Simon and Schuster, 1958.

———. *Chicken Inspector #23*. New York: Simon and Schuster, 1967.

Rascoe, Burton, and E. Conklin. *The Smart Set Anthology*. New York: Reynal & Hitchcock, 1934.

Seldes, George. *The Seven Lively Arts*. New York: Sagamore Press, 1957.

Stearns, H. *America Now*. New York: Charles Scribner's Sons, 1938.

Teichmann, Howard. *Smart Aleck*. New York: William Morrow and Co., 1976.

———. *G. S. Kaufman.* New York: Atheneum, 1972.

Thurber, James. *The Years with Ross.* Boston: The Atlantic Monthly Press, 1959.

White, E. B. *The Second Tree from the Corner.* New York: Harper & Row, 1965.

———. *Here Is New York.* New York: Harper Brothers, 1949.

Wilson, Edmund. *A Literary Chronicle.* Garden City, N.Y.: Garden City Publishing, Co., 1952.

Yates, N. W. *The American Humorist.* Ames: Iowa State University Press, 1964.

BOOKS BY OGDEN NASH*

(With Joseph Alger). *Cricket of Carador.* Garden City, N.Y.: Doubleday, 1925.

(With Christopher Morley and Cleon Throckmorton). *Born in a Beer Garden, or She Troupes to Conquer.* Rudge, 1930.

Hard Lines. New York: Simon and Schuster, 1931.

Free Wheeling. New York: Simon and Schuster, 1931.

(Editor). Wodehouse, Pelham Granville. *Nothing but Wodehouse.* Garden City, N.Y.: Doubleday, 1932.

Happy Days. New York: Simon & Schuster, 1933.

Four Prominent So and So's (music by Robert Armbruster). New York: Simon & Schuster, 1934.

The Primrose Path. New York: Simon & Schuster, 1935.

The Bad Parents' Garden of Verse. New York: Simon & Schuster, 1936.

I'm a Stranger Here Myself. Boston: Little, Brown, 1938.

The Face Is Familiar: The Selected Works of Ogden Nash. Boston: Little, Brown, 1940.

Good Intentions. Boston: Little, Brown, 1942.

The Ogden Nash Pocket Book. Blakiston, 1944.

Many Long Years Ago. Boston: Little, Brown, 1945.

The Selected Verse of Ogden Nash. New York: Random House, Modern Library, 1946.

Ogden Nash's Musical Zoo. Boston: Little, Brown, 1947.

Versus. Boston: Little, Brown, 1949.

Family Reunion. Boston: Little, Brown, 1950.

Parents Keep Out: Elderly Poems for Youngerly Readers. Boston: Little, Brown, 1951.

The Private Dining Room, and Other New Verses. Boston: Little, Brown, 1953.

The Moon Is Shining Bright As Day: An Anthology of Good-Humored Verse. Philadelphia: Lippincott, 1953.

The Pocket Book of Ogden Nash. New York: Pocket Books, 1954.

You Can't Get There from Here. Boston: Little, Brown, 1957.

The Boy Who Laughed at Santa Claus (pamphlet). London: Cooper & Beatty Ltd., 1957.

The Christmas That Almost Wasn't. Boston: Little, Brown, 1957.

(Editor). *I Couldn't Help Laughing: Stories Selected and Introduced by Ogden Nash.* Philadelphia: Lippincott, 1957.

Verses from 1929 On. Boston: Little, Brown, 1959. (Published in England as *Collected Verse from 1929 On.* London: Dent, 1961.)

*from *Contemporary Authors*

Custard the Dragon. Boston: Little, Brown, 1959.

A Boy Is a Boy: The Fun of Being a Boy. New York: Franklin Watts, 1960.

Everybody Ought to Know: Verses Selected and Introduced by Ogden Nash. Philadelphia: Lippincott, 1961.

Custard the Dragon and the Wicked Knight. Boston: Little, Brown, 1961.

The New Nutcracker Suite, and Other Innocent Verses. Boston: Little, Brown, 1962.

Girls Are Silly. New York: Franklin Watts, 1962.

Everyone but Thee and Me. Boston: Little, Brown, 1962.

A Boy and His Room. New York: Franklin Watts, 1963.

The Adventures of Isabel. Boston: Little, Brown, 1963.

The Untold Adventures of Santa Claus. Boston: Little, Brown, 1964.

Marriage Lines: Notes of a Student Husband. Boston: Little, Brown, 1964. (Published in England as *Notes of a Student Husband.* London: Dent, 1964.)

Santa Go Home: A Case History for Parents. Boston: Little, Brown, 1967.

The Cruise of the Aardvark. New York: M. Evans, 1967.

The Mysterious Ouphe. London: Robert Hale, 1967.

There's Always Another Windmill. Boston: Little, Brown, 1968.

I Wouldn't Have Missed It. Selected by Linell Nash Smith and Isabel Nash Eberstadt. Boston: Little, Brown, 1976. (post mortem)

Index